RANJI

RANJI

A Genius Rich and Strange

SIMON WILDE

THE KINGSWOOD PRESS

First published in Great Britain in 1990
by The Kingswood Press
an imprint of Methuen London
Michelin House, 81 Fulham Road, London SW3 6RB
First paperback edition 1991

Copyright © 1990 Simon Wilde

A CIP catalogue record for this book
is available from the British Library

ISBN 0 413 65350 1

Photoset by Rowland Phototypesetting Ltd
Bury St Edmunds, Suffolk
Printed in Great Britain by
Richard Clay Ltd, Bungay, Suffolk

To GAYLE

for her innings of support
and love

CONTENTS

ACKNOWLEDGEMENTS

I am extremely grateful to Ranji's great-nephew, Satrusalyasinhji, the present Jam Sahib of Nawanagar, for his hospitality during my visit to India. He placed all his resources at my disposal and without his help, or that of his staff and other members of his family, my researches would have been considerably the poorer

I would like to thank the staff at the India Office Library, who answered so many of my queries and guided me with such equanimity through its labyrinth of files towards numerous hidden treasures.

My thanks also go to the Cricket Society, for the use of its lending library; to Stephen Green, the librarian at Lord's; to Miss E. S. Leedham-Green, assistant keeper of the archives at Cambridge University; to H. A. Osborne, the Sussex CCC librarian; to the staff at the Newspaper Library, Colindale, at the East Sussex County Record Office, Lewes, and at the British Museum; to Mick Roffey and J. W. McKenzie, for photographic help, and to the late Sir George Allen, Peter Ball, various members of the Borissow family, Mihir Bose, Gerald Brodribb, Derek Deadman, Michael Down and W. J. Marwood.

For permission reproduce certain of the illustrations in this book I am grateful to the George Beldam Collection (nos. 2, 3, 4, 5), David Frith (no. 7), the India Office Library (no. 12) and *The Times* (nos. 1, 15).

Above all, I am indebted to Derek Wyatt, whose initial enthusiasm for the project spurred me on, and to Tony Pocock, whose gentle encouragement kept me going to the very end.

Simon Wilde

AUTHOR'S NOTES

In order to obtain the equivalent modern value of the sterling figures given in the text, it is necessary to multiply each sum by at least thirty-five; that is, today's pound would have been worth over £35 in the early years of this century.

Although the rates of exchange obviously varied throughout the years covered by this book, 1,000 rupees was worth approximately £58 in Ranji's time; 1,000 korees, a smaller and little-used unit of currency, about £17.

The Sussex CCC ground at Hove has been referred to throughout as the Brighton ground, the name by which it was generally known during Ranjitsinhji's playing career.

In quoted passages the spellings of some words, mostly Indian proper names, have, for the sake of consistency and clarity, been standardized.

INTRODUCTION

I feel there is a need to explain the reason for another book about Ranji. There have already been three full biographies of him: one during his playing career, one at the end of his life, and a third in 1983. Even for someone who was without doubt one of cricket's most important figures, and whose name still has the power to captivate fifty years after his death, this might have been thought sufficient.

But, of course, Ranjitsinhji was much more than simply a great cricketer. He was the first non-white sportsman ever to win international renown, while he also became, after almost twenty-five years of disputed succession, a ruling prince in India and one of the most famous men in the British Empire. How he achieved all this has never been adequately explained. There was not only a mystery – albeit an enchanting one – about the way he batted, there was also one about his courtly past, and how he eventually came to succeed to the Nawanagar throne. Chiefly through gaining access to a vast number of confidential government documents of the period, I believe I have got as close to the truth of the matter as is now reasonably possible.

And the truth is, the legend of Ranji is far removed from reality. A faintly perceived unreliability with money was in fact far more calculated and carried out on a far greater scale than has generally been understood (on his first visit to England as Jam Sahib, in 1908, he was practically hounded out of the country because of his numerous debts), while his ambitions towards the Nawanagar throne were not only based on an unfounded claim to being a prince, but were also pursued with equally measured step. Many of his off-the-field exploits with A. C. MacLaren and other leading English amateur cricketers will probably never be known, but it seems clear that sometimes they were not averse to conducting themselves in the fashion of E. W. Hornung's fictional character Raffles, the cricketing burglar. In late Victorian and early Edwardian society, there was not such a very great distance between the brilliantly illumined echelons of high society and the shadows and intrigues of the underworld.

Most importantly, however, such revelations only serve to demonstrate just what a great cricketer Ranji was. In the light of the fact that he was often in desperate financial straits, without the assurance of knowing that he had every right to present himself as a prince, or even of being sure that his claim to the Nawanagar throne was just and might one day be recognized, Ranjitsinhji's determination to make himself the dazzling monarch of the Englishman's national game takes on even more heroic proportions. He truly was a genius rich and strange.

Wimbledon
January 1990   Simon Wilde

1

THE GREAT ARTIST

'FROM THE MOMENT he stepped out of the pavilion he drew all eyes and held them. No one who saw him bat will ever forget it. He was the first man I ever knew who wore silk shirts, and there was something almost romantic about the very flow of his sleeves and the curves of his shoulders. He drew the crowds wherever he went, and at the height of his cricket days the shops in Brighton would empty if he passed along the street. Everyone wanted to see him. Whenever I bowled against him I felt as if he were impregnable. My impression was, "I shall never get this man out".'

These are the words of Gilbert Jessop, writing in a newspaper article in the 1920s, and they refer to Kumar Shri Ranjitsinhji, or Ranji as he was popularly known. Jessop thought Ranji was the most brilliant figure in what he believed had been cricket's most brilliant period, by which he meant the 1890s and the years shortly after, generally known as the Golden Age of Cricket. Jessop's remarks indicate the remarkable hold Ranji possessed over the public imagination: shops do not empty for just any passer-by, not even for quite well-known ones. Ranjitsinhji was one of the most famous figures in the Empire and even after he became His Highness the Jam Sahib of Nawanagar, a western Indian state situated beneath the Gulf of Kutch on the Kathiawar Peninsula, in 1907, people continued to call him Ranji.

His achievements were familiar to every cricket follower of the time, and to many who only took a passing interest in the game: his ten centuries and 2,780 runs in 1896, one equalling, the other establishing the record for a season; his aggregates of 3,159 in 1899 and 3,065 the following year, giving him the three leading totals then recorded; his five double centuries in 1900 when no one had previously

1

scored more than two in a season; his astonishing début for Sussex; his remarkable, defiant century against Australia on his first appearance in a Test; and, his unprecedented two centuries in the same match on the same day.

All these things helped establish Ranji as a phenomenon in the sporting world; as Sydney J. Southerton, editor of *Wisden*, wrote on his death, he 'was to become and to remain from 1895 until 1912 – with two breaks of four years each – the most talked-of man in cricket'. But his extraordinary hold over the British public went beyond the basic facts of his success, considerable though they were. There was the potent vision of a foreigner not only playing the English national game but doing so with such consummate skill that his method – his unerring use of cuts and glances, especially the leg-glance, a stroke of his own invention – was to cause a revolution in the way it was played. And there was also the perception of him as an Indian prince: the idea of a mysterious, fabulously wealthy Oriental in their midst proved irresistible to most people.

Neville Cardus, who was twelve years old in 1900 and watched cricket at Old Trafford at around that time, described something of this effect when he recalled in his *Autobiography* (1947): 'When the Sussex team came north, the imagination of Manchester boys ran riot . . . we beheld them like unto a cavalcade out of the warm south; and if it was not headed by Kumar Shri Ranjitsinhji on an elephant panoplied with gold and diademed with rubies, then a boy's fancy must not be counted more closely related to truth than obvious facts and appearance. Ranji cast his magic over all his team; we saw them in the glow of his Eastern splendour.'

Arthur Gilligan, who captained Sussex during the 1920s, also remembered, in *Sussex Cricket* (1933), being taken as a boy to see a county match at the Oval in 1908: 'Sussex were batting, and I waited for what seemed to be an interminable period till at last K. S. Ranjitsinhji came down the stone steps to a storm of cheers and applause. Naturally I was thrilled to the core, because the Jam Sahib had been my cricket hero since I was seven years old. I can visualize him now, with that elegant stance, that lightning control of the bowling, that glorious late cut, that superb leg-glance, and that perfectly wonderful eye, which seemed to indicate that he could see the ball in its flight a fraction of a second quicker than the average English player. What nectar of cricket it all was.'

Another thing that Jessop's comments reveal, and which Gilligan's account supports, was Ranji's complete mastery as a batsman. Jessop was, at his height, one of the best fast bowlers of his day and yet he felt that Ranji was impregnable, that he would never get him out. In *A Cricketer's Log* (1922), Jessop avowed that Ranjitsinhji was 'indisputably the greatest genius the cricket world has yet produced'. It is clear that here was no ordinary skill.

This is vouched for by others. C.B. Fry, who played alongside Ranji for Sussex and England and wrote perhaps the best assessment of his technique (in the *Windsor Magazine* in 1897), and A. G. Gardiner, who gave perhaps the best appreciation by an outside observer (in the *Daily News* in 1912), both regarded his ability as something that transcended the ordinary dictates of batsmanship. He was, they both agreed, an artist.

As will emerge, part of Ranjitsinhji's motivation for succeeding at cricket was a desire to promote himself in the eyes of the English and thus assist his ambitions to a prince's throne in India, but there was also a more aesthetic inspiration. Fry said he was 'an artist with an artist's eye for the game . . . Ranji's big innings please him in proportion as each stroke approaches perfection. He tries to make every stroke a thing of beauty in itself.' Gardiner was more explicit: 'If the supreme art is to achieve the maximum result with the minimum expenditure of effort, the Jam Sahib, as a batsman, is in a class by himself. We have no one to challenge with our coarser methods that curious refinement of style, which seems to have reduced action to its barest terms. It is the art of the great etcher who with a line reveals infinity. It is the art of the great dramatist who with a significant word shakes the soul. Schiller, said Coleridge, burns a city to create his effect of terror; Shakespeare drops a handkerchief and freezes our blood. The typical batsman performs a series of intricate evolutions in playing the ball; the Jam Sahib flicks his wrist and the ball bounds to the ropes. It is not jugglery, or magic; it is simply the perfect economy of means to an end.'

3

Gardiner felt obliged to stress that Ranji's batting was not jugglery or magic because that is what it was popularly supposed to be. There was an element of mystery in what he did, and how he did it, and some kind of conjuring trick seemed as good an explanation as any. He was commonly held to be a genius, who had come to England from India in about 1892, at the age of around twenty, who with barely any apprenticeship had become an almost instant and phenomenal success as a cricketer.

In fact, nothing could be further from the truth. Ranji's achievements were the fruits of years of hard and studious practice, and when he first began to attract attention for his performances, in Cambridge club matches in 1892, he had already been in England for four years, preparing the ground, in unexceptional anonymity, for his future triumphs. Those who played with him, like Jessop and Fry, testified to the amount of time he put in in the nets. He practised with as much purpose whether he had just been out for 100 or for 0. He was a severe critic of his own game, and if he was indeed a genius it was for his infinite capacity for taking pains, not for becoming a superlative cricketer overnight.

The one extraordinary gift he was born with was without a doubt his exceptional eye. This was confirmed by Jessop: 'I think that on the technical side his finest equipment was his eye. I played often with him and often against him, and it always seemed to me that his eye was infallible . . .' Fry and Gardiner also identified Ranji's wonderful power of sight as an important factor in his success, as it enabled him to judge the flight of the ball sooner and decide earlier which stroke to play. It was this, they both felt, that created the impression that with Ranji thought and action were one. The ball was certainly dispatched from his bat with unnerving speed. Sir Edwin Arnold, writing in the *Daily Telegraph* in 1896, likened his leg-glance to 'a shell from a seven-pounder – immense! audacious! unstoppable!' while Fry pointed out that the sheer rapidity with which Ranji executed his strokes may have suggested they were 'insolently careless' but in fact they were anything but.

Ranji thought deeply about cricket. Apart from working very hard at his batting, he did nothing blindly. He enjoyed theorizing about the game and putting those theories into practice. Fry said that some of his strokes had cost months of careful net practice. Even by 1897, when Ranji was in only his third full season of first-class cricket, Fry regarded his method as possessing 'a fine finish' with 'nothing crude or amateurish about it'. It was his free thinking, also, that led him to employ recognized strokes in original ways; to have, as Fry remembered in 1939, 'three strokes for every ball'.

It is difficult to imagine just how much of a shock Ranji's methods must have been to the cricketing public when he first arrived on the county scene in 1895. In *Good Days* (1934) Cardus attempted to express the impact of this fresh and incisive mind: 'In the 'nineties the game was absolutely English; it was even Victorian. W. G. Grace for years had stamped on cricket the English mark and the mark of the period. It was the age of simple first principles, of the stout respectability of straight bat and good-length balls; the flavours everywhere were John Bull's. And then suddenly this visitation of dusky, supple legerdemain happened; a man was seen playing cricket as nobody in England could possibly have played it. The honest length ball was not met by the honest straight bat, but there was a flick of the wrist, and lo! the straight ball was charmed away to the leg boundary. And nobody quite saw or understood how it all happened.' As H. S. Altham wrote in *A History of Cricket* (1926), 'the Jam Sahib . . . orientated afresh the setting of the cricket field'.

It was Ranji's ability to improvise that marked him out from his contemporaries. In this respect he was a disciple of Grace, who had been playing for thirty years and was forty-six when Ranji first appeared for Sussex, but whom Ranji himself described in *The Jubilee Book of Cricket* (1897) as 'the maker of modern batting'. He explained: 'What W. G. did was to unite in his mighty self all the good points of all the good players, and to make utility the criterion of style'. The guiding principles of batsmanship for both men were not to bat in what might be regarded as an elegant manner, as did so many players of their day, particularly those from the public schools, but to score runs and to score them safely.

Ranjitsinhji's methods were quite distinctive. Pelham Warner, describing them in *The Book of Cricket* (1944), wrote: 'With his wonderful eye and wrists, he could play back to almost any ball, however good a length, and however fast. Like Bradman, he seldom played a genuine forward stroke, for, again like Bradman, he found that balls to which he could not play back he could, with his quickness of foot, get to and drive.' Perhaps understandably, many players attempted to imitate Ranji's wonderfully successful technique, but with little comparable success. Indeed, his famous doctrine, 'Play back or drive', along with the vogue he established for an open, two-eyed stance, were unfairly blamed by some – particularly the old school, led by the influential Lord Harris, who had never liked what he had done – for English cricket's demise in the early 1920s, when eight consecutive Test matches were lost to Australia. Frank Iredale, the Australian batsman, confirmed in his *Thirty-Three Years of Cricket* (1920): 'He was a very fine player, but his style could never be copied.' It was a dangerous art.

What Ranji in fact did was to combine a safe and comprehensive method of scoring with beauty of execution. When the challenge of the bowlers had faded, an artist's desire for perfection continued to inspire him. The result was that he scored runs in greater numbers than ever before, greater even than Grace, though Ranji had the advantage of playing on better pitches, and his career average of 56.37 remained the highest for a batsman based in England until Boycott (56.84) retired in 1986.

A. G. Gardiner, in one of his most vivid images, and as we shall see one full of irony, conveyed what it must have been like to watch Ranji in full flow: 'He is not a miser hoarding up runs, but a millionaire spending them, with a splendid yet judicious prodigality. It is as though his pockets are bursting with runs that he wants to shower with his blessings upon the expectant multitude.' Fry, for his part, wondered why he ever got out. It was only the emergence in the late 1920s of Don Bradman, the ultimate run-scorer, that suggests Ranji had not quite reduced error to a practical minimum.

All of these things, considerable though they were, could not, however, fully explain Ranjitsinhji's achievement. His greatness came out of something that was rarely spoken of: that he succeeded as he did, when he did, despite the colour of his skin. And even he might not have managed it, had he not falsely laid claim to being a prince.

Jessop's appreciation of Ranji was not confined to his batting. In the same article as the one already quoted, he wrote: 'It was during the 'nineties that cricket reached its pinnacle as a national game and as a synonym of good sportsmanship. Ranji was one of the men who helped to put it there . . . I never heard him complain of a wicket, and I do not believe he ever did . . . I never heard him say an ill word of any player, whether on his own or on his opponents' side. That's a fine epitaph for a cricketer . . . behind all the superb brilliance of his technique and the glamour of his personality were supreme gifts of character. He was a perfect sportsman.'

Fry was equally effusive about Ranji's qualities as a man. 'He is mellow and kind and single-hearted, and has no spark of jealousy in his composition. No one has a keener eye for what is good in other people; the better they play the more he likes it.' Fry also referred to his 'genial ways'. A. A. Lilley, the Warwickshire and England wicket-keeper, recalled in his autobiography, published in 1912, that: 'The Jam was most loyal to this country, and had a great admiration both for England and the English people. That his good feelings towards us were fully reciprocated, was shown by the popularity he enjoyed on every cricket-field in the country'.

He received consistently glowing reports from people within the game. Open almost any book of reminiscences from the period and mention of Ranji will almost certainly be accompanied by reference to his modesty and his charm. Such praise, though, was not only confined to his life as a cricketer. Descriptions of him in his later years, when he was for over twenty-five years the ruler of Nawanagar, result in a similar sort of thing. When he died the newspapers were full of tributes to his regal qualities, and Lord Willingdon, the Viceroy of India, said that he had been 'an ambassador of co-operation, friendship and goodwill between the two races . . . A great ruler and a great gentleman.' More recently, Alan Ross, in his *Ranji: Prince of Cricketers* (1983), hailed him as 'an imaginative, conscientious and progressive administrator'.

There can be no doubt that Ranjitsinhji was, for the most part, an exceptionally charming man, who could provide wonderful company and was capable of acts of great generosity, but to read all this is to be given a vision of a man almost blindingly perfect. He seems almost too good to have been true. Which of course he was. Like everyone else, Ranji had faults. The difference was that in his case people appeared hardly ever to talk about them.

It is just possible to detect the occasional spot on the dazzling sun. Iredale, while admitting that Ranji 'was a cheery chap to his friends, and always had a jovial, free and easy character', also observed: 'He was strong in his likes and dislikes. He was sensitive of criticism, and had a profound dislike to be misunderstood.' Alfred Gaston, in his introduction to *With Stoddart's Team in Australia* (1898), alluded to Ranji's 'overpowering modesty' (can modesty really be modesty if it is overpowering?), while another posthumous assessment, by *The Times*, ventured to suggest that, though one of the most likeable of men, 'he could be ruthless in the pursuit of his aims and was uncannily adroit'. For this impertinence the newspaper was promptly pulled up by a friend and reverential admirer of Ranji, although, as we shall see, contemporary confidential government documents, monitoring his behaviour in India and Britain both before and after his succession as Jam Sahib, indicate that the description was, like Iredale's, at times hardly an exaggeration.

And then there was the well-concealed affair of him apparently relieving a childhood friend of what, at modern prices, was well over £350,000. We shall return to that business later, but it seems to reinforce the impression that Ranji's straightforwardly attractive public persona was complemented by a less well known and altogether less acceptable side.

There is one description of Ranji as a batsman that could have applied equally well to him as a man. It was one of his closest friends, C. B. Fry, who in 1897 wrote: 'Ranji has made a science of taking liberties.'

2

THE PRINCE WHO NEVER WAS

To GAIN A fuller understanding of the personality of this extra-ordinary cricketer, it is first necessary to go back to his childhood, particularly to one event when he was only nine years old which was to have a profound influence on his future. The unusual circumstances of Ranjitsinhji's childhood have quite rightly been recognized for the important bearing they had on his development, but they have nevertheless remained the subject of much confusion and dispute.

On the morning of 10 August 1882 in the ancient and sprawling palace in the heart of the state's capital, Jamnagar, Vibhaji, the then Jam of Nawanagar, was presented with a son and heir. Despite claims made later, there can be little doubt about the circumstances of the birth. The child, named Jaswantsinhji, was born to Janbai, a Muslim woman of Vibhaji's court. Vibhaji himself, though fifty-five years of age, was almost certainly the father. Although he had previously been given only one son, Kalubha, twenty-six years earlier, he had had daughters, and only the year before, in May 1881, Janbai had been pregnant but miscarried. There was, moreover, an important witness; the birth was attended by a European midwife, a Mrs McClelland, who had been living in the palace for five weeks (the baby was a month overdue) and whose services Vibhaji had specifically asked for. Once Jaswantsinhji was born, Mrs McClelland sent a certificate to the British Resident for the Western States of India, verifying the birth.

Another thing that cannot be contested, sadly, is that Vibhaji was a weak, ageing man and a poor ruler. Like every Indian prince, he was fond of regarding himself as a fine administrator, enlightened in

9

the spheres of education and justice, dedicated to public works, the possessor of a reputation for charity, and a distinguished sportsman. He was proud of having been appointed a Knight Commander of the Order of the Star of India, of having been among the first princes to welcome the Prince of Wales (later Edward VII) during his triumphal visit to India in 1875–76, and of having been a guest for the proclamation in Delhi of Queen Victoria as Empress of India, when he had received as a personal distinction an addition of four guns to Nawanagar's eleven-gun salute (the British awarded the leading states gun salutes, of anything up to twenty-one, as a reward for loyalty).

The reality was something different. His first son, Kalubha, had grown up a thoroughly unscrupulous and violent youth who, by the age of twenty, held the court at Jamnagar in terror. Vibhaji, shown scant respect by his son and his son's faction, had been at a loss as to how to control them. Warned to take care for his life, Vibhaji had furtively sought the assistance of the British, who began to take an interest after receiving reports of a multiple rape in the capital by Kalubha and some of his followers. In October 1877, Kalubha was exiled from the state and barred forever from the Nawanagar succession. After some debate, his eight wives and one young son were allowed to live on in the palace, but their lands were confiscated and they too were excluded from affairs of state. Thus, significantly, for almost five years before the birth of Jaswantsinhji, there had been no natural heir to the Nawanagar throne.

None of these events have seriously been disputed. What has always been in some doubt is whether or not Janbai, as a Muslim, could be a legitimate wife of Vibhaji, the head of a Hindu state. Even at the time Jaswantsinhji was born, British officials in the Resident's office at Rajkot were not certain as to her exact status.

However, what they were then probably unaware of, and what has not been acknowledged since, is that an almost identical situation had occurred in the state not so many years before. Kalubha's mother, Dhanbai, was also a Muslim (she and Janbai were, in fact, sisters) and the British, always wary of mixed marriages, had set up an inquiry to establish whether the leading families in Kathiawar objected to the Jadeja Rajputs of Nawanagar marrying Muslims, or to their issue succeeding to a princely throne. The inquiry, started in 1867 and carried out by the Resident's office, took five years to complete. It concluded that marriage between a Hindu and a Muslim was not invalid, nor was it contrary to past practices. Only three Kathiawar states had declared their disapproval of Vibhaji's marriage to Dhanbai and refused to recognize her son, Kalubha, as heir, and it transpired that two of those ruling houses had themselves contracted marriages with Muslims in recent times. The inquiry also alluded to the fact that Vibhaji had married Janbai, mother of the new baby, by an acceptable ceremony in 1862 and stated that he had, in all, four Muslim and eleven Rajput wives. Equally striking, it had established that the Jadeja Rajputs of Nawanagar had never had much regard or respect for any religion but in descent and custom were in close affinity with the Muslim faith. The founder of the state, Jam Rawal, who had emigrated from Kutch in 1535, had brought the Mohammadan religion with him and assumed the caste of a Rajput only for certain purposes. It emerged that Vibhaji's own father, Jam Ranmalji, had taken a Muslim as one of his wives.

This is not the version of events that has become accepted. Two books, *The Land of Ranji and Duleep* by Charles Kincaid (1931) and *The Biography of Colonel His Highness Shri Sir Ranjitsinhji* by Roland Wild (1934), either commissioned by Ranji or written with his or his family's co-operation for reasons which will become apparent, were subsequently to propagate an alternative account. They have been closely followed in their conclusions by Alan Ross, who accepted in his book, seemingly without question, that Wild's biography 'must be regarded as an authoritative, as well as an authorised, version'.

Kincaid and Wild raised doubts about Vibhaji's ability to be Jaswantsinhji's father; about Janbai being the child's mother; and about the status of their relationship. As far as the two authors were concerned, the influence of Vibhaji's four Muslim consorts was – could only be – totally pernicious. But the arguments they put forward were either contrary to the known facts or have no substantiation in the abundant British records that survive on the subject. They claimed that Vibhaji never produced any male issue, that Dhanbai was pregnant before he met her (he had in fact known her for two years before

11

Kalubha was born) but the 'old man' had been too overjoyed to ask any questions (he was only twenty-nine at the time!); while in Janbai's case, the infant Jaswantsinhji was 'almost certainly brought in from outside' (although Kincaid and Wild were not always consistent in this, for there were also ready references to Vibhaji's 'bastard'). Vibhaji, they said, had not gone through any marriage ceremony with Janbai and, although he had 'married' Dhanbai (who was described as a former prostitute) in an 'obsolete and illegal ceremony', Kalubha had been disinherited because he had attempted to poison Vibhaji's food, in a plot hatched by the malignant Muslim faction at court.

Such extreme and prejudiced views were of the kind normally associated only with the staunchest Rajputs, with the proud warriors of Udaipur, Jodhpur and Jaipur, among whom only marriage to another Rajput was acceptable, and Ranjitsinhji was indeed connected to these zealots, and received their assistance in his darkest days. But whatever the exact inspiration for the accounts of Kincaid and Wild, thus were the pedigrees destroyed of the only two men who ever threatened, directly or indirectly, Ranjitsinhji's chances of succeeding to the Nawanagar throne.

News of the birth of Janbai's child, and particularly whether or not she had produced a boy, was anxiously awaited in Sarodar, a small hillside village some thirty-five miles south of Jamnagar. It was the remote home of squires and their shepherds, although the villagers also farmed for wheat, millet and, when the rains were favourable, sugar cane. Overlooking the plains at the highest reach of the settlement was a stone fort, among the inhabitants of which was a branch of Nawanagar's ruling family.

Four years earlier, following Kalubha's disinheritance in 1877, when it had seemed important that he should find at least a temporary heir, Vibhaji had turned to these relations and asked them to provide him with an adoptive son. This was the practice of the ruling family in such circumstances; Ranmalji, Vibhaji's father, had come from there when an earlier Jam Sahib died without heir. This time, Jhalamsinhji, a cousin and an officer in Vibhaji's army, and the most senior member of the Sarodar family, met Vibhaji's request by giving a young son of his own, Umedsinhji. The formal ceremony had taken place one morning at Chela in March 1878 and the boy was given a new name, Raisinhji, to mark his new identity, but six months later he died of a fever at his father's house in Sarodar. (It was later claimed by Kincaid and Wild that he had been poisoned with arsenic in the palace by Dhanbai and that 'Vibhaji himself verified the traces of poison in his blood'.)

This episode had only made Vibhaji all the more determined to produce another son of his own, but nevertheless a few weeks later, in October 1878, as a temporary expedient, a grandson of Jhalamsinhji was picked out as the next, prospective heir. This was Ranjitsinhji. He was just six years old, a delicate child, not in the best of health; as a youngster he was to suffer from smallpox. Wild described him as a 'slim and frail' boy, and the irony of his name, which meant 'The Lion that Conquers in Battle', was not lost on many people. He had been born in one of the sparse ground-floor living quarters that faced into a small courtyard of the fort, on 10 September 1872, not to his father's senior wife but as the first son of a second – something generally unknown during Ranji's lifetime but vouched for by the present Jam Sahib's court historian. Had his later admirers in England been able to see the isolated spot in which he first caught the light of day they would have been even more amazed by him than they were. While still a small child he had been sent to live at the court of his uncle, the Raj Sahib of Dhrangadhara, 150 miles to the north-east of Sarodar, where he started to acquire the rudiments of his education and where he probably was when unexpectedly summoned home to see the Jam Sahib.

The youthful Ranjitsinhji must have made a satisfactory impression, because shortly afterwards Vibhaji took him to Rajkot to secure the approval of the Resident, Lt.–Col. Lionel Barton. This was to be the last recorded instance of Vibhaji and Ranjitsinhji – the middle-aged ruler and the young boy who would one day, by an unanticipated and extraordinary sequence of events, succeed to his position as Jam Sahib – being in each other's company. Shortly after, Ranjitsinhji returned to Rajkot, where he was provided with his own accommodation, a bungalow, as was the custom for a person about to join a royal court, and an allowance of 10,000 korees a year (about £165). For eighteen months he lived there, with a guardian, a tutor and an array of servants, before, in June 1880, at the age of seven, entering the Rajkumar College for princes in Rajkot, which had almost forty boys in attendance.

However, Vibhaji stalled from having the boy formally adopted as his heir. The reason, largely hidden until now, lies with Ranjitsinhji's family and, specifically, with the personality of his father. First of all, the Sarodar branch was connected by marriage not only with the state of Dhrangadhara but also with the mighty house of Jodhpur, and both these fiercely Rajput states frowned on the lax practices of the ruling Jadejas of Nawanagar (Dhrangadhara, the senior house of the Jhala Rajputs, had been one of the three Kathiawar states to refuse to recognize Kalubha because of his Muslim extraction). Very possibly the attitudes of one set of relatives had come to influence the opinions of another. Whatever the explanation, according to the account Vibhaji subsequently gave to the Resident, when he first asked the Sarodar branch to provide him with an adoptive heir they began to adopt unwelcome attitudes, and when he asked them to produce another heir, their naked ambition emerged: 'The whole family assumed an attitude as if their son was already the future ruler of my state irrespective of my wishes or my pleasure. They did not care to conceal their enmity . . .' Having been on the fringes of power for some time, Jhalamsinhji's family aspired to possessing influence of their own and appear to have interpreted Vibhaji's second request for an heir as a sign that they could not be denied the Nawanagar throne. They felt that, in Ranjitsinhji, a significant turn in their fortunes was as good as accomplished.

The worst offender – a man who came to inspire absolute loathing in Vibhaji – was Ranjitsinhji's father, Jiwansinhji. He was, ostensibly, a farmer; in reality he was a fearsome drunkard and the scourge of the district. According to the present Jam Sahib, the local bards had a song about him of how the thunder of his horse's hooves made the local women miscarry. His bearded figure became known to Vibhaji only as that of a man 'unprincipled and given to habitual intemperance and bad habits', who seemed to take pride in openly flouting his authority. If Jiwansinhji was the character Vibhaji said he was, it is possible that it was in order to give Ranjitsinhji refuge from his father's tyranny that he was sent away as a small boy to stay with his relations at Dhrangadhara.

Vibhaji, reluctant to complete the adoption of Ranjitsinhji after seeing the conduct of his immediate relations, thus allowed several years to pass without resolving the position of an heir and by August 1882, when, to his undisguised delight, Janbai presented him with a boy, he had long since determined never to be persuaded to proceed with his choice of Ranjitsinhji. When word of Jaswantsinhji's birth reached Sarodar, it must have been apparent to Jhalamsinhji and his family, if it had not already become so, that hopes of a child of theirs ever sitting on the Nawanagar throne had virtually disappeared beyond repair.

Meanwhile, Ranjitsinhji continued to be educated at the princes' college in Rajkot and to be treated with all the respect due an heir to a throne. Although he was to flourish in school life, his childhood must have been a pretty lonely and unhappy one. He appears to have had only one close friend from the time before he was ten, his half-brother, Devisinhji, who was eight years older than himself.

It was a traumatic period of his life, and it was to leave its mark. He was to grow up with an insatiable need for recognition and praise that was to show itself in a sensitivity to criticism of any kind and a constant need to test peoples' affections for him. Throughout his adult life, the area that found him most sensitive was his family background. He was to idolize and idealize both his mother (of whom he would have a relief made which resembled the Madonna) and his father ('by common consent the most splendid horseman in the province', according to another biography, *Ranjitsinhji Prince of Cricket*, by Percy Cross Standing, published in 1903).

In later life Ranjitsinhji encouraged a fictionalized account of his childhood. Roland Wild's biography, for instance, was to suggest that Vibhaji turned to his Sarodar relations for an heir not because it was simply a long-standing family practice but because they had proved themselves worthy of such a gesture; Jhalamsinhji was said to have shown heroic service in battle.

Ranjitsinhji's disappointment at coming so close to being heir to the throne, of being denied finally by Jaswantsinhji's birth, was never to leave him. It was so great that it led him to create a version of events that would account for the suspicion that his own adoption had never been completed, by claiming that it had in fact taken place in secret. Wild's opening passage, which is among the most graphic in his book and was presumably based on the testimony of Ranjitsinhji himself, described how the ceremony, binding in Hindu law, was conducted secretly: 'due to the fear of zenana jealousy . . . it took place outside Jamnagar, the capital, in a temple known as the Dwarka Puri, a mile from the city. An hour before dawn, a slowly-moving cavalcade left Jamnagar. Both the Jam Sahib and Ranjitsinhji travelled in "sigrans", the closed carts commonly used for purdah ladies. A circuitous route was taken, and the escort was formed of eighty lancers. The boy's father and grandfather watched the ceremony, which was officially recorded by the India Office, the Government of India, and the Bombay Government . . . No word was spoken at court regarding the adoption.' The theory of a secret ceremony first appeared in Kincaid's book and has been accepted without question ever since, but, contrary to Wild's claims, there is no evidence of such a ceremony in the files or ledgers (which record the existence and movement of all documents) of the India Office in London, the Government of India or the Bombay Government – which suggests, fairly conclusively, that it never happened.

In June 1884, an intriguing development took place: the British authorities in Rajkot attempted to dissuade Vibhaji from having Jaswantsinhji, now twenty-two months old, recognized as his heir. They did so not because of any doubts regarding the exact status of the boy or the boy's mother, but because the British *preferred* the choice of Ranjitsinhji.

There had been consternation in Bombay earlier that year when it was discovered, through Vibhaji's application for Jaswantsinhji to be officially named heir, that Ranjitsinhji's adoption had never been carried out. The governments of Bombay (in January 1879) and of India (in February 1879) had given their approval for his selection to

16

go ahead and they had assumed that the formal ceremony had long since been carried out. It appears however that, somewhat surprisingly, there had been no communication from the Resident's Rajkot office informing his superiors that no further steps had been taken in this direction. Bombay had not been pleased to learn that there had been no officially recognized heir in Nawanagar for almost six years.

Bombay, clearly annoyed at being placed in such a position of ignorance and at the dangerous situation that the absence of a successor presented, had written to the Resident's office stressing firmly the need to impress on the Jam Sahib the gravity of his latest request. The day after receiving the message, the Resident himself, Lt.–Col. Edward West, set out by horse from the spacious, comfortable environs of Rajkot on the fifty-mile journey to the capital of Nawanagar. He met Vibhaji at the Lal bungalow, on the outskirts of Jamnagar, where Vibhaji liked to go occasionally to get away from the bustle of court and where they were able to speak confidentially. West tried vigorously, but ultimately unsuccessfully, to persuade Vibhaji to go ahead with his adoption of Ranjitsinhji, which is noteworthy not least because, as West would have been only too well aware, Vibhaji was perfectly entitled to name as heir anyone he chose. West had already privately conceded, in a preliminary report to the government of Bombay, that, 'There can I suppose be little doubt that if looked at solely from a legal point of view the adoption of Ranjitsinhji is incomplete.'

West's motive behind his insistence on the choice of Ranjitsinhji, though, was not so much legal as what would be most convenient to the British, who were anxious, naturally, to have well-educated and intelligent men ruling the princely states. West had told Bombay: '. . . if personal character of his candidates is to be taken into consideration we know that Ranjitsinhji is a boy of remarkable promise . . . Of course we know nothing of the character of the infant Jaswantsinhji, but even if he is recognized as heir he is sure to be brought up in the zenana and subjected to influences which would spoil the most promising material. In the case of Kalubha we have a proof of how pernicious these influences may be.' West, though, was ignoring the fact that Jaswantsinhji would also one day enjoy the benefits of the Rajkumar College and that his upbringing need not resemble that of Kalubha, who had been twenty-four by the time the college opened in 1870 and was therefore unable to benefit from it.

West had concluded: 'I cannot acknowledge that the succession of Jaswantsinhji in preference to Ranjitsinhji would be for the good of the state or in accordance with the desires of the best part of the Jam's subjects . . . while I sympathise with the natural feelings which have led His Highness to take this action.'

West, however, could not say this to Vibhaji at their meeting. Instead, he suggested that even if Ranjitsinhji was to be overlooked it might not follow that Jaswantsinhji would be recognized as successor; another apparent change in the succession might encourage a claim to be made on behalf of Lakhuba, the twelve-year-old son of the disgraced Kalubha. This was an extremely speculative line of argument and even if a claim was to be made for Lakhuba, West had little evidence to support the idea that his case would prove stronger than Jaswantsinhji's. But West was clearly hoping that once the seeds of doubt were sown in Vibhaji's mind, he might prefer to drop the matter and 'be satisfied with the heir that he had himself selected, who had been approved by the Government and who united in himself so many desirable qualities'.

Vibhaji, however, was not to be moved. He answered, patiently but firmly, that Jaswantsinhji was his son and he wished him to be his successor. The case of Lakhuba, he said, had been settled at the time of Kalubha's disinheritance: he had been given a grant in recognition of his former position. When West attempted to persist with his arguments, Vibhaji grew angry. Was it not natural, he declared, that he should desire to be succeeded by his own son? He would never give up his rights, he added, and if necessary would take his case to the Viceroy.

West, muttering something about asking the Jam Sahib to think the matter over, took his leave, his mission a failure. Vibhaji, for once roused to boldness and defying the later theory of Kincaid and Wild that he only ever acted under the threat of poison from his Muslim women, promptly sent a letter after him, repudiating once more West's alarmist talk. If Lakhuba had not been disinherited along with

18

his father, he pointed out, there would have been no need to seek to adopt Ranjitsinhji in the first place.

Although West's attempt to dissuade Vibhaji from his course of action was thus unsuccessful, the episode illustrates the degree to which the British were prepared to interfere in a succession case in an effort to obtain what they saw as a desirable outcome, even if legally that outcome had little substance. It also shows how far back went their notion that Ranjitsinhji, if given the chance, would make a worthy ruler.

In October 1884, four months after West's visit to Jamnagar, Vibhaji learned that he had got his way: Jaswantsinhji was recognized as heir to the Nawanagar throne. Bombay had agreed to pass the decision over to the Government of India, and Lord Ripon, the Viceroy, after considering Vibhaji's lengthy application, had given his verdict on 3 October.

However, the Viceroy made a recommendation that was to have far-reaching and unlikely consequences. Although Ranjitsinhji had not been formally adopted, it was felt he should receive some sort of compensation: 'a suitable provision should be made for the maintenance of Ranjitsinhji, whose position under the altered circumstances constitutes a strong claim upon the generosity of H. H.'

Vibhaji, having achieved his most ardent wish, was quite happy to oblige. He wrote to West on 22 October:

. . . 'As the British Government has done me the honour to leave it to me to make suitable provision for Ranjitsinhji's maintenance, and has at the same time advised me that he has a strong claim upon my generosity, I have, while holding the same opinion as to his rights . . . decided to double the allowance mentioned in the agreement passed with Ranjitsinhji's father, and will grant him and the heirs male of his body in perpetuity a village yielding 20,000 korees a year . . . I wish it to be distinctly understood that Ranjitsinhji's father or his heirs will have no concern whatever with this grant . . .

I am sure you will not think it necessary that Ranjitsinhji should continue to have the same establishment as he has had hitherto. I do not propose to take upon myself the task of making the necessary alterations. It is my fixed intention to leave the entire management and control of Ranjitsinhji's education to the Agency, and wish in no way to be concerned with it farther than to arrange that the sum credited to Ranjitsinhji as above shall be always available either every month or every quarter . . . I am sure Ranjitsinhji's own interests will be best served by my leaving the control and guidance of his education to you . . . At the same time it shall be most agreeable to me to be relieved of all risk of any further discussion with his father or his family . . .'

West regarded Vibhaji's proposal as 'a very liberal act', adding that the 'arrangement, too, for placing at the disposal of the Political Agency the funds requisite for the boy's education and maintenance, has been made in the truest interests of the latter, for his father is addicted to drinking and, if trusted with the funds, would probably not employ them very judiciously'.

Life for the young Ranjitsinhji, who turned twelve a few weeks before Jaswantsinhji was officially recognized as heir, was, initially at any rate, little changed by the Government of India's decision. Although he no longer possessed the bungalow in Rajkot and although Vibhaji passed over the handling of all his affairs to the Resident's office, it seems to have been promptly decided that he should continue to be educated at the princes' college, with the fees being taken out of his increased allowance; his life was thus scarcely distinguishable from the time when he had been treated by most people as heir to a throne. But there was, of course, an important difference, one which the young man could not have been expected fully to appreciate immediately. He had seemingly been deprived once and for all of the chance of ever succeeding to the Nawanagar throne.

There are several indications that he gradually realized the full implications of what had happened, and that, once he did so, what Roland Wild was to describe as the 'theft' of his future was a severe and lasting blow.

The first recorded reference to Ranjitsinhji after the Viceroy's verdict was about a month later, at the college prizegiving at the end of November 1884, when Sir James Fergusson, the Governor of Bombay, was the guest of honour. During his report on the school's progress, Chester Macnaghten, the principal of the school, said: 'Ranjitsinhji of Nawanagar, whether as regards attention to study or general conduct, may be mentioned with special commendation . . . Your Excellency is aware that a great disappointment has recently befallen him, and nothing in his behaviour has been more admirable than the wisdom and fortitude with which he has borne his trial.' Interestingly, even as late as February 1888, well over three years after Jaswantsinhji's recognition and when Ranjitsinhji was about to leave the college, Macnaghten had cause to publicly return to this theme. He said then that '. . . a better or manlier boy has never resided within this college . . . Disappointments and troubles come to us all, and he has had his, and has borne them bravely. Looking back on his college career, I think he may look back without regret, and feel that the time he has wisely spent here has been a happy as well as useful time. It is a blessed thing for us all when we can look back and feel like that.'

There is more than a hint in these last remarks that Macnaghten was trying to assuage the oppression Ranjitsinhji may have been feeling at being, almost alone among the college's pupils, neither a prince nor an heir, and no longer with the prospects of becoming either. Although he was to excel academically and at sport, suggesting that he led a largely happy and stimulating existence at the college, it is possible to surmise that he was inclined to brood over the unfortunate series of events that had led to him being deprived of the promise of a princely throne, probably the greatest honour he could have imagined being bestowed on any young man. Perhaps he even kept, and rued over, the letter he had received from Vibhaji, dated 22 October 1884 (the same day the Jam Sahib had written to West with details of the settlement made for Ranjitsinhji), telling him of the altered arrangements.

We selected you to take you in adoption but the ceremony of adoption was not performed. In the meantime in our zenana, Kumar

Jaswantsinhji has been born to our wife Janbai and he has become the heir to the gadi [throne]; and it has been arranged to give you Khilos village [near Rajkot] out of our generosity and grace on the following conditions.

The right of enjoying the village rests only in you, your sons and grandsons, that is to heirs of your body successively. On failure of such a line the village would revert to our gadi. Your father or brothers or their heirs have no right whatsoever on the village.

You are a child at present and are studying at the Rajkumar College. Therefore the Khilos village has not been handed over to you in possession but will remain in the management of the state. When you attain majority, the village will be handed over to you. Meantime, korees 20,000 will be placed to your credit in the accounts annually and the expenses of your college education and maintenance will be defrayed therefrom; and when you attain majority, the village Khilos will be given over to you with the surplus if any that may be found to remain . . .

You and your heirs etc should conduct yourselves loyally and with fidelity with us and with our heirs and descendants who might succeed us to the Nawanagar gadi so that no doubt about it may arise . . .

Here, surely, is conclusive proof that Ranjitsinhji's formal adoption was never carried out.

The finality of this letter and the fact that only six years earlier Vibhaji had apparently wanted to be a father to him must have stung the adolescent Ranji to the quick. His disappointment was to reveal itself many years later in the opening pages of Wild's authorized biography, which interpreted the transfer of his care from Vibhaji to the Resident not as a sign that the Jam Sahib wanted nothing more to do with his Sarodar relatives but as due to the need to protect a secretly adopted heir.

If Ranji was indeed disappointed that Vibhaji had gone back on his intention to be to him the father he had never properly had, then he was fortunate (and so was English cricket) that another person stepped in to fulfil that role: Chester Macnaghten, the principal of the Rajkumar College. It was Macnaghten who inspired his pupil to persevere at the school and impressed on him that if he did well there he would be ultimately rewarded. It was a lesson that Ranji seems to have absorbed; he applied himself vigorously to everything he did while under the guidance of Macnaghten, while often in class photographs he is to be found with his eyes seemingly fixed intently on the horizon.

Macnaghten, who was thirty-seven when Ranji first became one of his pupils, had been in charge of the school since it had opened in 1870. The college was one of a number of schools set up by the Government of India specifically to 'fit the young chiefs and nobles of India physically, morally and intellectually for the responsibilities that lay before them'; instead of them being 'solitary suns in petty firmaments' they would become 'co-ordinate atoms in a larger whole'. In reproducing, as he did, all the character-building qualities of the British public school (it was possible to observe on the school's playing fields the curious spectacle of young Indian princes grappling with the complexities of English sports and games), Macnaghten was not only fulfilling this task but also recreating an environment he himself had never known; asthma had prevented him going to Harrow and he had been educated privately. Possibly this explained why he felt the strongest affinity to the pupil whose upbringing had been perhaps as lonely as his own.

Under Macnaghten's tutelage, Ranjitsinhji thrived. Although his days at school meant separation from Devisinhji, his half-brother, in about 1883 he met for the first time Mansur Khachar, a fellow-pupil, a prince and member of the ruling family in Jasdan, a minor state in western India. Mansur was his junior but they struck up such a friendship that they were to spend practically every subsequent long vacation together in Mansur's home state. It is uncertain when, if ever, Ranjitsinhji returned to his own home.

He had been at the school only two years when Macnaghten first declared him his most exceptional pupil and the one with the greatest promise. He was to accumulate a number of prizes and by the end of his fourth year, 1883–84, when he had risen to the top of the second class, Macnaghten, in his annual report, wrote of him as, 'by far the

23

cleverest and nearly the youngest boy in the college. He is as vigorous in body as in mind, and is an exceedingly promising kumar.'

This was only the first allusion Macnaghten was to make to Ranjit-sinhji's aptitude for sport. The following year, by when Ranjitsinhji knew he had been displaced in Vibhaji's affections, Macnaghten commented that he possessed 'that suppleness of mind combined with suppleness of body which no one can take from him but himself and which is the main condition of moral happiness'. When he had gone with Vibhaji as a six-year-old to see the Resident in Rajkot, Lt.–Col. Barton had given him his first kindergarten box, in which he had found six or seven wooden balls. That had possibly been the start of it all, with the solitary hours at the bungalow being filled with ball games, perhaps of his own invention. At school he was to become good at sport in general and by the time he left he had won gymnastics competitions and was the leading all-round player at both lawn tennis, which he had taken to at an early age, and cricket.

He had been taught the basics of cricket at the school by a Parsee when he was about ten or eleven years of age, and he represented the school for the first time in 1883. In 1884 he captained the side and was to do so again in his three subsequent years. In one of the last matches he played for the school, against Salaya in January 1888, he scored 81 not out (in a total of 126 all out) and 8 not out, and took 10 wickets. According to Standing's biography, during Ranjitsinhji's final year, in matches of the most rudimentary sort, he managed one score of just over 200 and several centuries, although Standing was to say elsewhere that an innings of 206 not out in a club match in 1895 was his first double century. Ranji himself, in a speech at Cambridge when he had become a celebrated batsman, admitted to having scored only two hundreds at school. Whatever the truth of the matter, it would be wrong to say that the ability for the game of this gifted, serious and rather proud young man had assumed any particular importance either for himself or for others (as has been suggested in the case of Macnaghten) while he was still at the school. Tennis was then his first love, and he later said that he had once played tennis better than he did cricket.

3

A STRANGE LIGHT OUT OF THE EAST

W HAT WAS TO happen to Ranjitsinhji when he left the college
was a problem that must have sorely vexed Macnaghten. Life
in Sarodar had little to offer the boy, while he would have had to
wait several years before he was of sufficient age to take over the
management of Khilos, even if that was what he wished. Realistically,
there was nowhere for him to go. However, before the matter could
acquire alarming proportions, his progress at the college became such
that a happy solution rapidly presented itself: he would go to England
to complete his education at Cambridge University.

This was a step that was to transform his life, although not in a
way that anyone could have anticipated when he sailed for Britain in
March 1888, accompanied by Macnaghten and two other boys of
similar promise, Ramsinhji of Bhavnagar and his friend Mansur
Khachar.

They had been in England only a few weeks when, in May,
Macnaghten took Ranjitsinhji to see a first-class cricket match. They
went to Kennington Oval, one of the most important sporting venues
in the world: county and Test cricket, international football and rugby
matches were staged there, as well as FA Cup finals. Moreover, they
went to watch Surrey playing the Australians, who were making the
first London appearance of their tour, and the crowd on the first day
was well over 6,000; curved banks of spectators enclosed the rounded
expanse of grass; row upon row of top-hatted and bowler-hatted
spectators watching fifteen white-clad figures roam the field in ritualis-
tic fashion.

It is only possible to speculate whether Ranji would have pursued
his interest in cricket had he not been taken to a game by Macnaghten,

or had they gone to a less impressive match. The fact remains that they did go, and Ranji was spellbound. The way the game was played would have been very different from anything he had experienced before. At college, the teams had usually consisted of fifteen a side rather than eleven, they dressed in native costume, and the bowling was always underarm. They had no net facilities; when they practised, they did so on the open field in front of the pavilion. It had often been necessary during their matches, which were either against local schools or regiments, or between teams within the college, to suspend play for two or three hours in the middle of the day because of the heat. Sometimes, too, they would not play on grass but used matting, which was never done in England. The masters had acted as umpires and the rules they applied were a rough and ready interpretation of the Laws of Cricket.

Did, perhaps, some of the finer points begin to be seen by him, that day? How, for example, when the Australian opening batsmen employed the cut stroke productively, the Surrey captain had effectively cut off this area of scoring by adjusting his field and instructing his bowlers to alter their line of attack. Such subtleties can have only rarely entered the school games. Another contrast was that, generally speaking, in county cricket the professionals were left to do most of the bowling, while the amateurs did the batting; at school, Ranjitsinhji had liked to take the lead in both. Also, he was probably surprised at the number of catches put down by the Surrey side, for he would later recall that one of the first things that struck him about the English game was the poor standard of fielding. Unusually, at Rajkot they had actually practised this aspect of the game, often for over an hour at a time, and Ranjitsinhji, even by the age fifteen, had become a brilliant fielder.

There were two things about the day that made it particularly memorable for him. First of all, during the lunch interval, Macnaghten took him round to the pavilion and introduced him to Charles Alcock, secretary of the Surrey club, who in turn took them to meet several members of the Australian touring team. Ranjitsinhji, understandably thrilled, shook hands with them and for several minutes chatted to them about cricket.

Secondly, he saw one of the Australians, C. T. B. Turner, who was by reputation a bowler, play a spectacular innings. Coming in with his side in some difficulty at 146 for 5, he wasted little time in taking the attack to the Surrey bowlers and even when wickets continued to fall at the other end kept the spectators entertained with a series of drives, cuts and leg-side hits to the boundary. With a straight drive for 4 Turner reached his 100 after only about two hours' batting, during which he had not made a serious error. Almost directly, he was caught at the wicket, and cheered all the way back to the pavilion by a bigger gathering of people than the youthful Ranjitsinhji can ever have seen before in his life.

Ranji was so impressed by this performance that he would write in his book *With Stoddart's Team in Australia* that he did not see an innings to equal it for almost ten years. He had seen to what heights of excellence cricket could be taken, learnt of the heroic proportions of which it was capable. And perhaps he began to think for the first time that here was something worth striving for.

Whether or not his visit to the Oval was the inspiration, very soon Ranjitsinhji began to hope that he might win a Blue at Cambridge – not at tennis, as had originally been his aim, but at cricket. No one at that time would have believed that an Indian was remotely capable of representing one of the two great nurseries of the first-class game, but it was something he began to work uncertainly towards.

His progress for a long time was slow, in fact virtually negligible. He took part in a few matches in London before leaving in October 1888 for Cambridge, where the following summer, according to Wild, he played occasionally at a local school, St Faith's. These matches were of the simplest kind and his knowledge of the game remained limited. During 1890, which he himself described as 'my first year of cricket' and when he occasionally played for Fitzwilliam Hall, a team of non-collegiate students but indifferent in quality, there was an embarrassing moment when he was given out because he did not understand one of the laws. He later described the incident in his *Jubilee Book of Cricket*: 'I was playing a game on Parker's Piece at Cambridge. I hit a ball to leg, and a couple of runs resulted. The ball

27

was thrown in by the fieldsman, and it hit the bowler's wicket. The ball having passed ten yards or so away, I immediately called upon the other batsman for a run. I trotted down the wicket very slowly, and very confident of my security. Meanwhile one of the fieldsmen sent the ball to the bowler, who pulled one of the stumps out of the ground. Much to my chagrin and disappointment, the umpire, on being appealed to, unhesitatingly gave me out.'

After they had spent six months in London, Macnaghten returned to India, having found tutors and guardians in Cambridge for his three charges. Ranjitsinhji and Ramsinhji were both to live with the Reverend Louis Borissow, chaplain of Trinity College since 1871 and possibly known to Macnaghten through their own days together at the university. Borissow was not Ranji's first tutor in England; according to E. H. D. Sewell, in *Cricket Wallah* (1945), the young man had already disliked and quarrelled with a previous one, which may suggest he was not finding it easy to make the transition to his new way of life.

Happily, there was companionship for the two boys at the vicarage in Chaucer Road, for Borissow had several sons (two of whom were of similar age to themselves: Clement, eighteen and about to go up to the university himself, and Harold, sixteen) and two teenage daughters (Edith, fifteen, with whom Ranji was later to form an intimate attachment, and Beatrice, eleven). It was originally intended that they should stay there until the end of their courses, but Ranji was not to do so. However, by the time he left, it was a home he had contentedly made his own and the ties he formed with the Borissow family were to remain among the strongest he ever made.

It seems that Ranjitsinhji spent part of the summer of 1889 with Mansur Khachar in the North Yorkshire village of Gilling East. There is a note to this effect in the visitors' guide to the parish church there, and as Trinity College was its patron it would have been quite simple for Borissow to arrange for them to stay at the rectory. The visit was probably made primarily for the sake of Mansur, who was not finding the English climate conducive to his health. It was to be the first of two long vacations that Ranji spent nursing his old schoolfriend.

In November 1889 Ranjitsinhji and Ramsinhji were allowed to enter

Trinity as 'youths of position'. Ramsinhji had passed the preliminary examination but Ranjitsinhji, surprisingly, had not. This is perhaps another sign that he had not yet adjusted to his new environment and that he was also missing the guidance of somebody like Macnaghten. Possibly too he was now more interested in playing sport. Whatever the reason, Borissow, according to Wild, started to accuse him of being both lazy and irresponsible. He was admitted to Trinity as a non-collegiate student, a short-term scheme and cheaper than paying college fees, but shortly afterwards he decided that the fees were, after all, worth paying. Thus, while many young men went up to Cambridge bearing fine reputations from famous public schools, Ranjitsinhji arrived rather ingloriously and unheralded.

The other long vacation he shared with Mansur was during the summer of 1890, which they spent in Bournemouth. By an irony, this chance trip to accompany his ailing friend, who had been on the south coast since March in the hope that its benign climate might speed his recuperation, was to play a significant part in Ranji's future. For, among Bournemouth's boarding-houses and pleasure gardens, its pine groves and steep ravines, its sandhills and promenades, amid its parades of nobility, Ranjitsinhji, for the first time, began to feel at home in England. He joined Mansur's party in mid-June and six weeks later they moved to better lodgings, in St Peter's Road. They also took the step of announcing themselves, as all the best people did, in the *Bournemouth Visitors Directory*, on 19 July. On the same day, there was also an item in another local newspaper, the *Observer and Chronicle for Hampshire and Dorset*:

Two Indian Princes are visiting Bournemouth, their Highnesses the Kumar Shri Mansur A. Khachar and the Kumar Ranjitsinhji. Their uncle, who during his present visit is simply styled Mr Desa Mala, and their tutor Mr H. J. Spenser, are also of the party. It may be noted Prince Kumar Ranjitsinhji played for Bournemouth on Tuesday. His Highness's brother [sic] is unfortunately an invalid, and it is for his benefit that the visit to Bournemouth has been made.

Thus Ranji began his life as a prince and social celebrity. Exactly how the impression came about that he was of royal lineage is impossible to ascertain but it is more than likely that it was assisted by him being in the company of a genuine prince, Mansur Khachar, and the fact that the English people they met were, through their fondness of romance, only too willing to accept the idea.

Once he had gained an introduction through Harry Spenser, the boys' tutor, he spent much of his time that summer at the Dean Park cricket and lawn tennis club. At first, it seems, he sought anonymity in the name K. S. ('Kumar Shri') Ranjitsinhji but, discovering the advantage of its rough English equivalent, was soon describing himself as 'Prince Ranjit'. He played a number of matches for Bournemouth, including a two-day game against MCC; appeared for Visitors v. Residents, in which he scored 88 before being run out; while, in another match, he captained his own XI at Sopley Park and lost by only 9 runs. In a match at Wareham, when he scored 76, one report said: 'The Prince's hitting was grand and would have been well worth double the number on a decent wicket.' All this confirms the impression that, although he had as yet had little formal training, he possessed some real, if raw, ability as a cricketer.

He also took part in a lawn tennis tournament, partnering a Miss Turner in the mixed doubles and Captain Wyld, a former Surrey cricketer, in the men's doubles, in which event they would have played against William Renshaw, a recent Wimbledon singles champion, had they not lost in the semi-finals. Interestingly, two of Ranjitsinhji's biographers, Standing (just thirteen years later) and Roland Wild, would claim that he beat Renshaw during this tournament, the first evidence that they were as dependent on the fanciful memories of their subject, his family and friends for sporting details as they were for affairs in Nawanagar.

By the end of September 1890, when he returned at the age of eighteen for his second year at Cambridge, his belief in both his ability as a cricketer and in the value of being seen in the eyes of others to be a person of importance, had grown immeasurably.

Ranji's development as a cricketer was greatly helped by the appearance of yet another family prepared to take him under their wing, although perhaps they never received the tribute that should have been theirs for doing so. The Haywards of Cambridge were a great cricketing family, trusty servants of a game to which they owed their livelihoods. They played cricket conventionally and patiently, they forged their trade as lovingly as any craftsmen, yet they, almost alone, were prepared to take the quiet, unassuming young Indian's clumsy efforts in earnest. And it was not insignificant that a Hayward was present when he added a new stroke to the batting repertoire.

A number of the Haywards were to play a part in Ranji's early struggles. In the early 1890s, Daniel Hayward, who was in his late fifties, ran a cricket outfitting business on the edge of Parker's Piece, an area of common land situated at the centre of Cambridge where for generations the townsfolk had played their sports, any number of matches simultaneously jostling for space between the numerous footpaths, and where in days gone by he himself had performed as player and then groundsman. Ranjitsinhji was to be one of his customers for several years. The Piece, meanwhile, was tended by one of Daniel's three sons, Arthur. Another son, Tom, occasionally helped in the shop, although he was already destined for greater things, having been engaged by the powerful Surrey club, primarily for his elegant and correct batting.

Tom was a firm friend of Ranjitsinhji, who was seventeen months his junior, and had joined him in Bournemouth for a time during the summer of 1890. They had bowled to each other in the nets there, but Tom did not play in any of the matches Ranjitsinhji had taken part in. Ranji wrote of him in *With Stoddart's Team in Australia*: ' "Tom" is an excellent fellow, and, although of a quiet disposition, is full of fun and merriment in his own particular way. He is a general favourite among all classes in England.' This unlikely couple would one day make their débuts against Australia within a month of each other.

The greatest cricketer in the Hayward family had been Daniel's brother, Thomas, who, in the 1860s, when Cambridgeshire were one of the strongest teams in the land, had been regarded the equal of any batsman playing. Never blessed with great strength or good health, his forte had been on-side play, especially the shot that forced the ball off the leg stump between mid-on and short-leg. It was a way he had of conserving energy. He also excelled on fiery pitches, when he would get his small frame behind the rising balls and play them down. There was to be more than a passing resemblance between his methods and those that Ranji was to adopt under the tutelage of Thomas's near-relations.

The person who gave Ranjitsinhji most help, with coaching and net practice, was Daniel's third son, also called Dan, who was the professional at Corpus Christi College. He was also one of two bowlers available for hire by members of the Cambridgeshire club, which had recently been re-formed as a 'second-class' county in June 1891. Ranji, impatient to learn, had been among the first to enrol with the new club, along with his friend Ramsinhji. It is important, however, not to misinterpret Dan Hayward's influence on Ranji: he did nothing more than to help make the most of what was already there. Ranji was perhaps thinking of his own experiences when he wrote in his *Jubilee Book of Cricket*: 'If a boy shows a tendency to play a stroke in an effective way but unlike others, he ought to be encouraged to do that stroke and not have his natural style cramped. Nothing is more detrimental than to check the natural strokes of a boy. Nor should a coach try to make his pupil too steady a bat if he shows an inclination to hit out. Let him make the best of his material, and not try to change the boy's natural style, attributes, or gifts by forcing them into a fixed groove.' He added: 'Too much coaching is bad. Half an hour a day once or twice a week is quite sufficient, added to the practice which he gets at the nets by himself and in games.'

Two trial matches were organized in August 1891 to assess Cambridgeshire's strength, and scores of 4, 18 and 23 were enough for Ranjitsinhji to win a place in the first fixture against Leicestershire in September. In the first innings he was out for 0 to Woodcock, who was to gain a reputation as one of the fastest bowlers in the country, but in the second he played some fine strokes in his 23 not out and was at the wicket when the winning runs were scored. A couple of weeks later, he braved bitter weather to appear for a South of England

XI, containing a number of Surrey players, against a local XIX at St Ives in Huntingdonshire and top-scored with 34, perhaps his most notable performance to date.

At this time, his ambition and courage can have known few bounds, for not only did his method remain raw, but his slight build meant he still did not have the physical strength to play a full range of strokes. He had only a few shots at his disposal, relying on the unfailing instinct of his eye to play either a wristy cut or pull, although he would sometimes undercut fast and high balls on the off-side over the heads of the astonished slip fielders for 4. These strokes were always to remain a vital part of his repertoire, even after he had acquired more traditional lines of attack, for reasons that he outlined in the *Jubilee Book of Cricket*: 'The pace already imparted to the ball by the bowler is helped on and added to by a flick of the bat, executed either with the wrist or some movement of the arms. Consequently, the faster the bowler the easier it is to make hard cuts and glances. Putting "beef" into strokes in front of the wicket is a different matter. Besides hitting the ball at exactly the right moment and in the right way, it is necessary to utilise the weight of the body, the swing of the arms, and the flick of the wrist. Timing, in the more restricted sense of the word, means bringing all these means of propulsion to bear on the ball in combination.'

When Dan Hayward began coaching him, the most serious fault with his game was that he would often step out of the line of the ball. As a fast delivery came towards him, his first impulse was to move out of the way. This was fraught with danger; not only would the stumps be exposed, but the stroke attempted would not be played with a vertical bat, which was therefore less likely to meet its target. Unusually, his movement was not towards square-leg, but towards point. He himself was to confess, in possibly the first interview he ever gave, published in *The Cricket Field* for 2 June 1892, that in the end, during a net at Fenner's, the university cricket ground, one of the professionals, Jack Sharpe, had exclaimed to him in frustration: 'Look here, you know, sir, if you can't keep those legs of yours still, I shall have to peg them down.'

And that had proved to be the solution: if Ranjitsinhji could not remain in the path of the ball of his own accord, he would have to be made to do so until he could unaided. Nature had to give way to art until art became nature. Ranji, who conceded that he could not play properly before 1891, was later to admit, in the *Jubilee Book of Cricket*: 'I had to have my right leg pegged down almost every time I practised during my first two years at serious cricket.' Although it was probably Sharpe's comment that inspired the idea, it is almost impossible to imagine this embarrassing exercise ever taking place during university nets; the likelihood is, therefore, that it happened only in the less public sessions he enjoyed with Dan Hayward. According to Wild, Ranji was certainly coached by Hayward with his right leg pegged down, and Wild actually attributes the idea to Hayward rather than Sharpe.

There were several consequences of this regimen. It made him adopt a relaxed, open stance at the crease – the bowler, as usual for the period, was given a fairly generous view of the stumps – that left him looking straight down the pitch. It also taught him, in the end, to stand without reservation in the line of the ball, although initially he could not resist the temptation to move his unshackled left leg across towards point, and one day this resulted in the most celebrated consequence of all, the creation of a stroke that was to become forever associated with Ranjitsinhji.

The leg-glance, as it eventually became known, was used to a delivery on or around the leg stump. Dan Hayward might have been expecting Ranjitsinhji to try to push the ball between mid-on and short-leg; what he in fact did was to improve the argument, to refine the logic, by once more flouting the rules. C. B. Fry, in 1897, described the process best: with his free left leg 'he used . . . to slip across the wicket towards point. Suddenly he found out that by moving the left leg across towards the off, keeping his bat on the leg side of it and facing the ball quite squarely with his body, he could watch the ball on the bat and play it away to leg with a twist of the wrist.'

With a modicum of effort the ball could be sent flashing behind his leg for a certain 4. It was a dangerous stroke; undoubtedly the slightest error in judgement would have resulted in downfall, but Ranjitsinhji, as Jessop would testify, was not prone to such error: 'It was the speed and judgement of his eye that enabled him to reach such perfection in his leg-glide.' And, once he mastered the stroke, Ranji was able to make back play as potent a means of attack as forward play had traditionally been: he set in motion a revolution by demonstrating that runs could be scored to any and to all parts of the field.

Although Wild vouches that the stroke came about during practice with Hayward, there is nothing to suggest precisely when the event took place. The circumstantial evidence, however, is that it happened on Parker's Piece in the spring of 1892. Before then, Ranjitsinhji's scoring had been distinctly limited: in 1891 he had made only a few appearances, for Fitzwilliam Hall, before July because of quinsy and he had not yet scored a century in England; afterwards, his scoring increased dramatically to around 2,000 runs in all matches during 1892. Clearly, he had come across some new means of accumulating runs freely and relentlessly, and as Macnaghten had said it would, perseverance was having its reward.

Although he was thus making good progress in Cambridge club matches in his efforts to turn himself into a cricketer, within the university he was receiving frustratingly little encouragement. Another well known incident from this period has been used regularly, and correctly, to illustrate just how far from being accepted as a serious batsman he then was in the circles that mattered most.

It took place one day in the spring of 1892, at roughly the same time as the practice session with Dan Hayward. It involved Stanley Jackson, the university captain, who had already played for his county, Yorkshire, and within eighteen months would represent England and score 91 and 103 in his first two matches against Australia; in 1905 he would captain England to the Ashes. On Ranjitsinhji's death he described the incident in *Wisden*.

He was walking across the Piece when a nearby cricket match caught his eye. What was unusual about it was that it had attracted quite a large gathering of spectators. Jackson found his curiosity sufficiently aroused to go over and join them.

The minor commotion, it transpired, concerned one of the batsmen, a dark-skinned, slim man of around 5' 10" who was employing such

35

extraordinary methods that Jackson was able to recount them quite clearly over forty years later. At the time, he could have quickly dismissed them as absurd and continued on his way had they not been so outrageously successful. The batsman was gathering runs as readily as he did applause.

In Jackson's eyes, there was nothing correct in his play. It was technically unsound; body not erect, neither legs nor bat ever straight; and the result was a variety of unorthodox strokes, among them one where the batsman almost went down on his knees to pull a ball round to the leg side. Jackson, tutored in the game at Harrow, would, like any other public school cricketer of the period, have regarded it as near-immoral to play such a stroke. It went without saying that a ball pitching on the off-side should be hit only to the off, a straight ball hit within the arc from mid-on to mid-off, and only a ball pitched on or outside the leg stump could, with decency, be hit to the leg-side. Jackson himself gave ample proof of the value of this style.

He played his cricket according to such principles because they had been laid down for him when he learnt the game at school. What he saw on the Piece offended these principles and his response took no account of the fact that at this time an increasing number of techniques were coming into vogue that defied public school doctrine. Not all batsmen could be judged by the same set of rules, especially as these new methods were being used to greater and greater advantage; it was only necessary to watch W. G. Grace, the most successful of all batsmen up until then, to understand that. Not a product of one of the big public schools or universities, Grace did what he saw fit and would not be confined by any predetermined notions.

Grace had elaborated on his theory of batting in his book *Cricket*, published in 1891. In it, he rejected style for the sake of style alone. 'Some of the players I have met,' he said, 'possessed a beautifully free style, and gave the impression of being able to score largely; but somehow the runs never came. Some had a cramped and ungainly style, which provoked severe comments; but nevertheless the runs did come. Then there were others who kept up their wickets for hours for very small scores; while opposite them were free-hitters who made runs in a tenth part of the time. Now it will not do to say that all of them may not be described as first-class batsmen . . . It may be safely laid down that the duty of a batsman is to make runs, and that he who can make them quickly or slowly as the occasion requires belongs to the very highest class.'

Grace's book, and perhaps this passage in particular, were to be studied with interest by the batsman on Parker's Piece, and when he himself came to write a treatise on the game he supported what Grace had said: 'There is a certain class of batsman nowadays who sacrifices effectiveness in order to attain what is called a pretty style. But a style which is not so effective as it might be can hardly claim to be either good or beautiful.' He also summarized neatly the only theory of batting that had ever really mattered to Grace, or to himself: 'utility was the criterion of style'.

The other things that need to be remembered in examining Jackson's response to what he saw that day on Parker's Piece are that he had probably never seen anyone bat in quite such an extraordinary way before, nor could he have been expected to realize that the batsman he was watching was someone of unique talents, who could not be measured by normal yardsticks. Neville Cardus expressed this perfectly when he wrote in *Good Days*: 'His style was a remarkable instance of the way a man can express personal genius in a game – nay, not only a personal genius but the genius of a whole race. For Ranjitsinhji's cricket was of his own country; when he batted a strange light was seen for the first time on English fields, a light out of the East. It was lovely magic, and not prepared for by anything that had happened in cricket before Ranji came to us.'

Although he did not say so in his account, Jackson must have found the figure at the crease unusual in another respect, and it was something that would not have gone unnoticed by others present, if his face had not already become familiar to them on the Piece. He had jet-black hair and a moustache after the fashion of the period, but his strange, rather ethereal presence was accentuated by a large silk shirt that flapped and billowed against his movements. This, again, was exaggerated by the fact that the shirt was buttoned at the neck and wrists, where it met the gloves covering his hands. Jackson knew, as he looked on, who it was; he had heard of an Indian playing college cricket the previous year.

He watched the batsman step down the wicket once again, attempting another unorthodox stroke, but for once the bat failed to find its target and the wicket-keeper collected the ball and whipped off the bails. Jackson, from where he was standing, thought the batsman was out, but the umpire decided otherwise.

Jackson walked on, confirmed of the reports he had received that here was a resourceful but untutored player.

It can be contended that Jackson was in fact to receive too much credit for the advancement of Ranji's cricket career. Although he was the man who eventually gave him the first cricket Blue ever awarded to an Indian, he arguably did so a year later than he should have done, and only overcame a lengthy period of doubt after he was persuaded by others. Although it is hard to be sure, it looks suspiciously as though Jackson, who was incidentally the son of one of the Marquess of Salisbury's cabinet ministers and would one day hold the position of Governor of Bengal, was simply prejudiced against Ranjitsinhji. Jackson himself was later to admit that his original assessment of Ranji's ability was mistaken and that this was partly due to him not then possessing a 'sympathetic interest for Indians'.

The first university man Ranjitsinhji made a favourable impression on was not Jackson but C. M. Wells, a scholar and all-round athlete and one of Jackson's more experienced players in 1892. That year, Wells believed Ranjitsinhji was good enough to be tried in the 1st XI but Jackson played him only in the two early season trial games. His scores hardly suggest he was a failure – 3, 29 not out, 0 (run out) and 58 – but they could not sway the Cambridge captain from his opinion that, 'It is all right on Parker's Piece and in college matches, but when he comes to be pitched against first-class professional bowlers he will have a very short innings.'

Ranjitsinhji experiences in trying to win a place in the admittedly strong Trinity College XI were even more illuminating. Jackson was a prominent figure in the college's cricket team at that time and would have had a large say in the selection of the side, but even though he had made some useful scores in his few matches for Fitzwilliam Hall he had to wait until 1892 before being given a place by Trinity (Jackson later said, incorrectly, that Ranjitsinhji first played for the college in 1891). Even then, his first appearance for Trinity was only as a last-minute stand-in against St John's, but he ensured his retention by scoring 79 not out. A few weeks later he hit a century against Selwyn but neither that, nor his performances in the trial matches, were enough to persuade Jackson to give him a try in the 1st XI. Wild said that, in his early matches for Trinity, Ranji 'was ignored by other members of the team, and sometimes sat alone and friendless in the pavilion'. It is worth recording that Wells, apparently an admirer of his batting, was also a member of the Trinity side.

At the end of June 1892, Ranjitsinhji, who throughout all of this appears to have simply gritted his teeth and resolved to show all the doubters that they were wrong, went up to Lord's to watch the University match, and what he saw was perhaps partly indicative of his own dilemma. M. R. Jardine, the Oxford batsman, employed a stroke of his own making, a leg-glance that sent the ball just behind square-leg. Jackson refused to alter his field against such tactics, continued to bowl to an orthodox setting of seven fieldsmen on the off-side and two to leg, and Jardine went on to score 140.

At about this time he moved out of the Borissow home. Now receiving financial assistance from his Jodhpur relations, he looked around for rooms and found some in Sidney Street. He also began to concentrate all his energies on playing regular cricket for Cambridge-shire and for any club side that would have him, and the following two months saw him score prolifically with an expanding repertoire of strokes.

He was now playing several matches a week, and during 1892 as a whole scored at least nine and possibly as many as twelve centuries in all matches, the majority of them after June. During one spell of six days he scored three centuries, for three different teams: on 10 August, he made 141 for Victoria against Bedford; on 12 August, 142 not out for Trinity Long Vacation Club against St John's LVC; and on 15 August, 111 not out for Bassinettes against Jesus LVC.

It might be imagined that this sequence was the origin of one of the most common stories about Ranji: that once, on Parker's Piece, he scored three centuries in three separate matches during the same day. However, this story apparently made its first appearance in Wild's biography and there is evidence that it is no more than an elaboration of an earlier, less startling story. In March 1933, one A. E. Reeve, in the *Cambridge Chronicle and University Journal*, remembered, in an article entitled 'Memories of "Ranji" and his Times', the tale that: 'While at Cambridge he [Ranjitsinhji] was so keen on the game that on one occasion he played in two matches at the same time. Having been dismissed in one match, he strolled round to where another match was being played. The side batting, being one man short, asked him to bat and he could not resist the temptation to do so.'

Towards the end of August 1892, the Cassandra club, for which Ranji principally played, made a short tour of Yorkshire and an incident during the match at Bridlington gives a further indication of the sort of unpleasantness that Ranjitsinhji, as an Indian, occasionally had to contend with. The other Cassandra players had told the opposition that he knew only a few words of English, which encouraged them to refer to him in offensive terms when he was at the crease in the belief that he would not understand them. When it became evident that he could bat well, the bowlers began spicing things up for him. One delivery hit him in the face, and he heard a fieldsman say he hoped that would 'knock some of the steam out of the joker' – or words to that effect. There was considerable embarrassment among the opposition when they heard him communicating perfectly adequately with his companions during lunch (other, later, versions of the story state that the opposition only discovered the truth when Ranji made a speech after dinner that evening). He scored 142 that day.

Unlikely occasion though it was, it was during the Cassandra tour that he first made the acquaintance of the athletic, handsome figure of C. B. Fry, whose cricket career was to be so inextricably bound with his. Fry was staying in Beverley during his first long vacation from Oxford and appeared against the Cassandra team in a one-day match. Never one to shy from embroidering fact with fiction, Fry, fifty-five years later, described his earliest encounter with Ranjitsinhji: 'A slim young Indian was bowling. I hit him over the wall into a shunting-yard. An engine was slowly puffing around. The ball hit the barrel of the engine, cannoned forward off the brass beehive, and went into the funnel. The engine puffed away with the ball in its belly.'

Importantly, Jackson spent the winter of 1892–93 touring India with a team of amateur cricketers, his first visit to the subcontinent. He did not score as many runs as perhaps he thought he would, several Indians made their mark against the Englishmen, and Jackson returned deeply impressed by the natives' ability.

Then one day in April 1893, he had just completed one of his first practice sessions of the season at Fenner's when he noticed Ranjitsinhji was batting. Before he had begun his own practice, Jackson had seen him in the nets, and noted that the two bowlers he had chosen to serve him were Lockwood, the great Surrey bowler, and his protégé Richardson. They were at Cambridge, along with other county professionals, to spend a month getting fit for the new season and supplement their hard-earned summer wages with rewards for the simpler task of getting the students into shape. Now, some while later, Ranjitsinhji was still hard at it, having dispensed with Lockwood and Richardson and got himself two fresh bowlers. Wells was standing nearby and Jackson went over to speak to him. He pointed out that Ranjitsinhji, who had become a regular sight at net practices during the previous two years, seemed to be overdoing it. As he probably never showed himself to be anything less than enthusiastic, it must have been an intensive workout indeed. It was said of him, as it had been of Grace when he was a young man, that he began his net practice in March; his eagerness was also apparent in his fielding, which was agile and effortless and made a sad contrast to the average cricketer, who regarded a spell in the field with indifference.

Wells made his way over to Ranjitsinhji, still rapt in concentration at his wicket, to suggest that perhaps he should take it easier. Wells walked back to tell Jackson what the reply had been: 'I find I am all right for half an hour but I cannot last. I must now master endurance.'

Lockwood recalled in an interview with *Cricket: a Weekly Record of*

41

the Game for 28 July 1898, how, not long after this episode, he was again bowling in the nets to Ranjitsinhji. Jackson came up and looked on, and asked Lockwood what he thought of him.

Lockwood could remember when he and his fellow professionals first bowled at Ranji in the nets, when he hardly knew how to bat at all, at least against anything like first-class bowlers. He had practically no defence, though he was very quick to pick up hints, and nearly always tried to pull to the on-side, although he was by no means certain to make the stroke successfully. But whenever he was batting, if he made a mistake, or if a ball jumped quickly, he would never make any remark, but would whistle quietly to himself. As time had gone on, they had got him out less frequently. Lockwood knew that he and Richardson would find themselves bowling to him quite frequently because he invariably asked for the fastest bowlers he could get, whatever the state of the pitch might be, whereas others were not so anxious to play against them unless it was perfect. He also recalled that the other undergraduates never seemed to take any notice of him.

Lockwood considered Jackson's question. 'Well, sir, you're playing two or three worse Blues than he is,' he ventured.

'Can he *really* play?'

'Sir, you come and try to bowl him out!'

Jackson had laughed, and started to walk away.

Lockwood himself believed that it was from that moment that Stanley Jackson took proper notice of Ranjitsinhji.

He began May 1893 with scores of 102 not out and 91 for Trinity, did adequately in the first trial match, and three days later was making his first-class début against C. I. Thornton's team at Fenner's. It was a twelve-a-side match and he batted at number nine, and his cutting drew comment before he was bowled by Mold, the Lancashire fast bowler, for 18.

Later the same week, for Trinity, he shared a stand of 136 with Jackson effectively to win the match against their strongest college rivals, Jesus. Retained for the university's next match, against the Gentlemen of England, and confronted by an attack including Woods, of Somerset, and J. T. Hearne, of Middlesex, he established his place in the side for several matches by making 40 in one and a half hours (during which his cutting was again remarked on) and a calm 11 not out as the university struggled to complete victory. He was by now undoubtedly growing in confidence and although he was a little careless to be run out cheaply against Yorkshire, he scored 55 against MCC, adding 91 in less than an hour with Perkins, who was to secure his place against Oxford on the same day as Ranjitsinhji, and 38 against Surrey, when he and Jackson put on 81 in an hour.

His appearances in the Cambridge XI were to transform his life. Having grown accustomed, through his unsettled background, to a lack of companionship, he found that success at cricket won him both the acceptance and friendship of his university contemporaries. It would hardly be surprising if during this process he did nothing to scotch rumours either that he was a prince of fabulous wealth or that his father (some said his uncle) was the ruling sovereign of an Indian state. This would seem to be supported by the stories that, according to Reeve's article of 1933, grew up around him: 'Many were the romantic tales bandied about among the sporting fans of his times. Of how elaborately the rooms he occupied in Sidney Street "over the little baker's shop" were furnished, the sheets of his bed being of the finest silk! Then, the professional bowlers employed by him at the nets on Parker's Piece – the county net among others – must have looked upon those days as the Golden Age, for a golden half, and even a whole, sovereign was placed by "Ranji" on the tops of the stumps, the same going to the bowler *if* he dislodged them. Tales were current, too, of the handsome presents received by those who helped to polish the rough diamond that later shone with such great splendour.'

Ranji certainly began to adopt a luxuriant lifestyle: he took a hansom cab where before he would have cycled or walked; he became an occasional smoker (he was to smoke more often after his days as a regular county cricketer were over); and he developed a special love of fine clothes and objects with which to fill his dark and cluttered sitting-room at 22 Sidney Street. At around this time he acquired Popsey, a parrot, who was to be a life-long companion. It must be considered unlikely, however, that he ever felt well enough off to reward net bowlers with even a half gold sovereign.

His room became the venue for bibulous supper parties which regularly ended in songs around the piano or a game of poker extending into the small hours. Sometimes the conversation would turn to cricket and Ranjitsinhji would give his own theories on the art of batting, a subject he studied as diligently and with as perceptive a mind as any academic studied his books. His new-found friends, finding 'Ranjitsinhji' something of a mouthful, originally dubbed him 'Smith' but later reduced his name to a manageable, if irreverent, 'Ranji'.

By now he had begun to encounter a new problem, although it was one with which he was subsequently to become familiar. He began to get into financial difficulties, for his supposedly boundless resources were in fact distinctly limited. He was keeping terms at Lincoln's Inn, and in the spring of 1893 had written to Sir Charles Ollivant, the Resident in Rajkot, to ask Vibhaji for money to help cover the expense of being called to the Bar in November and to pay off his debts. To his delight, a remittance of £500 arrived in May. The money, it was stressed, was an advance on his allowance and was sent only on condition that he returned to India after passing his Bar examinations.

The knowledge that he must shortly go back to his homeland must have heightened Ranji's determination to do well at his cricket. His fielding at slip for Cambridge University was quite exceptional and he told *The Cricket Field* (1 July 1893) with obvious delight of the occasion, in the match a few weeks earlier with Yorkshire, when he took a snick from Tunnicliffe left-handed in the slips with such lightning speed (initially he had moved to the right, thinking it was going that way) that Gay, the wicket-keeper, had turned round, expecting to see the ball on the way to the boundary, and called out sharply: 'Don't stand there grinning like that; go and fetch it!' This incident has been regularly re-told, although often with the irate fieldsman erroneously identified as Jackson. It is probably safe to discount the story related by Reeve that he once, while standing in the slips, caught a swallow in flight.

Another player, though, was driven to exasperation by Ranji's ability in the field. In 1892, when Ranji was fielding as substitute for the university during the match with MCC at Fenner's, Charles Wright had hit a half-volley from Jackson very hard in his direction and he had caught it spectacularly, high up with one hand. Wright had already started running and was turning for a second when Jackson pointed out to him as he passed: 'Charles, I'm afraid that your energy is wasted.' In 1893 Ranjitsinhji again caught out Wright, who was playing for the Gentlemen of England, and at the close of play Wright went across to him, physically shook him and declared that the next time they met Ranji was not to take the field!

He was still, of course, occasionally the butt of jokes. According to Alfred Gaston, in his introduction to *With Stoddart's Team in Australia*, there was a tale current at Cambridge that Ranji's father had, on receiving news that his son had scored another century, ordered three more slaves to be sacrificed in tribute. The concept Ranji's peers had of his supposed father was a striking and painful contrast to the actual person and it must have been difficult for him to laugh off this particular story.

Ranji learnt from Jackson on 10 June 1893, after the match with the Australians, that he would be getting his Blue. He had batted one and three-quarter hours for 58 in the first innings and two hours, on a badly worn pitch, for 37 not out in the second, against the finest bowlers possessed by Australia. This double performance suggested that he was finally beginning to 'master endurance' and it may have been this that clinched the matter for Jackson, who possibly held to the view expressed by Lord Harris, a former England captain, as late as 1905, in his introduction to *Stray Thoughts on Indian Cricket* by J. M. Framjee Patel, that, 'To wear down good bowling, and patiently wait for many overs for a run here and a run there, is easier for the phlegmatic Anglo-Saxon than for the excitable Asiatic.'

It was certainly a magnificent display by Ranji, who was still only twenty years old. S. J. Southerton, in 1934, remembered being present at the match and said he had never forgotten the impression the young batsman created. Another student of the game, J. N. Pentelow, the journalist and author, also recalled, in *Cricket* in 1896, being struck

45

by the ease and grace of his style. During the match, Ranji successfully brought off his leg-glance a number of times, and the shot clearly did not go unnoticed. Pentelow said: 'An old farmer from the Fens, out Ely way, sat next to me open-mouthed for a time; but one of Ranji's glances at last elicited from him this remark, "Whoy, he only tooch it and it go to th' boundary!"' It was the first first-class match in which Ranji was known to have employed the stroke, although Pentelow said he remembered seeing him use it in a minor match at the end of the 1892 season.

At the end of the match a large crowd gathered outside the pavilion and gave him an ovation, although this was more likely for his defiant batting that day than for the achievement of winning his Blue, about which they were probably not yet aware. This more notable news seems to have been greeted with general approval, although the following week, when he played for the South of England against the Australians at the Oval (he was run out going for a fourth run off one of his 'pretty' leg hits), the Oxford colleagues he dined with at Lincoln's Inn after the game were still speculating whether he would actually play at Lord's. The *Cambridge Review* offered its congratulations to 'our dark Blue' and was moved to observe effusively: 'An Indian playing against the Australians on Fenner's ground in our national game of cricket, is surely a remarkable sign of the times. Three parts of the world, each remote from one another, were represented, yet each was a part of the British Empire. Peace and prosperity must likewise exist before such a thing could be.'

As far as Ranji was concerned, winning his Blue was the culmination of his immediate desires. He was not unaware of the magnitude of his achievement and realized that it could not have been achieved without the help of others. As Jackson would recall: 'For some years after we first met at Cambridge in 1892 I had the pleasure of his close friendship, and many indications of a confidence and goodwill which in later years I realized was but a natural return of a high caste Indian gentleman for what he regarded as some special act of friendship or service.'

Ranjitsinhji prepared for the University match with Cambridge's first away fixtures of the season, against Sussex at Brighton (the first of his many appearances on the ground), where he hit a bright 40, and MCC at Lord's, where he scored 54 in eighty minutes. There was more than a suggestion in the second of these innings that, with the most important game of his life imminent, he was making strenuous efforts at orthodoxy, playing forward and scoring runs in front of the wicket on the off-side. But, as had happened in the previous match with MCC, after he reached 50 his concentration seemed to go and he resorted to many wild and risky shots before soon getting out.

The match against Oxford proved an anti-climax. The fixture in those days was a great sporting and social occasion, and as Ranji made his way to the wicket on the first day, he was given an overwhelming reception by the 19,000 spectators. His first runs came when he dispatched the ball past point for 4, but he could add only 5 more runs before a good-length ball took the top of his stumps. In the second innings, when he was again cheered to the wicket, he had not scored when he hit a ball hard into the hands of mid-off. However, he had the satisfaction of taking three catches as Cambridge achieved an emphatic victory by 266 runs. Although his highest score in nine matches for the university had been only 58, he had made five scores of 40 or more and taken nineteen catches. As *Wisden* said, 'Ranji's introduction into the XI was abundantly justified . . . Not even the captain worked more keenly for the well-being of the side . . . the young Indian made himself highly popular.'

No sooner had his great ambition been realized than another honour came his way. The Surrey committee, who were having difficulty getting together an amateur side to meet the Players, sought to conscript a number of men from the University match. Ranjitsinhji was due to be playing for Cambridgeshire against MCC but promptly told them by telegram the day before that he would no longer be available (he was to appear, with mixed success, in their five other two-day matches later that summer, on one occasion as captain). And so it was that, two days after the match at Lord's, he found himself stepping out to represent the Gentlemen at the Oval, where five years earlier he had been an enraptured member of the crowd. In fiction he would have made a century; in fact he made 6 and 0.

Reluctantly, Ranji knew that, once he had passed his Bar examinations, he ought to abide by Vibhaji's wishes and return to India, and in the autumn of 1893 he began making his farewells. There were incentives to stay. Two or three county sides had shown an interest in him during the season, including Surrey, outright champions in six of the previous eight years and the club of Wells, Lockwood and Tom Hayward. What plans he had for himself once he reached India is unclear, for he had never intended to pursue a career at the Bar, and he may have meant it when he told his friends that he would try to return as soon as possible.

On 26 September he was invited to speak at the annual dinner of one of the Cambridge club sides, Old Higher Grade. It was attended by many of the county's eminent cricketing figures and townsfolk who had become Ranjitsinhji's acquaintances either on the cricket field, at the Liberal Club in St Andrew's Street, where he went most evenings to play billiards, or on fishing and shooting expeditions. Ranji's speech, full of charm and eloquence, indicated how sorry he was to be leaving and just how happy had been his most recent months in Cambridge. No one present, perhaps, could imagine what a contrast it had been for him from his childhood existence.

'I would like to thank everyone,' he began, 'for the great sympathy shown to me during this year in the great event of my life – getting the Blue. I think that your sympathy, in no small degree, made the university men give me my Blue – more than the little I have done myself. I shall always consider the reception given me by Cambridge men as not the least flattering and, at the same time, the most undeserving.

'I do not consider myself a foreigner in Cambridge. I don't think Indians are foreigners in England; that distinction has passed away long, long ago and I think that in time to come we shall look upon each other as absolutely the same subjects under Her Majesty the Queen.

'I am sure I also owe the fact I got my Blue to the kindness of the Cambridge press . . . I shall, as I have always done, try my best to promote Cambridge cricket and I give you my word I will try to get my own people to let me come back to England as soon after next June as possible.'

Although it must have taken a certain degree of boldness to state that Indians were no longer considered foreigners in England, Ranji had probably been attempting to say no more than the right thing, and may have been startled by the response with which these words were met. The *Cambridge Weekly News* published a lengthy article, under the heading 'Mr Ranjitsinhji on Imperial Federation', which included the following remarks:

> At the Old Higher Grade Cricket Club dinner last Tuesday Mr K. S. Ranjitsinhji contributed a few remarks which merit something more than a mere passing notice. The speaker struck a chord that will find a responsive echo wherever the English language is spoken . . . Not often do Cambridge people have the opportunity of hearing one of the Queen's Indian subjects pleading eloquently for Indian Federation. That, if we mistake not, is the true inwardness of Mr Ranjitsinhji's remarks. The speaker may rest assured that in Cambridge at any rate he is not looked upon as a foreigner. He has developed qualities that appeal straight to the heart of the average Englishman. During his residence at the University of Cambridge he has unconsciously perhaps provided a powerful argument for Imperial Federation. Englishmen can appreciate and admire the qualities that have won for Mr Ranjitsinhji his Blue and although it is too much to expect that he is typical of his race it proves they have qualities dormant but which only need stimulating . . .

In view of Ranji's later attitude towards federation, these were ironic comments indeed. However, they must have shown him, if he had not already realized it, that the British people seemed prepared to hang not only on his every deed, but on his every word.

4

AN ENGLISH GENTLEMAN

RANJITSINHJI DID NOT return to India as intended, however. He was kept in England because, at a fairly late stage, he found that his debts were larger than anticipated and he could not afford the costs of being called to the Bar. In the spring of 1894, unable to meet his various college fees and numerous personal expenses, he left Cambridge University. He had been there four and a half years. He must have departed with reluctance, for he did so not long before the start of the cricket season. He continued to live on in his rooms at Sidney Street.

Shortly after he came down, when it was realized he was not returning to India, his quarterly remittances from Nawanagar were stopped, to recover the £500 advanced him the previous year. It is interesting to note that Kincaid and Wild (and Ross in turn) attributed Ranjitsinhji's departure from Cambridge and the halt in his allowance to the death of Vibhaji, though in fact that happened more than a year later.

By September 1894 Ranjitsinhji was once more writing to Ollivant, the British Resident. 'I am writing to you again,' he pleaded, 'to help me to get the Jam Sahib's assistance as to my getting called to the Bar and for the money required for my return home. I may write here that this will be my final appeal to him. I fully regret that my liabilities of last year did not enable me to use His Highness's previous loan for the purpose for which it was granted. It would be unseemly for me to write to you and ask His Highness to give me the sum as a loan, so I will beg of him to give me his help in whatever way he thinks it best. The sum I require is £250. I shall get called in November on passing one more paper next month and I hope to be in India in

December.' He asked for the withheld payments of his allowance to be sent, along with December's in advance. It had now been agreed that £300 of the original loan was to be regarded as a gift.

Although he claimed that all he required was £250, Ranji, unbeknown to the authorities in Nawanagar, was borrowing money from other sources in order to keep himself solvent. He borrowed £30 from Chester Macnaghten, who also asked a London friend to keep an eye on his former pupil's welfare and 'help him with a loan if not more than £50'. Ranjitsinhji accepted an offer of £25 and promised to try to settle his affairs, but this was not a simple task. He owed money to many local Cambridge tradesmen, several of whom, fortunately, were his friends, and when eventually challenged by one of them, his tailor, with 'But can you *pay*, sir?', he had had to reply, 'Of course I can't, but you will get your money one day.'

Vibhaji agreed to send the money he asked for. Although he laid down 'the distinct understanding that he returns to India, by the end of December next, and makes no further application for any advance', this was undoubtedly a mistake, and one which was to have serious consequences. Had Vibhaji refused this second request for financial assistance, he might well have killed off what was to became an almost insatiable desire on the part of Ranjitsinhji for reparative favours from the Nawanagar state. Instead, Ranji must have been encouraged in thinking that he could do as he wished and somebody else would always foot the bill. But Vibhaji, while not as feeble or as vacillating as his critics would have us believe, seems to have been rarely far-sighted or prudent.

The £250 made little difference. By the autumn of 1894, Ranjitsinhji was once more unable, or unwilling, to find the money to pay for being called to Bar, and he was never in fact to be called. (It was later a common mistake that he was a qualified barrister, but the entry in Venn's *Alumni Cantabrigiensis*, which states he was called to the Bar on 26 January 1894, is incorrect.) Whether or not he had a serious prospect of passing his examinations can only be guessed at, but he did not seem to spend much time attending to his studies. Ranji ought to have begun making preparations to return to India as instructed, but he was perhaps no longer in awe of the Jam Sahib's wishes; moreover, other factors had begun to play their part.

He had been developing the acquaintance of the amateur members of the Sussex cricket team, particularly Billy Murdoch and Charles Fry. Fry, just a few months older than Ranji, and Murdoch, who was forty in 1895, had in common a self-confidence and zest for life. They knew what they wanted and were sure of getting it. Murdoch, though past his best, was then considered the greatest batsman produced by Australia. He had settled in England in 1891 and began playing for Sussex two years later, chiefly through the efforts of Lord Sheffield, a generous benefactor of Sussex cricket and president of the county club since 1879. Murdoch had been made captain from the start.

Fry had first played for Sussex in 1894 while still at Oxford, where he had gone with a fine academic reputation but had become celebrated more as an outstanding all-round sportsman, winning three Blues as a Freshman and equalling the world long-jump record.

Possibly the three-sided friendship blossomed through a mutual passion for shooting; certainly they did not play much cricket together at first. Ranji's first experience of shooting had been in Bournemouth, and with his quick eye he had learnt rapidly. He seems to have spent much of the winter of 1894 shooting in and around Cambridgeshire and Wild says that once, on a visit to Fulbourne, the head keeper had come along and ordered the party off the estate unless he was paid by Ranji. Fortunately, one of his friends had come to the rescue and they were able to continue, Ranji apparently doing so without the least embarrassment.

At some stage Murdoch became keen for Ranji to play for Sussex, who had never been a strong side and would have welcomed any addition to their strength. Murdoch's interest made Ranji hesitate further over returning to India. Finance was most probably a highly persuasive factor. Amateur cricketers were not as self-sufficient as the name suggested; Murdoch, for one, liked to be rewarded for his work and had been dropped by Australia in the 1880s for demanding, with others, 50 per cent of the gate money. A first-class county club was expected to pay an amateur's out-of-pocket expenses, such as hotel bills and railway fares, and a secure place in the side practically amounted to subsistence throughout the summer months. And the more valuable an amateur, the more his club would endeavour to accommodate his needs. Walter Read, for example, one of Murdoch's circle of friends and in his day one of the best batsmen in England, had been made assistant secretary by Surrey, with an annual salary of about £400 for what amounted to a sinecure, to enable him to give up his schoolteaching and play regularly for the county. What arrangements, if any, were made either directly or indirectly for Ranjitsinhji during his Sussex career are not known, but it would be surprising if such a superlative batsman and manifest crowd-puller – and someone who could only rarely have afforded to turn down an offer of help – did not receive any financial rewards.

For Ranjitsinhji, for whom a return home can have held little attraction and only a number of painful memories, the offer was too enticing to pass up. During 1894 he had kept in practice against first-class bowling with three matches at Lord's for MCC; two benefit games, at Trent Bridge, where he kept wicket for some of the time (the only known occasion of him doing so), and at the Oval, where he scored 62 in an hour and forty minutes; an appearance in Cambridge University's last fixture of the season, in Aigburth; and two matches at the Scarborough Festival, in the second of which he made 42 and 52 not out. These matches were too sporadic for him to run into any rich vein of form. For MCC against Oxford University he was bowled by Fry for 0, while Lord Hawke, the Yorkshire captain, later recalled in his autobiography how, in the first match at Scarborough, he was at a complete loss as to how to play the off-breaks of Wainwright. He must, though, have gained valuable experience when he played for MCC against his old university and partnered W. G. Grace for two hours. Grace was well set and the bowlers already tired when Ranji went in and together they added 200 runs, Ranji scoring a chanceless 94 and 'The Champion' 196. Though it has been said that this was the first time the two of them batted together, they had in fact done so for the Gentlemen in 1893, although only briefly.

At a lower level, he had continued to play in Cambridge: as late as the second week in June he was taking part in a college game, while he also appeared for Cassandra, with whom he made a short tour of

Kent in late August. In a non first-class match against the touring South Africans, at Portsmouth, he hit 53 and 146 not out.

In 1895, he was in the Cambridge nets from March. He prepared even more assiduously and with far greater belief than when trying for his Blue. He even promised Tom Hayward, who in particular helped him in practice, that he would give him a signet ring when he scored his first hundred in an important match. As the season drew near, he played in a couple of club matches and scored 85 and 174 not out.

There was, of course, no guarantee that he would appear for Sussex regularly; perhaps that was why no one worried too much about his qualification. To play for a first-class county in which you had not been born it was necessary to have resided in the county for the previous two years, but it was a difficult thing to establish and had led to heated disputes in the past. It was really down to another side to protest if they felt a rival club had infringed the rule. Would anyone object to the Indian in Sussex's XI? Murdoch and Ranjitsinhji, clearly, were prepared to take the chance. There was, after all, a lot to be gained and nothing to lose.

Only when the Sussex team for their first match, against MCC at Lord's, was announced four days beforehand did Ranji's association with the county club become public. Murdoch's version of events, which he gave during a speech at Cambridge in September 1896, was that Ranji had written to him, saying he would like to play for Sussex and was qualified to do so. However, the player himself told the press prior to the opening game, with characteristic ingenuousness, that he would be taking up residence in Eastbourne shortly. The following year *Wisden* hinted at the true state of affairs when it observed, 'Ranji's appearance in the team took most people by surprise, as the fact of his qualifying for Sussex was practically unknown until the early part of May', but if any eyebrows were raised at the time, nothing actually seems to have been said.

On 28 April 1895, in the Lal bungalow at Jamnagar, Vibhaji, the Jam Sahib of Nawanagar, lay dying in his bed. For almost a week he had been in the grip of a fever, which over the previous two days had gradually increased in severity. He was being attended by doctors but his temperature had risen steadily and it became only a matter of time before the inevitable happened. He had been ruler of his state for forty-three years, and was just ten days short of his sixty-ninth year. In the palace, amid hushed corridors, preparations were made for his death. In the zenana, His Highness's wives mourned; elsewhere, his many valued retainers – regular beneficiaries of the old man's benevolence – attended to their obsequies. As afternoon turned to evening, Vibhaji lost consciousness, and as the palace clocks moved on to 7.20, he died.

Vibhaji departed the world content in the knowledge that, through his untiring efforts, his 12-year-old son Jaswantsinhji would succeed him to the throne. Five days after he died, some 300 miles to the north-east, the Resident in Jodhpur was asked to wire to Rajkot: 'Jodhpur protests against obstruction to Rajput succession of illegitimate son by Mohammadan mistress succeeds late Jam of Jamnagar.' But had Vibhaji been able to read it, he would have laughed, for it was a futile objection. The official ceremony of succession, which by custom had to occur within thirteen days of the death of the previous ruler, took place on Friday 10 May in the state capital. Jaswantsinhji, grieving the loss of his father, arrived in procession at the durbar under an eleven-gun salute. As he was shortly to enter the Rajkumar College, the British decided an Administrator should be appointed to govern the state until he reached an age appropriate with his assuming full power. As Jam Sahib he would adopt a new name, Jassaji. At precisely a quarter to nine in the morning, attended by Agency officials and officers of state, he ascended the dais.

The sun was a good deal higher some 5,000 miles to the north-west, over the very heart of the British Empire. It was afternoon in London and a beautifully fine day. At Lord's cricket ground, the baronial seat of the game, the capital's first important fixture of the season was taking place; flags were flying and the new spacious, tiered pavilion looked magnificent. It was the second day of the match between MCC and Sussex. At the very time that Jassaji formally succeeded to the Nawanagar throne, the young man whose life had been so dramatically changed by his birth was playing in a cricket match that was possibly to alter both their futures.

MCC had batted first, and Sussex's latest recruit displayed some smart early work in the field, in particular a brilliant catch at short-slip to dismiss Grace, who was captaining MCC. He also bowled a few overs of medium-slow off-breaks shortly before the innings ended. Down at number five in the batting order, he found himself going out to take the place of his captain, Murdoch, not long after a shower at 5.30 p.m. had delayed play for ten minutes. The score was 83 for 3. He began uncertainly, with a cut for 3 only just out of reach of Grace at point; a younger and more athletic fieldsman might have completed the catch. Two more wickets fell and he was joined by George Brann, another amateur and one of Sussex's more experienced players. They batted until stumps, when Ranji was 22 not out, with four boundaries to his credit, including a leg-side shot off J. T. Hearne, MCC's leading bowler.

On the second morning, Brann and he stayed together for a further hour, putting on 101 in all, but once Brann was out the remaining wickets fell quickly; Ranji ran-out one partner with a bad call. He carried out his bat for 77 in a total of 219, and in two hours at the crease displayed both sound defence and brilliant hitting, especially his cuts. When he returned to the amateurs' room in the pavilion, he was congratulated warmly, Murdoch, knowing of his high scores in pre-season matches in Cambridge, jocularly adding, 'I suppose you won't let yourself be disposed of for under 80!'

MCC set about increasing their lead of 74. Grace, huge of frame and with a grandfatherly grey beard, showed all his old skill with another century, but shortly after he had reached his hundred Ranjitsinhji, who had been brought on only a little earlier, had him caught. After that, Ranji was kept on and finished with 6 wickets for 109, but by then Sussex had the apparently hopeless task of scoring 405 to win. They lost a wicket before the close of play.

Scarcely one hundred spectators turned up for the start on the final day. Ranji, promoted to number four, came in at 37 for 2. The match had already proved a personal success for him, and nothing was going to hold him back now, certainly not the prospect of his side's defeat. He made two hits over the boundary, in those days worth 5 each; gave a difficult chance, his first of the match, to J. T. Hearne at cover slip when 41, and, unperturbed, raced on to his fifty in forty minutes. He quite overshadowed Murdoch, who scored only 9 out of the 46 they put on for the third wicket. With Brann the score ran on from 117 for 5 to 185 for 5 at the lunch interval, when Ranji was 112 not out. His first century in first-class cricket had come in one session of play.

By the time the game was resumed, at ten minutes to three, the crowd had greatly increased. Brann, however, was soon bowled. Heasman took his place and eventually settled in. Ranji hit out relentlessly and with a new certainty. There was scarcely anything the bowlers could provide that was new to him; he had met it all before, either in practice or in the solitude of his mind's eye. He batted more dazzlingly than he had ever done before, scoring 150 of the 208 runs Sussex added in two hours thirty-five minutes, before the simplicity of a straight, good-length ball from Grace undid him. He walked back to the pavilion to prolonged applause.

After the match, which MCC won by only 19 runs, the crowd gathered in front of the pavilion to congratulate Sussex and their new-found hero on a memorable performance. Across the land the telegraphs hummed with the news. Tom Hayward would, after all, be getting his signet ring: it was going to be more necessary than ever to be seen as The Prince.

The next four months were a triumphal progress round the county grounds of England. Although he finished as high as fourth in the first-class averages, with an impressive aggregate of 1,775 runs at 49.31, it was more by his presence and by what he represented that he made such an impact on the British public. His magic apparently had the power to precede him wherever he went. People who had never seen him knew of him from the mouths of those who had, and for all of them he had an aura of romance. When he appeared on a ground he had not played at before, invariably a large crowd would gather, a phenomenon that stayed with him throughout his career, while his reception from spectators was said to equal that reserved for W. G. himself, who enjoyed a glorious return to form that year at the age of forty-seven.

Wisden said that he, 'scarcely ever looked back from his brilliant start; he quickly accustomed himself to the strange surroundings of county cricket, and scored heavily against all classes of bowling, his wonderful placing on the leg-side quite disheartening many of the leading professionals, who were unaccustomed to see perhaps their best ball turned to the boundary for four.' Although he did quickly accustom himself to county cricket, his actual introduction to the county championship was a severe one. Five days after his success at Lord's, he was at Trent Bridge, where the weather was so bitter that, when fielding, he kept his hands in his pockets and stopped the ball with his feet. Nottinghamshire amassed 726, then the record first-class total by a county, and Sussex suffered a crushing defeat. Ranji's scores in this match (29 and 27) were sound if unstartling, as they were in his next, against Lancashire at Old Trafford (35 and 46), which Sussex also lost comfortably.

Wild's comments on these games once again illustrate the exaggerated and inaccurate nature of much of his reportage. Although, characteristically, he does not identify the match exactly, he was undoubtedly talking of the first game when he said Ranji 'was on the point of collapse when a sudden snow storm overtook a match at Trent Bridge. The Sussex team had to wrap him in blankets and hurriedly light a fire in the pavilion, plying him with brandy until he recovered. This incident occurred just after he had delighted the Nottingham crowd by making a sparkling century.' What he wrote of the second match created a myth about Ranji's treatment of Mold, the fast bowler: 'Facing the most dangerous bowling in the country, Ranji showed no fear, and quickly made Mold's efforts look ridiculous. Time after time he flicked the ball to leg for a boundary.' While not doubting that Ranji did hand out this kind of punishment, especially to the faster bowlers, this match was not such an occasion. Mold's analyses do not suggest such a thing, nor do contemporary reports confirm it; indeed, *Cricket* described Sussex's first innings as 'slow and uninteresting'. Ranjitsinhji, who took forty minutes for his 35 and one and a quarter hours in poor light over his 46, in fact reserved more of what aggression he showed for Briggs's off-spin.

Sussex's results and Ranjitsinhji's own performances improved after they moved on to the more benign pitches of the Brighton ground, where the county played most of their home matches. There, a few hundred yards from the seafront, Ranjitsinhji was to become one of the day's chief attractions. The crowds would stroll the outfield during the intervals in play, beneath sea breezes full of shrill gulls, at a loss to explain what he did: the most disdainful flick of the wrists, and he could exasperate some of England's finest bowlers; the most rapid sweep of the arms, and the ball was charmed to any part of the field he chose, as though he had in his hands not a bat but a wizard's wand. It cannot have seemed unnatural that he should provide them with enchantment; few had ever seen a black man before, let alone one supposedly a prince.

High scoring was common at Brighton, particularly as the square boundaries were relatively small, and in four of Ranjitsinhji's first five games for Sussex on the ground the match aggregates exceeded 1,000 runs, one being the highest until that time for a fixture in England. In the first of these games, watched on the bank holiday Monday by a then record Brighton crowd of almost 10,000, he failed twice, but in the others, in which the cricket was often attritional, he accumulated over 500 runs, with four half-centuries and a chanceless 137 not out in about three hours on a crumbling pitch to save the match against Oxford University. The game with Yorkshire at Hastings, where he made 59 in only an hour and 74 in two and a quarter hours, hitting a total of twenty-five 4s, got him back to his most fluent, after which he returned to Brighton to face Hampshire (whom he chose to oppose rather than accept an invitation to play for the Gentlemen against the Players at Lord's) and reeled off 83 in eighty minutes, with fifteen 4s. During a few free days in this period, he returned to Cambridge and scored 206 not out for Cassandra in a club match on Parker's Piece, his first confirmed double century.

Ranji was now in fine form and soon produced two exceptional displays. The first was against Middlesex at Lord's, where he steered Sussex to victory with 110 and 72, the top scores of the match on a pitch of unreliable and lively bounce; the second was against Nottinghamshire at Brighton, where for once conditions were far from ideal, rain having made the pitch on the last day baffling to all the home batsmen except Ranji, who scored 100 in three and a quarter hours out of a total of 171. During the second innings of the Middlesex match, he shared his first century stand with Fry, 117 in only seventy minutes; it has not been generally appreciated that this was the first time they had batted together in a first-class match.

The Cricket Field described the hundred against Nottinghamshire as 'almost the finest innings of the year', but it was to be Ranji's last performance of substance during the season. From the final week of July he found his best touch elusive, and frequent interruptions for rain did not help him rediscover it. An innings of 41 against Lancashire occupied two hours, with only one scoring stroke in the first half-hour, as did his 51 against Kent, which contained the unusually high number of twenty-seven singles. The spell began and ended with modest scores against Surrey, Lockwood and Richardson showing, not for the last time, that they knew his methods as well as anyone.

Possibly he was also beginning to suffer from the mental and physical exhaustion of being expected to make runs throughout an unfamiliarly arduous season. This might have partly explained why, at Bristol early in August, after his dismissal in the second innings, he immediately changed and left the ground, presumably to catch a convenient train for Taunton, where the county were playing the next day. There was an embarrassing consequence to this when Sussex's last wicket fell with the scores level thirteen minutes from the end of the match and Jessop, with no more than one over available to him, was able to turn the third ball for the winning run towards point and the unhurried figure of Grace, the Gloucestershire captain, who had agreed to act as substitute for the absent Ranjitsinhji.

During a season in which he captured the hearts of the British public, Ranji, as he was becoming widely known, was naturally enough regularly sought out for interviews. He seems to have accepted the publicity with humility; indeed many people were impressed by his modesty. The questions must have become only too predictable for him: When did he first take up the game? What was it like playing cricket in India? Did he play any other sports? Who was the most difficult bowler he had faced? Questioners were also particularly inquisitive about his education, as though seeking an explanation for

his talent. They appeared to find comfort in the fact that the principal
of the school where he learnt cricket was an Englishman; almost,
indeed, saw it as proof of the beneficial effects of the Empire. Had
they been told that it was not an Englishman but a Parsee who taught
him the game, they might have been forced to re-examine their sense
of superiority. During these interrogations, Ranji adopted the habit
of saying he had come to England in 1892, four years later than was
actually the case. It made his rise to fame sound less of a struggle than
it had in fact been. Other things he often stressed to them were that
his initials stood for Kumar Shri, that this was a title meaning Prince,
and that it was wrong to call him '*Mr* Ranjitsinhji'.

This led to a revealing exchange with a Wiltshire journalist during
a country-house match in mid-August. After being informed that
Ranji's return to India depended on family affairs, the journalist
commented: 'A report has been circulated in some papers that you
are about to figure as the hero in an Indian succession question, which
involves delicate and important issues of high policy; that you had
according to the recognized custom been selected as the lawful successor to the chieftainship by the then reigning Prince, Sir Shri Vibhaji;
that you had since been passed over for a youth, who is illegitimate
by every established rule and therefore not entitled to succeed to the
gadi, and furthermore that, briefly, this was due to the thoughtless
acts of the Radical who at that time happened to be the Viceroy.'

'Ah, I have heard that report before,' answered Ranjitsinhji. 'It's
totally wrong and incorrect, and therefore I hope you won't notice
it. It has evidently been taken from some of the Indian papers and
they have got into a bungle in interpreting it. They do not understand
it.'

However, the journalist was to write that he then 'further gathered
that "Kumar Shri" was the title of the sons of the reigning prince of
his father's state to which he is the lawful heir. His father, who is a
Knight Commander of the Star of India, is Jam (or ruler) of Nawanagar in Kathiawar which is situate in West India and is a small state
about the size of Devon and Cornwall put together. The state is under
the protection of the British Government. It is now a well known
fact that Ranjitsinhji is a Jadeja of the Rajput race, a Hindu nation,

which, almost alone among the original inhabitants, offered a successful resistance to the Mohammadan invaders of India, and has never been subdued by anyone in their native hills . . .'

This barrage of detail, apparently volunteered by Ranji, suggests that, contrary to what he had said just previously, he was not in total disagreement with the version of events circulating in the press – that he may indeed have been its source. But the truth was that he was not the lawful heir in Nawanagar and his father was not ruler of the state, while the remarks about having resisted Muslim invasion tellingly indicate a Rajput pride more in keeping with a Jodhpur warrior than a kinsman of Nawanagar. Certainly, none of it suggested that he was conducting himself 'loyally and with fidelity' towards his state, as Vibhaji had asked.

These were among the first signs that Ranjitsinhji, beneath his jovial, carefree exterior, was beginning to harbour a determination to dispute the Nawanagar succession. What had brought this resolve nearer to the surface can only be speculated upon, but the constant enquiries about his background must have made him realize that his claim to be a prince was only tenable if he was actually contesting the Government of India's decision eleven years earlier to recognize Jaswantsinhji as heir. His fierce pride may also have been stirred by two other things. One was Vibhaji's death; the other, just possibly, the death of his father. Neither Standing, Kincaid nor Wild refer to Jiwansinhji's death; it is an event that has been allowed to disappear into the mists of time, but when Ranjitsinhji went back to India and visited his family in 1898, nothing was heard of his father, neither then nor subsequently.

Ranji's form in the early weeks of 1896 was even more impressive than it had been the previous year. There was nothing, of course, to match the sensation of his first appearance for Sussex, but he was more consistently uninhibited and brilliant in his play than he could have realistically hoped. By mid-June he already had four centuries to his name: a majestic 138 in two and a half hours against the powerful Yorkshire side, hundreds that saved matches against Gloucestershire and Somerset, and an innings of 146 at Fenner's that Jessop, who was bowling for Cambridge University, described later as 'just about as perfect a specimen of the art of batsmanship as one could desire'. At three hours forty minutes it was his longest innings to date. On 19 June he became the first amateur to reach one thousand first-class runs for the season, only a few hours after Abel of Surrey had become the first professional.

By that stage, he had had several encounters with the touring Australians. He had captained an Eleven of the South against them at Eastbourne and been a member of the MCC side that had inflicted on them their first, crushing defeat, which included the touring team being bowled out for just 18, their lowest-ever total. More importantly, he had amply demonstrated that he could cope with their bowling, in particular that of Ernest Jones, who spearheaded their attack and had gained a considerable reputation since the tour began. Jones's commanding physique enabled him to unleash deliveries at great speed off a short run and to get the ball to kick nastily off the pitch.

Ranji had first encountered him in early May, in a match on Lord Sheffield's estate, near Fletching in East Sussex; Ranji was a member of Sheffield's house party. It was a magnificent occasion attended by that great friend of India, the Prince of Wales, with huge crowds which totalled 50,000. The pitch was awkward and Jones bowled well and with hostility but Ranji was able to cope with him by working the leg-side effectively – as he did to all the bowlers, even after they had realized what his tactics were – and by steering him through the slip region. Jones took his wicket in both innings but only after he had scored 79 and 42, and he was not hit by him in the process; others on his side, including Grace, were.

These were the events, as far as Ranji was concerned, that preceded the MCC committee's meeting to select the England side to play Australia in the first Test at Lord's from 22 to 24 June. The main subject of debate, without question, was whether or not to include K. S. Ranjitsinhji. If the decision could have been made by popular concensus, or on cricketing ability alone, there would have been no argument: Ranji was one of the most celebrated figures in the country and quite clearly a good enough player, but there were other considerations.

No official explanation was ever given for the committee's decision not to choose him, but the reason that gained widest credence was that one of its members, George Canning, the fourth Lord Harris, the previous year's president of the club and a former captain of England, opposed the idea because Ranjitsinhji was not of British stock but a temporary resident in Britain who would one day return to his proper homeland. The Committee would probably have rejected him on the grounds that he had not been born in Britain except for the awkward fact that neither had Harris, who was the son of a colonial officer and had been born in Trinidad.

The reasons generally believed to be behind Harris's opposition have probably been mistaken. Harris, then in his mid-forties, was to enjoy a long playing career and for much of his adult life was an important figure in cricket's administration, but by 1896 he had just spent several years in politics and out of the game; after serving as an under-secretary during Salisbury's first two ministries, he had been Governor of Bombay from 1890 until 1895. It is more likely that he won the day in the MCC meeting not because his influence within the game was such that what he said went, but because he understood and conveyed to the meeting the 'international implications' which the press acknowledged.

It cannot be discounted that these implications had been impressed on Harris by Salisbury's latest Conservative government, keen to avoid what it would have seen as a dangerous precedent. Apart from a reluctance to see Englishmen interchangeable with or indistinguishable from other races – even if those races were members of the Empire – it had been growing increasingly concerned about the rise of Indian involvement in domestic British affairs. In 1892 the first Indian had been elected to the House of Commons in Dadabhai Naoroji, who while unable to take part in the administration of his own country was determined to represent the interests of India and its people from within the parliament of Britain. The government had been extremely anxious to prevent him winning a seat and when, during his campaign, he allied himself with the Liberal party in advocating Home Rule for Ireland in an effort to forge a link between the Indian cause and the Irish question, it began to cover him with scorn. The plan misfired when the Prime Minister himself, in a speech in Edinburgh, dismissed him as 'a black man', and the ensuing wave of public indignation had resulted in Naoroji achieving his aim of taking a seat in Westminster.

Harris's task of persuading the other committee members to share his point of view was not, however, easy. In fact they prevaricated over the decision so long that the MCC secretary was obliged to ask Ranji to 'hold himself in readiness' for the Test, and two days before the match the constitution of the team was still not publicly known. Finally, the secretary had written to Ranji again and explained why he would not be chosen. Whatever the reason for the decision, it was certainly a generally unpopular one, for the crowds wanted nothing more than to see Ranji bat. *The Field*, on 27 June, while not actually making specific mention of the case, must have had his exclusion in mind when it observed in its editorial: 'It would be hard indeed if the stranger electing to live in our country, of his own free will, should be debarred from taking part in the highest form of the game.'

Although his absence from the England party for Lord's created considerable public debate, the issue was far from finally settled because in those days Test sides were chosen, not by a permanent selection panel, but by the club staging the match. When it came to the Lancashire committee picking the side for the second Test at Old Trafford in mid-July, the decision was again not known until almost the last minute, but no lofty considerations were taken into account. Ranjitsinhji was clearly a financial draw-card and was continuing to produce spectacular form. He had just followed an innings of 171 not out, which had carried his side within ten runs of a remote target of 339 in three and a half hours against Oxford University, with scores of 69 and 73 against Kent on a bumpy pitch at Hastings, when the next highest score for Sussex had been only 37.

Lancashire sent a telegram inviting him to play. The modest reply came back: he would be glad to take part, provided that his selection was unanimously agreed and that the Australians offered no objection. It would have been difficult in the circumstances for Harry Trott, the Australian captain, to withhold his agreement, and he gracefully acceded. After what had happened, the Lancashire decision only served to draw attention to the earlier one by MCC. As *The Field* again pointed out, on 18 July: 'In asking Mr Ranjitsinhji to play the Lancashire club undoubtedly cast a reflection upon the MCC . . . Whether the MCC acted rightly or wrongly, the attitude they took upon the matter should not have been lightly set aside by one of the most prominent county clubs in the country, and the course adopted by Lancashire emphasizes the necessity for a specially appointed committee to select the England teams for representative matches.'

However, in this particular instance, there could be no going back and it was effectively settled that, 'as far as cricket is concerned', Ranji was an Englishman. But the controversy, which had rumbled on for three weeks, still did not go away. For one thing, it required a singular act of imagination for most Englishmen to think of the Indian as the same as themselves. After his successful first Test appearance, for example, the *Manchester Guardian* could not refrain from pointedly observing, 'had it not been for the magnificent hitting of Ranjitsinhji and Lilley, "England" would have cut a sorry figure indeed . . . Our Indian ally showed us how the Australian bowling should be met'. Then, in early August, when it was rumoured that Ranji had already been sounded out about his availability for a tour of Australia in 1897–98, feelings on the issue in the Australian states were sought. Responses were varied but generally favourable to him playing for England, except in South Australia, 'the racial difference appearing to local critics a very material point'. That, in itself, was to have repercussions.

Ranji's personal opinion of the view taken of him by MCC never became known but, on the day the first Test began in front of huge crowds, in the relative solitude of the Brighton ground he played his first ball, from Jessop, into his stumps, his first duck in first-class cricket for almost two years. Perhaps more tellingly still, on his next appearance at Lord's, directly before the second Test and in front of 10,000 people (Harris and the rest of the MCC committee no doubt among them), he gave an astonishing exhibition of batting.

He was playing for the Gentlemen against the Players, the first time he had appeared in the fixture at Lord's, which was considered one of the great occasions of the year. Coming in at 39 for 1 on the first morning, he made what must have been a premeditated assault on the powerful attack, which included Lohmann, the great Surrey medium-pacer, Richardson and Hearne, the three bowlers who had shared the Australian wickets in the first Test. Forsaking the customary initial caution, he began by hitting 24 out of 26 runs in just ten minutes, all from boundary strokes in two overs from Richardson: one cut, two drives and three of his inimitable leg-glances. He made 47 out of 70 in forty minutes, with ten 4s, two 2s and three singles, before being leg-before going down the pitch to drive Briggs, who two overs earlier had missed a caught-and-bowled chance from him, the ball going on to hit the umpire in the chest.

Within seven years Standing's biography would state that the whole innings lasted only ten minutes, and Wild's book made other extravagant claims on behalf of this performance: that Ranji reeled off eleven 4s and a 3 before being out to the thirteenth ball he received, which hit him in the stomach. This would have been a noteworthy achievement in a minor game, let alone in one the stature of Gentlemen v. Players at Lord's, and it is incredible that respected cricket writers have allowed themselves to repeat these unlikely details.

The public flocked to the Old Trafford Test: 20,000 on the first day, 18,000 on the second, when the weather was glorious, and 5–6,000 for the beginning of play on the third day, when rain and an English defeat threatened.

With MacLaren as well as Ranji brought in, amateurs occupied five of England's seven batting places. From the start the match went badly for England. Late injuries led them to play only three front-line bowlers; the pitch was perfect and Trott, not Grace, won the toss; Australia, having endured a crushing reversal in the Lord's Test, batted into the second day for a total of over 400. On that same second day, England surrendered fourteen wickets to an attack that possessed greater depth and versatility than their own. It was a catalogue of errors, though some fine catches were taken too.

Ranji fielded as he was to bat, not like an Englishman at all; keen and athletic in the field, he resembled more the Australians themselves. Then, in the first innings, he compiled a cautious 62 in an hour and three-quarters, during which he again employed his now well known strokes to leg, before being caught by Trott. Jones had come off soon after he went in. His dismissal, though, was not without its controversy. The *Sussex Daily News* reported: 'The Prince was secured very low down indeed at point, and appeared to doubt the decision against him so much that before leaving the crease he appealed to the second umpire.' When England followed on, 181 runs behind, he once more went in first wicket down, and with great care made 41 not out in an hour by close of play. The overall deficit had then been reduced to 72, with six wickets remaining.

On the last morning, Jones started by bowling very short and Ranji concentrated on surviving the onslaught and getting thoroughly played in. Jones bowled his fastest; Ranji, no doubt to the bowler's frustration, never flinched, stood up straight and played the rising deliveries down. Dan Hayward would have been proud of him. A. A. Lilley recalled in his autobiography that in 1908 Ranjitsinhji had told him that Jones got one through his defences during the innings, striking him a painful glancing blow and splitting the lobe of his ear, but it is surprising that Lilley, who was playing for England in this match, should not have known of the incident earlier. Ranji's partner, J. T. Brown, scored 19 of the day's first 23 runs before falling to Jones. Having taken twenty-five minutes to advance the nine runs to his 50, Ranji began to play some magnificent strokes on the leg-side, although admittedly George Giffen bowled loosely to him. With England still two runs in arrears, MacLaren was also out, but Ranji, unperturbed, took his score to 80 and his side into the lead with a drive to the boundary, 'a beautiful stroke in front of cover – one of the finest hits in a magnificent series', according to the *Manchester Guardian*. Now, barely an over was going by without him producing at least one fine hit, and only one or two could have been described as chancy or unsafe. On 98, he put a ball up within a couple of yards of point, but then a fine drive to the boundary off Trumble gave him his hundred. It was the first century the Australians had conceded on their tour and he had progressed from fifty to his century in just forty-five minutes.

Lilley stayed while 53 runs were added but once he was out Australia were into the tail and Trott brought back Jones for a final burst. Ranji clipped him to the square-leg boundary and in his next over straight drove him to the sightscreen. Ranji was all there was between the Australians and victory, but for almost another hour he kept their attack at bay, continuing to cut, drive but above all work the leg-side relentlessly. Trott was quickly forced to bring back the accurate and artful Trumble, who eventually drew from Ranji the first signs that he was beginning to tire. The *Manchester Guardian* said: 'Ranjitsinhji had dealt mercilessly with Jones, whose bowling caused him no difficulty whatever; but off Trumble he made the only faulty stroke of his innings. He seemed to give a difficult chance at the wicket, but the ball beat Kelly and went to the rails.' That took his score to 148 and later in the same over a 4 to square-leg brought up his own 150 and his side's 300, but Hearne and Richardson fell soon after that and England were all out for 305.

Ranji finished with 154 not out. During two hours ten minutes that morning he had hit seventeen of his twenty-three 4s and scored 113 of his runs. Australia took three hours ten minutes to score the 125 runs they needed to win, losing seven wickets in the process. Richardson, bowling throughout in an heroic display of stamina, claimed six of those wickets, three caught by Lilley, the wicket-keeper, and another, brilliantly, by Ranji in the slips. It was a desperately tense finish, and Trott, unable to watch, left the ground and took a ride in a hansom cab.

Shortly after six o'clock, the crowds wended their ways home, disappointed at the outcome but thrilled by the memory of Ranji, his unique methods and the revival in England's fortunes they had wrought. The man himself was bitterly disappointed at the final result, but he had succeeded on his first appearance for England and had shown himself equal to the hour of crisis.

The Australians, while readily admitting that he was a superb cricketer, were clearly still baffled by his methods. After the match, Lilley remarked to one of them, Clem Hill, what a fine batsman Ranji was. 'A fine batsman, eh?' replied Hill, ruefully. 'He's more than a batsman – he's nothing less than a juggler!' Giffen, looking back on the match in the *Windsor Magazine* in March 1898, reflected: 'Ranji is the batting wonder of the age. His play was a revelation to us, with his marvellous cutting and his extraordinary hitting to leg. I have never seen anything to equal it.' Pelham Warner, who was to play in several later Test matches against Australia, was to say that Hill, Trumble and Jones 'were always talking of that innings'.

Another member of the Australian side, Frank Iredale, described in more detail what it was like trying to contain Ranji: '. . . we did all in our power to keep the bowling away from him. In the whole course of my cricket career I never saw a man play the game in the manner that Ranjitsinhji did in his second innings of this match. He simply played with our fellows, and though we tried to block his strokes, especially on the leg side, he seemed to take a fiendish delight in putting the ball from where we had moved a fieldsman. Well, we managed to get Jackson caught, but in doing so Ranjitsinhji and he crossed, and instead of having Brown, the newcomer, to bowl at, Ranjitsinhji took up the strike, and so well did he manage the bowling that it was six overs before Brown got a strike! By that time he had warmed up, and was quite ready for his turn. Twice again Ranjitsinhji did the same thing, and each incoming batsman had a good sight of the ball before being called upon to play.'

The Times said there had never been so flawless an exhibition of scoring in an important match, while the *Manchester Guardian* was more voluminous in its praise: 'No man now living has ever seen finer batting than Ranjitsinhji showed us in this match . . . when we remember that the young Indian had never seen cricket played until a few years ago, his achievement excites not only our own strongest admiration, but also astonishment. Grace has nothing to teach him as a batsman; and none of the men of renown of thirty years ago could have exhibited a more thorough mastery of every point in the game . . . No matter what kind of ball was sent down to him – fast or medium, pitched up or pitched short, on the off stump or the leg – they were all served alike. He seemed aware of every change in the field, and they were numerous; and wherever the fielder was not, there the ball was sure to be. The force he put into his drives was not more remarkable than the ease and elegance of his wristwork. Altogether, his innings was a masterpiece.'

Such accounts as these, particularly those of the Australians, re-inforce the impression that Ranji's style was radically different from anything that had been seen before. But what was it that struck observers as so unusual about him?

One of the most striking things was that his build was seemingly too insubstantial to meet the demands made of it; the way he walked out to the wicket swinging his bat back and forth from the wrist, too indolent; the very way he moved, too languid. Everything conspired to suggest a complete absence of effort or concentration. One commentator was to observe: 'The shirt, always of silk, always fully large, was his most distinctive feature. It bellied and flapped round his body like a sail at every movement of the breeze. And there he stood at the wicket, the very embodiment of grace and elegance, almost careless and lazy in attitude, so perfect and relaxed was the whole poise of the slight delicate figure.' But whatever his appearance, he left nothing to chance.

Gardiner described another, fundamental difference between Ranjit-sinhji and other batsmen: 'There is extraordinarily little display in his methods . . . He has none of the fine flourishes of our own stylists, but a quite startling economy of action. The normal batsman, obeying a natural impulse, gets into motion as the bowler starts his run . . . The style of the Jam Sahib is entirely different. He stands moveless as the bowler approaches the wicket. He remains moveless as the ball is delivered. It seems to be on him before he takes action. Then, without any preliminary flourish, the bat flashes to the ball, and the stroke is over. The body seems never to have changed its position, the feet are unmoved, the bat is as before. Nothing has happened except that one sudden flash – swift, perfectly timed, indisputable.'

Ranji's method was based on an economy of movement; on a principle of conserving energy. It was a way of mastering endurance. This, of course, was the origin of his preference for shots behind or square to the wicket, not only his leg-glances but also his cutting, which required so much less physical exertion. This reached the stage that he would often play these strokes to balls which other batsmen would have had to drive; he could even play the leg-glance off good-length deliveries on the middle stump, and off front or back

71

foot. His skill was so consummate that he was becoming able to place his shots between fieldsmen with a high degree of accuracy, while the rapidity with which the ball would travel to the boundary was always to be a feature of his play. He hardly ever missed a ball he played at, he timed the ball perfectly and rarely lifted it off the ground. As Jessop wrote, in 1922: 'One rarely saw a bad shot from him when he was in regular practice.' It was no wonder the bowlers became demoralized.

His ability to make fine adjustments to strokes only came to him through practice, as it had only come to Grace and Arthur Shrewsbury, of Nottinghamshire, one of the leading professional batsmen in England, whom he rivalled in the art. The year after this, in 1897, Ranjitsinhji was to write in *The Jubilee Book of Cricket*: 'The art of placing is now, and always has been, at a premium. There are not more than ten players in the country who pay much attention to it. The Champion made a speciality of placing. He himself attributes much of his success to the ease which assiduous practice gave him in the art. The way to acquire the art of placing is never to make a stroke without thinking where the ball is meant to go.' Ranjitsinhji's skill in this area stemmed from his powerful wrists and nimble footwork. Instead of gripping the bat in the flats of his hands, he used almost entirely his slim fingers and thumbs, with the top of the handle pressed against the base of the left thumb, holding the bat, unlike Grace, with hands apart. He varied his precise grip according to the stroke he was going to play and his wrists were always free to give sting and finish to a stroke. This was assisted by the use of a bat (usually a Gunn & Moore) that was long in the handle and not heavy for its period – about 2lb 5oz. The result was a uniquely uninhibited technique that allowed him to score runs in almost any direction.

All this occurred because he was preoccupied with eliminating error. He took nothing on trust. Of course, he might be deceived if a ball deviated unexpectedly through some quirk of the pitch, but everything else he regarded as within his control. He would not only watch the ball in flight but even as it left the bowler's hand, for any early indication of imparted spin or swing, and would make a point of taking a closer examination while standing at the non-striker's end. After studying the back-play of Shrewsbury he became convinced of its superior safety. This was to lead to accusations of him sometimes defending the stumps with his pads, but his method was based on attack rather than defence. Jephson, the Surrey lob bowler, wrote: 'By their consummate placing Shrewsbury and Ranji could score off any ball I had the temerity to suggest to them. They played back or were up the pitch and smothered everything! I once hit Shrewsbury on the leg, and Ranji I hit on the pads! I was as pleased as if I had got them out, for, of all the men I have ever bowled at or seen bowled at, these two made the fewest mistakes. They so rarely missed a ball they played at.'

Ranjitsinhji was reluctant to go forward to deliveries, and sometimes did so only to smother, because he knew there was a moment in a front-foot stroke when the ball was out of sight and had to be played on faith. He would, though, occasionally jump down the pitch to slow or lob bowling. He rejected the argument that all strokes not played with a straight bat must be unsafe, saying that in the case of the cut, the pull or the hook it was simply a matter of choosing the right ball to hit (he was to make this quite clear in *The Jubilee Book of Cricket*: 'The old-fashioned theory that any stroke played with a cross-bat must be bad cricket does not hold water. A stroke which is safe and effective cannot be bad cricket'). He would even sometimes avoid wearing a sweater, regardless of the weather conditions, for fear it might cramp his movements. He had, quite simply, thought of everything.

By the relatively early stage in his career of 1896, perhaps the greatest flaw in his game was that, if he was to apply himself properly, he often needed a suitable spur. His most notable successes had invariably occurred not when he felt free to play his shots but when his side were in difficulty or the situation demanded some measure of self-restraint. Thirteen of his fourteen centuries in first-class cricket before 1897 were to be made in just such circumstances.

Despite his successes, he still had some way to go to win the support of certain sections of English society. Among those who watched the Old Trafford Test of 1896 was Sir Home Gordon, a journalist and publisher and a passionate cricket-lover. Afterwards, he recalled in his *Background of Cricket* (1939), he returned to London and met an old acquaintance, a long-standing member of MCC who had served on the club's committee and played for the Gentlemen. Home Gordon enthused to him over Ranjitsinhji's wonderful performance. The veteran turned on him and told him that if it were possible he would have him expelled from MCC for having 'the disgusting degeneracy to praise a dirty black'.

Home Gordon found this was not an isolated sentiment. He heard other MCC members decry 'a nigger showing us how to play the game of cricket'.

Ranji suffered something of a reaction to his phenomenal Test début. In his next match, which started five days later, he again played the Australians, for MCC at Lord's, and made just 1 and 3 (the least productive match, in which he batted twice, of his career), followed by scores of 2 and 18 against Middlesex at Brighton. Although in five innings he then hit three half-centuries and an unbeaten century, which saved the match against Nottinghamshire, he endured another double failure in the third and final Test at the Oval, when he was dismissed cheaply twice on the second day.

The Test was overshadowed by a strike by five of the selected professionals, who demanded that their fees be doubled to £20 plus bonus money. One of the professionals' chief complaints was that the popularity of cricket had risen sharply in recent years while their wages had not, but the other, more significantly, was that they were finding themselves little better off than the amateurs, who were of course receiving liberal expenses. Considerable controversy was aroused and there must have been a strained atmosphere among the England players. Three of the rebels in fact backed down before play began and the demands were not to be met for another three years.

England nevertheless won the match and the series, bowling Australia out for just 44 on the last day, when Ranji did not take the field. Fry, who was attending the match as a spectator, described what happened, in his *Life Worth Living* (1939): 'Ranji, who had had a bad night with asthma, indulged in a leisurely uprising, and we were driving past the oak palings of the Oval about an hour after the start of play. Standing up in the hansom cab I saw on the scoreboard:

Total 14 for seven wickets down. Heavens! This could not be England, because England had scored more than that overnight. Again Heavens! When we drew up at the main entrance gates I helped Ranji out of the cab and lent him my arm as support. It appeared that he had trodden on an upturned carpet-nail at the hotel on his way to the bath.'

This is the earliest match in which asthma is said to have hampered Ranji, although it was to do so more consistently and more seriously the following year and intermittently for the rest of his playing career. Standing stated he first contracted it after night-fishing in Huntingdonshire. It is possible that on this specific matter Fry, whose autobiography is in any case a far from accurate document, was let down by his memory (he was an hour out over their arrival, which from the score was in fact about two hours after the start of play). It is also possible that Ranji had little wrong with him and had simply 'indulged in a leisurely uprising' in the belief that England, who were 60 for 5 overnight, would still be batting when he got to the ground, only to find they had collapsed to 84 all out and a professional was substituting for him in the field. Ranji certainly appears to have had a poor reputation among his captains for punctuality and was to admit that when he met up in Naples with the rest of the party for Australia in September 1897, Stoddart 'was much relieved and gratified to find me safe on board, inasmuch as the knowledge of a certain amount of forgetfulness in my character made him anxious as to my being able to arrive on the appointed day'.

If this was the true reason for his absence during the Oval Test, it might explain why Ranji, mindful of the sensitive position existing with the professionals, later acted with such generosity towards one of them, Lilley, over an incident earlier in the match. Ranji had received much acclaim for chasing the ball to the boundary's edge and effecting a run out with a throw into Lilley's gloves over the stumps, a distance said to be well over 100 yards (the batsmen were on a fifth run when his return came in). For what was, after all, a very minor role in the dismissal, Lilley received from him a gold cigarette case. Although Ranji was to present other players with extravagant gifts – he gave Killick, the Sussex professional, a gold watch and chain, and Richardson an Indian tea and coffee service as a wedding present, this was generosity indeed.

An end to the Test series and all the attentions that had gone with it seemed to act as a release to Ranjitsinhji, who enjoyed spectacular form over the next ten days at Brighton. As he had after the second Test, he promptly met up again with the Australians, but did so with greater success for Sussex than he had for MCC. The touring team won comfortably, but in the second innings Ranjitsinhji, who scored 74, and Fry produced the best partnership of the match, 123 in seventy minutes. Then, against Lancashire, he gave a remarkable performance. Batting at number seven in the first innings because of a finger injury, he hit 40 out of 65 added in an hour and then, in the second, 165 out of 216 added in three and a quarter hours to almost single-handedly save the match for his side. When Sussex had gone in again they were 192 behind with four and a half hours remaining. Ranji went in after the early loss of Fry and quickly assumed control during a second-wicket partnership of 71 with Marlow, who scored 25. He made a point of seeing off the dangerous Mold, whom he punished severely on the leg-side, although the fast bowler later returned to have him missed at third man when 65. He added 43 with Newham (whose share was just 10), and 52 with Vine (who made only 9). As the *Manchester Guardian* said, 'It was nearly all Ranjitsinhji's work'. He was finally stumped, easily, off Sugg's lob bowling, having hit twenty-six 4s, while his forty-three singles were a clear indication of how he had again controlled the strike.

Lancashire were to finish second in the championship that year and Ranji's next match was against the side that won it, Yorkshire. The encounter resulted in one of the most celebrated feats of his career. On the second day Yorkshire had gained a position of command when rain brought play to a close early in the afternoon with Sussex 23 for 2 in reply to a total of 407; Ranji, batting in his usual position of number three, had been in less than three overs and had yet to score. The next morning Sussex were all out for 191, of which Ranji's share was 100, made out of 132 while at the wicket in ninety minutes. After being asked to follow-on they held out for a draw, scoring 260 for 2, Ranjitsinhji unbeaten with 125 out of 199 in two hours ten minutes. He had not only scored a century in each innings, a feat only four batsmen had previously achieved in England, but he had done so on the same day, which remains without parallel. He was able to bring off this unique performance partly because of the way he monopolized the scoring, as he had against Lancashire, and partly because of the speed with which he made his runs, scoring twice as fast as his partners. He was, in turn, able to score so quickly because of the high proportion of his runs that came in boundaries; eighteen in the first innings and twenty-one in the second, when he also had an all-run 4 and a hit for 3 supplemented by an overthrow.

His first-innings century was a feat of technical skill, his second one of physical endurance. Murdoch had been out to the first ball of the third day, leaving Sussex struggling at 23 for 3, but Ranji and Newham, who also batted extremely well but could score only 37 in two hours, then shared a remarkable stand of 132 in less than eighty minutes. Ranji's second fifty came in just half an hour. At 12.55 he was out, caught at extra slip off Ernest Smith, off whom he had earlier nearly lofted catches to Hawke at mid-on and Brown at deep point. Just how awkward conditions were was shown by the fact that, after he was out, Sussex's remaining 6 wickets fell for 36 to Hirst and Smith, who bowled short and got several balls to rear dangerously. Hawke, looking for the breakthrough that would effectively win the match, continued with the same bowlers after lunch, when Sussex followed-on 216 behind, but conditions were easing, Smith and Hirst were growing tired and the batsmen were taking no risks. After an hour Fry was out at 61, which, at about a quarter to four, brought in Ranjitsinhji again, less than three hours since he was last batting. From then until twenty-five minutes to seven, during which there was a tea interval of half an hour, Ranji occupied the crease, his only escape being an early stumping chance off Brown. For the first fifty-five minutes he was partnered by the imperturbable Marlow, then by Killick, with whom he played out the last eighty minutes and put on 127. Hawke used eight bowlers in the innings but Yorkshire had resigned themselves to a draw and to Ranjitsinhji taking easy runs off the occasional bowling when, at 6.20, he scampered a single off Hirst to reach his second hundred.

77

The crowd, which had grown from 1,000 to 3,000 since the start of play, clapped, shouted, waved hats and handkerchiefs, and generally displayed what *Wisden* was to describe as the 'wildest excitement'. This continued when Ranji ran from the field at the end of the match and when he later emerged from the amateur dressing-room to acknowledge the acclaim of the large gathering outside the pavilion.

His strokeplay that day seems to have been brilliant all round; reports comment on his superb wristwork, his marvellous placing on the leg-side, his grand driving and his crisp cutting. It is interesting to note that of his thirty-nine boundaries only five (four of them off Jackson) were behind the wicket on the leg-side, while as many as twelve came from the cut, a stroke of which he obviously had particular mastery but which received less public attention than his more original leg shots. The only members of Yorkshire's championship-winning attack that appeared to cause him any real trouble were, in the first innings, Smith and, in the second, Brown, whose slow right-arm bowling to a strong leg-side field was not played with ease by any of the Sussex batsmen. Ranji hit eleven 4s off Jackson, on whom he was particularly severe, six off Peel, five off both Hirst and Smith, four off Denton, three off both Wainwright and Brown, and two off Moorhouse. *Wisden* said, 'It is not often that the Yorkshire bowlers have been treated with so little respect', but it has to be remembered that, being in with a chance of victory and in no danger of defeat themselves, they were more concerned with taking wickets than saving runs.

The *Yorkshire Post* was not inclined to be as enthusiastic over Ranji's great performance as the Brighton crowd, commenting that the match ended in a draw 'chiefly because the period of play was curtailed by rain'. Elsewhere, noting that he was not the first batsman that season to have scored a century in each innings against the county (Storer, of Derbyshire, having done so in June), it added: 'The dual performance may suggest some weakness in the Yorkshire attack, and possibly the suggestion may not be quite groundless, though on the other hand, without disparaging either batsman's efforts, it should be mentioned that on each occasion the second hundred was made when an abortive result of the match was a foregone conclusion.'

Ranji's second hundred in the match was in fact his tenth of the season, equalling the first-class record, held inevitably by Grace, and took his run aggregate to 2,578, only 161 short of the highest-ever for one season, also held by Grace. He had three matches left to him and although he was unable to play another innings of fifty, let alone one of a hundred which would have allowed him to beat outright Grace's total, he scored solidly, so that by his final match, against Surrey at Brighton, he needed only a further eight runs to claim the aggregate record. He made them on the first day, with very great caution. Apart from equalling one major batting record and establishing another, he also had the satisfaction of finishing top of the averages, with 2,780 runs at 57.92 an innings.

The 1896 season had proved to be a succession of cricketing triumphs for Ranji. As a mark of their appreciation, Sussex were to present him with a silver shield bearing his scores during his two seasons with the club, and at the end of September Cambridge paid tribute to its new son – and England at large saluted its most unlikely hero – with a dinner in the great banqueting room of the town's Guildhall.

There were 300 guests: town and borough dignitaries, eminent figures from the university, representatives from the leading cricket clubs, and many of Ranjitsinhji's friends. Dr Butler, the Master of Trinity, proposed his health and several other speakers were to lavish him with praise. Naturally, the guest of honour was also called on to speak, and he frankly admitted his nervousness at having to do so, feelings which cannot have been alleviated by the whole company singing 'For He's a Jolly Good Fellow', accompanied by handkerchief-waving from the ladies in the gallery, as he rose to his feet. The cheering went on for several minutes.

The occasion was, of course, meant to be primarily a cricketing one, yet judging by some of the speeches, and the press response the following day, it represented more the possible beginning of Ranjitsinhji's political career. Two local MPs spoke. One said that Ranji had gained the support of both Houses of Parliament by helping to 'establish that solidarity and good feeling which ought to subsist between all the subjects of the Queen . . . and which is the real security of our Empire'; the other said that if Ranji was contemplating standing for a seat in the Commons, 'he would find as hearty a welcome as on the cricket fields of England'.

In his own speech, Ranji endorsed the opinion of the first MP. 'It has always been, and will always be,' he said, 'my endeavour in my humble way to bring about real brotherly love between the two nations . . . From the very beginning I have been connected with English people, and have a great liking and admiration for their high social and intellectual qualities.' He added that he hoped it would not be long before all Her Majesty's dominions could live together happily and trust each other in a way they had not done before. 'I trust that the wrongs done in the past by Her Majesty's Indian subjects and the injustice, if any, which they have suffered in days gone by, will be forgotten and that England and India may in future form one united country.'

The national press, while alluding to Ranji in their usual clumsy, embarrassing images of the jungle, responded by hailing him as a true friend of the Empire. One newspaper, the *Star*, reiterated that, 'if Prince Ranjitsinhji had any ambitions in the political line, he would have no difficulty in securing a nomination from some enthusiastic constituency, for at this moment he is the most popular man in England'.

In view of the fact that Indian representation in Parliament was still an extremely sensitive issue, these remarks are interesting indeed. Naoroji still held his seat in the Commons and had been seen as sufficiently dangerous by Salisbury's Conservative party to have warranted installing an Indian puppet, M. M. Bhownagree, to counterbalance him. The notion of Ranjitsinhji entering Parliament was certainly an earnest one and, even before the Cambridge dinner, there had been talk that he had political ambitions in England and that he was nearly persuaded to address a meeting at the Dome in Brighton during the previous general election of July 1895. Indeed, within a year it was to be reported, in the *Windsor Magazine* in August 1897, that he intended to stand for a parliamentary seat in Brighton as a Liberal. In the event, this proved to be a wish unfulfilled but it can be imagined that in government circles there was anxiety as to exactly where his political sympathies lay and at the power his widespread popularity might bring to the Indian nationalist movement.

However, although it was fairly clear to others that he possessed loftier ambitions than simply to be a successful sportsman, it is probable that he flirted with politics in Britain simply to satisfy their preconceived ideas of what those ambitions were. His real ambition, as he himself had gradually come to realize, lay in the Nawanagar succession and had probably been shaping itself more firmly since he had first discussed the issue with the British press the previous year.

The more celebrated he became in Britain, it seemed, the more bitter he became about his past treatment in India. In a letter to Lt.-Col. Willoughby Kennedy, the Administrator of Nawanagar, ten days after the Cambridge dinner, he pointedly referred to 'the adoption deed, by which I was years ago made heir apparent' and, perhaps encouraged by Kennedy's admiring remarks ('I must congratulate you most heartily on your cricket form this last season and that you came off so well against the Australians at Manchester the other day'), declared that he was thinking of petitioning the Government of India on the Nawanagar succession and on his 'exact status'. He also intended to enquire,

'. . . whether I could not have a suitable allowance considering the peculiar circumstances of my case and as befitting the dignity of Jamnagar, not that Jamnagar would care to think very much of me. I think you will not consider that I am doing anything that is wrong in this as I think it high time that I did something for my future prospects, for I cannot long continue to live on so small an income of my own and be dependent on my generous relatives who have so far treated me to the best of their means . . . I thank you for your kind congratulations regarding my success at cricket. The English people here have been most kind and generous in their hospitality towards me. They generously gave a banquet to celebrate my being at the top of the English averages but the greatest success which I consider is the honour of being chosen to represent England v. Australia.

I often long to be back but there are many things to prevent me carrying out my intention. I cannot think I can put up with the worry which I should be put to nor do I think I should feel quite safe being there, knowing different durbars as I do. I daresay I am encroaching on your valuable time in the management and improvement of Jamnagar. I feel sure you must have had a great deal to improve.'

All this talk, however, had a more practical inspiration than simply harboured feelings of injustice: during his first two seasons in county cricket, Ranji's financial plight had grown worse rather than better, and he had been acquiring new debts and failing to pay off old.

He had still not, for example, repaid the £30 he owed to Chester Macnaghten. Macnaghten had died in the spring of 1896 but when his widow twice wrote to Ranji about the money, her letters were ignored. Kennedy had been obliged to inform Ranji that the money would be deducted from his allowance, which was already being withheld to recover his two sizeable advances. Ranji was desperate for the payments of his allowance to be resumed and claimed, in his letter to Kennedy (whom he addressed as 'Major'), that it had been agreed with the late Jam Sahib that one of the advances was entirely a gift, while the other was to be repaid only when he returned to India. He also asked Kennedy to meet a draft for some £450 – 'I am quite sure the state (through you) could well afford to be generous in a matter of this sort rather than make me a sufferer' – but when he tried to draw it, in London towards the end of October, he was refused. About a month after that, he at last received the latest payment of his allowance, but once the various deductions had been made, he got only £82.

Ranjitsinhji's batting achievements of 1896 were some of the most remarkable in cricket history. They were so not least because they were made against a background of indifferent health and shameless, though very necessary, pleas for money.

5

A WIDER FAME

ON A SNOWY day during the winter of 1896, Ranjitsinhji was shooting on the estate of a local landowner, Henry Wright, at Royston, some fifteen miles from Cambridge, when he was taken seriously ill with congestion of the lungs. Through the hospitality of his host, he was confined to Wright's house there, Kneesworth Hall, for the next ten weeks and attended upon with the greatest care.

This is the version of events given by Percy Standing and Roland Wild, although Alfred Gaston, in his introduction to *With Stoddart's Team in Australia*, published two years after the events, told of how he had visited Ranji's rooms shortly before and had noticed that he was not well then. Remembering the desperate financial difficulties Ranji was in at the time, the chance to live at somebody else's expense must have held considerable attraction, and this may have been an instance of him availing himself of such an opportunity.

Whatever the exact circumstances, Ranji's stay with Wright also, happily, presented him with the opportunity to earn some money and produce one of the classic works on cricket. Some time before this, a publisher had asked Fry to edit a series of handbooks for schoolboys on various athletic pursuits, and Ranji had been invited to contribute one on cricket. He had, accordingly, begun work on a manuscript. However, more recently another firm, Blackwood and Sons, had approached him with a proposal for a larger work, a textbook dealing with all aspects of the game, but although they offered more money and the idea must have had greater appeal, it was a large undertaking and he had not seen how he could find the time: that is, until he was laid up at Kneesworth Hall.

As soon as he was able to sit up, he dictated his share of the book to a typist – six technical chapters, subjecting each department of the game to an unprecedented analysis, and a concluding chapter on the development of cricket during the Victorian era. Further chapters, giving histories of the game at the great public schools and universities and for each of the major county clubs, were provided by other writers. Fry, whose series of handbooks never materialized, helped with final revisions when they travelled together in Europe in the spring of 1897, probably paying particular attention to the last chapter, which has a more literary bias. Though the final work was addressed to the young reader, in form it resembled Grace's *Cricket*. There has been much unfounded speculation about Ranji's ability to write such a book and about Fry's precise contribution, but the author's explanation of his involvement in its production, in an interview with the *Windsor Magazine* for October 1897, is persuasive in its detail and leaves little doubt that Ranji was the principal contributor.

Profusely illustrated, it was published in August 1897, during Victoria's Diamond Jubilee celebrations. Ranjitsinhji and his publisher did not miss the opportunity to entitle it *The Jubilee Book of Cricket* or to add, 'Dedicated, By Her Gracious Permission, To Her Majesty The Queen-Empress'. His consummate knowledge of the art and science of the game guaranteed it would be a masterly treatise; devoured by a public who suspected its creator was touched by genius, it rapidly went through several editions and has survived the years with its reputation intact.

Refreshed after his European trip with Fry, Ranji quickly picked up where he had left off the previous season when he returned to the cricket field with two of the longest innings he had then played. In his second match, for Sussex against MCC at Lord's, he hit 260, by 89 runs the highest score of his career until then, and five days later on the same ground made 157 for MCC against Lancashire. In the second of these innings he batted three and a half hours; in the first, four hours five minutes. He had written, 'It is impossible to train for long scores in a few days. It may be years before a man can combine enough proficiency with enough strength to play a really long innings.' These two innings suggest that his regime of regular pre-season practice was starting to reap its reward. He was slow to settle during his double century, perhaps hampered by chilly early May weather, but he then unleashed a series of glorious shots, including an uncharacteristic number of powerful drives, and in all hit one 6 and thirty-six 4s. His score came out of a total of 418 (but Sussex lost the match) and was only 18 runs short of the record for an innings at Lord's.

This glorious beginning opened up seemingly boundless possibilities for his season, but it was to prove a false dawn. His next sixteen innings realized just four half-centuries and the highest of these, 79 against Essex, contained several chances. One of his best displays was the 74 he made against the Philadelphians at Brighton, after earlier being bowled for 0 by the first ball he received from J. B. King, the fast bowler, who was largely responsible for Sussex's dismissal in less than an hour for 46. Afterwards, King was reminded of the magnitude of his achievement when Ranji presented him with his bat.

Although there was little wrong with the pitch on this occasion, Ranji had to bat on some awkward strips during this spell and it was the first match in July, against Middlesex at Eastbourne, before Sussex were able to reach 300 in the championship. Conditions there were ideal for occupying the crease and Ranji played himself back into form with an unbeaten 129 in the second innings. A fortnight later began a sequence of three matches in which he was able to bat on firm, true pitches. It started at Old Trafford, where large crowds watched a high-scoring draw with Lancashire in which Ranji, the chief object of attention, hit 87 in a stand of 140 with Brann, and it continued at Brighton, where he took a fluent 149 off a weak Hampshire side and scored 170 as Sussex comfortably saved the match with Essex after being made to follow-on.

On the second evening of the fixture at Old Trafford, he had to travel down to London and back and, with the game certain to end in a draw, batted again the following afternoon, Saturday, only because of the many spectators, most of whom had come to see him bat. Sadly, going in at 128 for 1, he was out for 0. However, Wild may have been again relying on an ageing man's indistinct and fanciful memories when he described the occasion thus: 'The crowd demanded that Ranji go in first wicket down, and so insistent were they on seeing him bat that he was sent for from his hotel on the last day of the match. When the wicket fell and it was learnt that he would make a personal appearance, the crowd waiting outside the gates paid their money gladly and filled the stand. There was an anti–climax. Ranji was out first ball and the stands were suddenly empty again.'

In Britain for the celebrations of Queen Victoria's Diamond Jubilee, were Devisinhji, Ranji's half–brother, and Pratap Singh, Regent of Jodhpur since the death two years earlier of his elder brother, Jaswant Singh, and a relative of Ranjitsinhji, although they had almost certainly never met before. Pratap was a short, powerfully built man in his fifties, displaying all the traditional Rajput virtues, and fond of saying, 'For a Rajput, war is an open door to Heaven.' A man of few words, he had a natural talent for upstaging other people. Ten years previously, in 1887, he had attended Queen Victoria's Golden Jubilee and had laid his sword at her feet, taken the hand extended for the customary kiss and put it across his eyes, signifying the surrender of the warrior's greatest treasure, his sight. It must have been clear to Ranjitsinhji that Pratap, possessing considerable influence in both British and Indian court circles, was a man worth cultivating and he was soon not only presenting Devisinhji as his brother but the Regent of Jodhpur as his uncle.

It was perhaps no coincidence that it was about now that Ranji began to show signs of restlessness with his position. His fame was making him keenly aware of what circumstances had denied him. The British public, believing him to be a prince, expected his daily extravagances, expected him to bestow exotic gifts on friends while treating himself to the best of everything, but such even–handed generosity was only serving to put him on the brink of bankruptcy. It is revealing that a profile of him in *Vanity Fair* in August 1897 referred to him having a 'violent temper' and to a well–publicized argument he had had recently with 'Teddy' Wynyard, the Hampshire captain, after helping himself to some of Wynyard's grapes. Although others were to remark on his impatience and a reputation he had for not suffering fools gladly, he seems to have been generally of good humour, but around this time there were further, more telling indications that he felt unfulfilled, in the shape of continuing rumours that shortly he would be forsaking cricket for politics.

Before the 1897 season was even over, Ranji had resolved that the time had come to act, no doubt after listening to the advice of Pratap Singh and Devisinhji, who would have informed him that Lakhuba, Vibhaji's grandson, had begun the previous year to dispute the Nawanagar succession. He decided to return to India at the next available opportunity, which was to be after the forthcoming five-month tour of Australia.

All this, of course, distracted Ranji from his cricket, and he produced only one score of over fifty after July. He appeared to lack application and throw his wicket away, although this was partly due to the effects of asthma, which inconvenienced him more during the last two months of this season than at any other stage of his cricket career in England. He suffered so severe an attack during his last match, against Surrey at Brighton, that he had to retire and resume his innings later. At the end of the season, *Cricket* observed that he had 'not been himself for some time' and attributed his loss of form to the rigours of authorship and claims to a kingdom. His overall figures – 1,940 runs at 45.12 – rivalled the best of other batsmen, but he was dismissed for a single-figure score fourteen times (including four ducks), a tally he never approached either before or after.

Unfortunately, his final poor spell of form coincided with the *Sussex Daily News* setting up a subscription fund for him, which it was hoped would match Grace's £4,000 testimonial of 1895, but it was rather late in the season and his absence from the headlines meant that all he received was a gift of plate and a portrait of himself by H. J. Brooks, a Royal Academy painter.

The England tour of Australia in 1897–98, led by A. E. Stoddart, was, in terms of results, a disaster. Beaten by four matches to one in the Test series, several of the players failed to find any sort of form and the Australians were not only superior all round in technique but also demonstrated themselves more sophisticated tactically, studying carefully the individual weaknesses of their opponents. The only successes among the visitors were MacLaren and Ranjitsinhji, whose close friendship can be dated from this time.

Ranji scored 1,157 runs in twelve first-class matches, 457 of them in the Tests, and perhaps as a result of his Indian past was able to adjust quickly to the heat, the brighter light and faster pitches. His rapid acclimatization was especially praiseworthy as sea travel never agreed with him and although he had shortened the journey by meeting the main party on the south of the Continent he was ill during the month-long voyage. He had the consolation, however, of stopping over at Colombo on the way and was clearly moved by his first sight of Asia in almost ten years.

Only three days after the team arrived they began their first match, against South Australia in Adelaide. Having fielded into the second day, Ranji was nearly out to the first ball he received, from Jones, but, enjoying a good deal of fortune, survived for almost four and a half hours and scored 189. He must have shown some assurance, because he hit twenty-three 4s and thirteen 3s, but he also gave at least six chances, not including the ball rolling into his stumps without disturbing a bail when he was on 78. After the match, the touring side moved on to Melbourne, where they were received by the mayor at the town hall. J. T. Hearne, a member of Stoddart's team, noted in his diary the 'large crowd of people outside, all to see Ranji'.

Although the tour was a personal triumph on several fronts for Ranjitsinhji, his achievements were even greater than may at first be realized, because of the extent to which he was hindered by poor health and fitness. Everything had appeared to be going well in his preparations for the first Test in Sydney, scheduled to start on 10 December. He scored a half-century against Victoria and a chanceless unbeaten hundred as his side raced to victory over New South Wales (he and MacLaren put on 180 in one hour fifty-five minutes); but during a game in Brisbane near the end of November he was taken ill. The illness worsened on the journey to Toowoomba, where he made only 0 and 8 against a local XVIII, and was diagnosed as quinsy, which he had previously suffered in 1891. He missed the next fixture, another minor match, at Armidale, and was so poorly that when the party was due to go on to Sydney he was unable to accompany them.

Had the first Test begun on the appointed day, Ranji would certainly have been unable to take part, but heavy rain encouraged the trustees of the ground to chance the ensuing controversy and delay the start until the weather improved. Perhaps the possibility that the popular Indian would recover was also a factor in their decision, for the Australian public was so keen to see him that the New South Wales government had even waived in his case a tax on coloured persons entering the colony. In the event the Test was postponed from Friday until Monday, and by the Sunday there was talk that Ranji would be well enough to play.

He eventually decided that he was fit, and his first innings has claims to be the greatest performance he ever gave. It presented him with the ultimate test of his abiding principle, of playing within one's means in order to conserve energy; for somebody playing in a Test match, having spent most of the previous fortnight in bed, this was absolutely vital. Though aided by his innings being spread over two days, he nevertheless demonstrated his faithful observance of his rule during a masterly and lengthy stay at the crease. The *South Australia Advertiser* declared: 'Under any circumstances it would have been a great innings, but as it was it was sensational . . . After this it will be difficult to assign a limit to his powers.'

In making their decision to delay the start of the match, the trustees did so without consulting the captains; with Stoddart unavailable (his mother had recently died) and Ranjitsinhji ill, MacLaren, the acting England captain, had wanted to start the match on the appointed day, perhaps with the view that playing on a rain-affected pitch gave his side their best chance. Anyway, three days late, he won the toss and chose to bat, and it was his chanceless century that enabled Ranji to be kept back until late in the day. When he went in, at number seven, the score was 258 for 5, the weather glorious, the outfield a lush green and the pitch, though a little slow, ideal for batting. Earlier in the day, Ranji had practised briefly, but did not look in good shape, and it was a surprise when he began to shape confidently. He did not bat with his usual fluency, but perhaps concentrated the more fiercely because of his illness, and justified his decision to play by his sheer pluck. He repeatedly looked for the less strenuous openings behind square on the leg-side, but Hill patrolled the area efficiently; just occasionally he unleashed a dazzling shot to remind everyone what he was ordinarily capable of. He kept pace with Hirst, his partner, until stumps, by which time he was judging the flight of the ball better and placing his shots with his customary precision. When he came off the field, 39 not out, he was exhausted and unable to speak.

The next day promised to be even more difficult for him. Before play he underwent a minor operation on his throat and was in pain for hours. He began quietly, sparing himself, while the attack was maintained by Hirst. Then, with two successive 4s off Trott, he brought up first his own fifty and then the century partnership. Throughout most of the morning session and into the afternoon period, when Trumble and Jones shared the attack, he confined his scoring to occasional bursts of activity; both were bowling tight, while Ranji was to say later that the first few overs he received from Jones were among the fastest he ever faced. He cut Trumble for 4 twice in the same over and shortly after broke a bat driving at Jones, whom he then cut for 4, but he began to show signs of weakening. As the interval approached his strength manifestly failed; it seemed he would achieve his hundred only if he had the stamina to do so. He reached the haven of lunch with his score 94, and on resuming showed renewed strength. Soon, he was able to hook Trumble to square-leg for 4 runs and the century was his.

Hirst had been bowled by Jones less than half an hour into the morning, after the sixth wicket had realized 124 in only one hour thirty-five minutes. Now it was up to the tailenders, although there would have been little point in them staying there if Ranji did not attack while he still felt refreshed. He took the withdrawal of Trumble from the attack as the signal to begin. Though he sometimes straight-drove McLeod, in the period that followed he was to score chiefly from leg-side hits and brilliant cuts. Trott was forced to place an extra fielder between point and third-man, but Ranji still cut with success. Hearne stayed while 49 runs were added and though Briggs fell quickly, Richardson played unexpectedly well in a last-wicket partnership that produced 74. Ranji took most of the strike and treated the bowling with little mercy: in the same over that saw the 500 come up, Ranji gave a very difficult return chance that split McLeod's hand on the way to the boundary. Eventually, through sheer exhaustion, at 551 Ranjitsinhji hit a good-length ball from McKibbin straight to

Gregory at cover-point. He had batted three hours thirty-five minutes for 175, and hit twenty-four 4s. Half his boundaries and 75 of his runs came in the last sixty-five minutes. It was then the highest Test innings played for England and remained the record until R. E. Foster reached 287 on the same ground six years later to the day.

Largely because of his remarkable display, England won the match by 9 wickets (he was at the wicket when the winning runs were hit). But he was still far from well. It was rumoured that he would miss the second Test at Melbourne a fortnight later and only avoided doing so when the Australians, who batted first, agreed to him being absent for most of the opening day in order to visit a doctor for the lancing of his quinsy. Two days after the Test ended, he suffered a severe attack of asthma and did not bat against an XVIII of Ballarat, and in the following match at Stawell went in only at number nine. It was Fry's recollection that Ranji was plagued by asthma throughout the tour and perhaps it was in this respect alone that he found the Australian climate did not suit him. As if all this was not enough, in the third Test at Adelaide he was to have the misfortune to bruise a finger badly while fielding.

During the Melbourne Test and the one that followed at Adelaide, it emerged just how dependent England's batting was on MacLaren and Ranji. Both matches followed a similar course, with Australia batting into the sixth session for 520 at Melbourne, and into the seventh at Adelaide for 573, and were decided by England's inadequate responses (they were made to follow-on both times and lost each match by an innings). Even by Australian standards the summer was proving hot, and Ranji found himself going in to bat in the first innings of each game in crippling temperatures. At Melbourne, he was again kept back in order to prevent him having to bat late on the second day, when the pitch had already begun to deteriorate. Next morning, when he went in, he showed early signs of uneasiness – Australian journalists were to identify him as an uncertain starter – but gradually he settled to his task of grafting it out as the Australian batsmen had done. In Storer, who helped him add 70, he found a like-minded partner and he had hardly played a false stroke in two hours twenty minutes when Trumble, with the fifth ball after tea, bowled him for 71. His dismissal led to a minor collapse and England batted again 205 behind. Then he assumed his usual position of number three and tried to get down the pitch to the bowlers as much as possible, although tight bowling kept him in check. MacLaren had just got out for 38 when Ranji, having played the previous ball into his stumps without disturbing a bail for the second time during the tour, played forward too soon and was clean bowled by Noble for 27. After this double blow, England slipped quietly to defeat.

At Adelaide, Jones, bowling superbly, had already got him to snick one which Kelly almost knocked up for first slip, when Trumble came on for the last over before lunch on the third day and with his third ball had Ranji caught for 6. England slumped to 105 for 5 and although they made a slight recovery were 295 behind on first innings. Next day, with the added distraction of winds carrying kiln dust from a nearby factory across the field, Ranji and MacLaren made a tremendous but futile effort to save the match. Ranji, far from at ease initially, was dropped at long-off on 19, but the two of them, judiciously waiting for the right balls to hit, survived to reach well-earned fifties. Ranjitsinhji was beginning to open up when he miscued an off-drive against McLeod and was caught for 77. In two and a half hours he and MacLaren had added 142, but the other nine batsmen were to muster only 68 between them as the touring party's fortunes slid into an irreversible decline.

Having seen all his efforts in the previous two matches go to waste, Ranji's spirit was near breaking point during the disastrous fourth Test at Melbourne, when the English team's batting was so poor that he was moved to describe it shortly after as 'the tamest batting I have ever seen'. In the first innings, he had struck Howell for three 4s and moved briskly into the twenties when Trumble, for the second successive Test, came on and promptly claimed his wicket, this time to a slip catch as he tried to repeat his favourite cut stroke. England followed-on for the third successive Test, 149 behind, and on the third day, when visibility around the ground was hindered by the smoke from bush fires, Ranji's luck finally deserted him. Having almost been yorked first ball by Howell, he had battled grimly but successfully for one hour forty minutes in an effort to wear down the bowling when he dragged the ball into his stumps after it had hit his left boot. His dogged 55 was England's only half-century of the match.

The fifth Test at Sydney was lost by 6 wickets after England had led by 96 runs on first innings. Ranji suffered his only double failure of the series, but in each case could have had better fortune. He was dismissed in the first innings by a brilliant catch at extra-cover by Gregory off a high-flighted slow ball from Trott and in the second was given out leg-before to Jones after a questionable decision – Ranjitsinhji believed he had hit the ball first, while the bowler only appealed after the ball had been returned to him. Between the last two Tests, he had received more treatment for his throat.

There was not much consolation for the touring side from the return matches with the three state sides. Admittedly Victoria were beaten comfortably by 7 wickets, Ranjitsinhji scoring two half-centuries, but South Australia had the better of a draw while New South Wales had an emphatic win by 239 runs in a game at Sydney that produced a record match aggregate of 1,739 runs. Stoddart's XI, set 603 to win, felt they still had a chance after the fifth day, when they were 258 for 1 (MacLaren 135 not out, Ranji 42 not out), but both batsmen were soon out next morning, events which the losers were inclined to blame on one of the South Australians supposedly cutting up the pitch with his studs.

Ranji showed his disappointment at England's four successive Test defeats in a series of articles he rather unwisely agreed to write about the tour for a national magazine, the *Australian Review of Reviews*. With the assistance of a journalist, Alfred Gaston, these were put together in book form and published in England by James Bowden in August 1898 under the title *With Stoddart's Team in Australia*, which went through at least four editions that year. His writing on the game displayed its usual mastery and typically alluded to his own achievements only fleetingly, but several of his explanations for the team's losses and his fearless criticisms of aspects of their treatment exasperated some of his Australian admirers, who suspected him of whingeing, although some of his remarks may have represented no more than a continuation of the general frustration he had shown during the previous season in England. On a variety of matters he let his feelings be known in no uncertain terms, from the reluctance of Australians to accept that England had had the worst of a deteriorating pitch during the second Test and the 'disgraceful' barracking on the last day of the series at Sydney, to inadequate arrangements on a shooting expedition and their hosts' failure at a local dance to introduce the visiting cricketers to any partners: 'We watched the dancing with much interest for an hour and a half.'

For such opinions he was satirized mercilessly by the newspaper cartoonists, but his commentaries were actually far from one-sided. When he did refer to his own performances, it was never with smugness. He described his 77 in the Adelaide Test thus: 'Owing to an injury to my left hand I started rather wildly, and after attempting to force the game, was missed in the outfield when my score stood somewhat about 20. After that, however, both he [MacLaren] and I raised the score safely to the extent of 142, when, in attempting to place McLeod between two fields in the country, I spooned one up in the slips, which Trumble safely held. It was a wretched piece of judgment for me to have attempted the stroke at such a critical period of the game . . .' He also candidly admitted to several errors in the field during the tour: at least three dropped catches in matches at Adelaide and 'six misses out of seven easy catches' at Melbourne, where surrounding trees created an awkward background. Moreover, he was full of praise for the Australian fielding and for the skills of Trott, who, by his timely bowling changes and subtle field settings, 'demonstrated what a great captain he is'.

Feelings all round might have remained amicable had it not been for the hornet's nest Ranji had had stirred up through his comments on the first match of the tour, at Adelaide. Ernest Jones, bowling for South Australia, was no-balled for throwing by Jim Phillips, the touring team's Australian-born umpire, and Ranji was asked to give his opinions of the episode for the *Australian Review of Reviews* (it was after this original, controversial piece, that the magazine had asked him to write commentaries for the rest of the tour). He did so, upholding the umpire's decision and making several adverse remarks about opposing players and ground facilities. Perhaps he was aware of, and had taken exception to, the antipathy in the state towards him as an Indian; perhaps the local population was simply looking for the opportunity to make their feelings clear; whatever the reason, the press, the *South Australian Advertiser* in particular, turned on him and doubts about his right to play for England resurfaced. The accusation was also made that he was afraid to face a Jones permitted to bowl at his fastest – it was certainly true that while he had made a big score in that opening match he had never been fully in command against the pace bowler – but to this he had produced an appropriate riposte by hitting his match-winning 175 in the first Test at Sydney and handling Jones, who perhaps bowled as fast as he did because of the doubts raised over his action, well enough. On his two subsequent visits to Adelaide, however, Ranji was nevertheless remorselessly barracked by the crowds, particularly in his first innings of the return state match ('I was at the wickets for about a quarter of an hour, and during the whole of that time uncomplimentary and insulting remarks were hurled at me from all parts of the field'), and he had felt it necessary, as the tour moved to its close, to write to the *South Australian Advertiser* a letter of farewell and good wishes in an attempt to make his peace with the public there.

Frank Iredale had his own opinion of why his countrymen reacted as they did. He later said that Ranjitsinhji 'was never understood in this country. Australians will never know a man of his blood, because so few people in this country rightly understand what the blue-blood of India really means. The people here view all people not actually white as alien, and they think that the proper conversation to indulge in when they address them is pidgin English. They never realize how cultured an Indian really is amongst the blue-bloods. This will explain why so much umbrage was taken at some of Ranjitsinhji's remarks about Australia.' What would Iredale have said if he had known that Ranji was not a 'blue-blood' at all?

Although Ranji himself may have taken too much notice of the affair, nothing could detract from his immense standing in Australia, which was as spontaneous and heartfelt as anything he ever knew. During the early weeks of the tour he had created a sensation. He was admired by women, courted by society, and found a host of unlikely

95

products being sold under his apparently magical name. Shortly before he departed the country, the Melbourne Cricket Club, which had made a healthy profit out of the tour and witnessed what a potent attraction he could be, invited him to return with a side of his own during 1900–01. He promised to cable them a reply when he reached Colombo, but although he continued to talk of the scheme while in India, no cable, it seems, was ever received.

6

STAKING HIS CLAIM

RANJITSINHJI ARRIVED BACK in Colombo on the *Ormuz* in the second week of April 1898. According to *Cricket*, before disembarking and leaving his colleagues he promised them that he would be in England again in time for the September festival matches, but in a newspaper interview in Madras shortly after, he said he would miss the entire English season. Certainly his only contribution to Sussex's championship campaign proved to be an early telegram wishing them luck. His travelling companion in Asia was Arthur Priestley, who was a friend of MacLaren and had been with the touring team in Australia as a spectator. Thirty-two to Ranjitsinhji's twenty-five, he seems to have shared the Indian's gift for exuding charm and eloquence. After several days' rest in Ceylon, during which they played in a cricket match between the Lancashire Regiment and the Royal Artillery and had meetings with the infamous exile Colonel Arabi Pasha, who had shattered Anglo-French control in Egypt by leading a nationalist revolt there in 1881, they set out on their long route north.

It was Ranji's first visit to India since he had boarded a steamer at Bombay with Macnaghten, Ramsinhji and Mansur Khachar early in 1888 as an impressionable and unworldly youth, and he must have had mixed feelings about what lay ahead now, but as he and Priestley made their progress he was feted by people who had heard he could excel the greatest of English cricketers.

Their journey was broken in central India by a stay with the Maharaja of Ratlam, a Rathor Rajput, who received them magnificently and entertained them with panther and buck shooting, pig-sticking and polo. Here too Ranji met his half-brother Devisinhji,

97

who had been preparing the ground for his return. While Ranji was in Australia, Devisinhji, using Dhrangadhara as his base, had taken a letter to the ruler of its powerful northerly neighbour, the Maharao of Kutch, chief of the Jadeja Rajputs. The letter disputed the Nawanagar succession, adopting the objection to Jassaji already put forward by Jodhpur – that he was illegitimate – and claiming that Ranjitsinhji was a thoroughbred Rajput and, as such, a suitable alternative.

In May, Devisinhji took Ranji to see Pratap Singh in Mount Abu, the summer capital of Jodhpur. Pratap, too, had not been idle. As Regent he had, two months earlier, appointed Ranji a sirdar, or nobleman, of Jodhpur and ensured that he would continue to receive financial help from the state, now through an annual grant of Rs30,000 (about £1,750), although as we shall see this considerable sum was probably not paid regularly. Pratap also informed him he had arranged for an introduction to Rajinder Singh, the Maharaja of Patiala, Sikh head of the premier state in the Punjab and one of the wealthiest men in India.

Rajinder was then in Simla, the northern hill station used by the British during the hot, sultry months, and the summer residence of the Government of India. It was a fashionable place for important and influential people to gather and Rajinder, who was assiduously pro-British, liked to be seen there. His anglophilia extended to an enthusiasm for English sports (he was only twenty-two years old, not 'aged' or 'old' as Wild and Ross were to state) and this had come to encompass cricket. By 1898, he had imported two professional county players, Brockwell, of Surrey, and J. T. Hearne, of Middlesex, to coach himself and his men and he was apparently most anxious to meet the famous Ranji.

No sooner had they met than Ranji was playing in the green and yellow colours of the young Maharaja's cricket team. In front of large crowds, the side played a three-day fixture against the British residents in Simla and beat them in a closely contested match. The Maharaja's new favourite, on an unfamiliar matting pitch, top-scored for his side in both innings with 40 and 74 and took 7 wickets; he also caused a stir by resorting to what some regarded as sharp practice when, as he came up to bowl, he ran-out a batsman (a sergeant-major) standing out of his ground at the non-striker's end. Moreover, he shared in an entertaining partnership with His Highness, who liked to hit out and who scored – was perhaps *allowed* to score – the majority of the runs while they were together.

The two men quickly struck up a great friendship and before long Rajinder Singh was established as Ranji's latest benefactor, probably his most generous to date.

Unbeknown to Ranjitsinhji, while he was touring Australia his position was being closely monitored by the British authorities in India. Aware of his impending return, they were concerned about his future plans and debated them among themselves at length. At a time when he was only just beginning to take steps to promote his remote and relatively undeveloped claims to the Nawanagar succession, it is revealing to learn from their discussions that while some of them regarded his prospects in India as modest, others, probably disliking the political-undertones of his speech in Cambridge, saw him as a potentially disruptive and dangerous influence within the state.

Fortunately for Ranjitsinhji, he seems to have had a number of sympathetic admirers among the British in India, chief among them Lt.-Col. Kennedy, the Administrator of Nawanagar. Kennedy, an experienced member of the Indian Civil Service, had been deeply moved by their correspondence towards the end of 1896 and the sorry financial plight the famous young cricketer found himself in. About a year after that Kennedy had been in touch with both the Resident in Rajkot, Lt.-Col. John Hunter, and the India Office in London to make known his desire to propose to the Government of Bombay that Ranjitsinhji should receive an increase in his allowance. Whitehall, perhaps with an eye on Ranji's history since coming to England, had demurred and considered that Rs11,400 (about £700), or double the previous figure, would be an acceptable rise.

There was, of course, no justification for such an increase, but as Kennedy had said in his letter to the India Office on 8 November 1897, 'I understand the people at home will be only too glad if Ranji the popular idol of the hour gets plenty.' Hunter gave a more considered assessment of the situation when he wrote shortly after to the Government of Bombay: 'Colonel Kennedy proposes . . . to again double Ranjitsinhji's allowance – which means quadrupling the sum originally stipulated for by the Kumar's father. There can be no question that this is a very generous provision to which the Kumar has no actual right, but which under the peculiar circumstances of his case may be sanctioned not as a compensation for the Kumar's disappointment at being set aside (for he already received a solatium when the original provision was doubled) but in view of the surroundings and mode of life into which the young man has been educated, which perhaps render it difficult for him to maintain himself comfortably even on the originally enhanced allowance.'

Part of Kennedy's reasoning had been that Ranjitsinhji's allowance was greatly inferior to that accorded to Lakhuba, the grandson of Vibhaji, who had been awarded an annual grant of Rs50,000 and given a good education by the late Jam Sahib. (Lakhuba, who was the same age as Ranji, had since had his allowance reduced to Rs25,000 for contesting his disqualification from the succession and then refusing to sign a declaration that he had no personal interest in the throne.) Kennedy had originally wanted Ranjitsinhji to have parity with Lakhuba (that is, an increase to Rs25,000 rather than to Rs11,400), fearing that otherwise his claim to the throne – if ever the case arose – would be prejudiced, but this dangerously flawed reasoning was rejected by both Hunter and the India Office. Hunter pointed out that to accept it would be to show little respect for Vibhaji's wishes in the matter, while the India Office thought that 'Ranji might be content with his £700', although even it was persuaded to suggest that Kennedy should record clearly that an increase to this smaller sum did not imply any prejudgement of his relative claims to the succession.

Kennedy's revised proposal was rejected in unequivocal terms by Sir Steyning Edgerley, secretary to the Government of Bombay, on 27 January 1898. The firmness of his reply suggests just how serious a view the government was taking of Ranjitsinhji's impending visit to India, about which there had been speculation in England since the previous September. Although he did not say so initially, Edgerley shared Hunter's doubts about the correctness of what was being proposed. (Several months later, after it had been agreed to increase

Ranji's allowance to £700 provided certain conditions were met, he wrote: 'Kumar Ranjitsinhji was but a somewhat distant relative of His Highness conditionally adopted, and it is not difficult to understand why His Highness should have been inclined to portion Kumar Lakhuba more liberally. But whatever the reason the record of what he actually did remains, and it is entitled to respect, while the action of the British officers who had to deal with the matter has reduced the provision for Kumar Lakhuba by one half and increased that of Kumar Ranjitsinhji four-fold.') Edgerley wanted Ranji to be made to agree to take a life annuity in place of the grant of land he then possessed. His fear was that, although Ranji had not, on coming of age, taken over the village of Khilos (continuing instead to receive in cash its estimated yield), he would one day decide to do so, and that if he ever came to Kathiawar he would be a divisive influence, creating friction and fostering intrigue. 'It is, in the opinion of government,' read Edgerley's reply to Kennedy, 'not good policy to encourage him to settle in Jamnagar or even to be a landed proprietor in Jamnagar . . . give him direct encouragement to stay away.'

Edgerley thought that Ranji should be offered the increased allowance of RS 11,400 only on condition that he agreed never to settle in or around Nawanagar's capital and that, since he had acquired English tastes, he would probably be quite amenable to this considerable addition to his fixed income. If, however, this proposition proved unsatisfactory, Edgerley suggested offering him, subject to his good conduct, half his allowance again in consideration of his greater expenditure in Europe, thereby encouraging him to stay away from India altogether.

Hunter wrote back to Edgerley on 31 March: 'I would respectfully express my doubts whether it is desirable to hold out to Ranjitsinhji an inducement to expatriate himself and live for the day as this might result in his contracting an European marriage, which is not desirable, and in leaving behind him a destitute family. Ranjitsinhji has a delicate constitution and his present reputation at cricket will probably be short-lived, when his popularity will wane and he will probably gradually drop out of English society, when he will be barred by the proposed settlement from returning to his native land. It seems to me better that the door should be left open to him to return to India (though not perhaps Kathiawar), where he will be able probably to contract a marriage in the family of one of the chiefs of Rajputana from whom he would receive a marriage settlement in land.' Some five weeks after this and not long after Ranji's arrival in India, Hunter told Kennedy: 'I hear he has gone or is going to Jodhpur to his so-called uncle and I hope will get married there', and added, commenting on the scenario he had put to Edgerley: 'I expect Ranjitsinhji will oscillate between Rajputana and Lord's and Brighton cricket ground.'

Eventually a compromise was reached, and on 5 May Kennedy wrote to Ranjitsinhji and informed him that the Nawanagar state, in consideration of his life style and as an act of grace, would double his allowance to Rs11,400 (£700) per annum provided he agreed to certain conditions. These were that, if he was found to be involved in any intrigue, he would be allowed to reside in Jamnagar territory only at the discretion of the head of state, or in Kathiawar with the permission of the government; that the grant was not an hereditary one; and, that it was to be considered a final settlement of his case. It is interesting that at just about this time Kennedy began receiving reports of Devisinhji's activity on behalf of Ranji in Kutch and that Ranji's purpose in coming to India was to stake a claim to the Nawanagar throne. Edgerley was adamant that the allowance should be withdrawn if Ranjitsinhji failed to conform.

Kennedy had asked for a prompt answer. Ranji was travelling between Delhi and Simla when he received the letter, forwarded by his agents, Messrs King and Co. of Bombay. He did give a prompt reply – from 'Kumar Shri Ranjitsinhji of Jamnagar' – but only one that begged for more time to consider the matter. He assured Kennedy he would let him know the moment he made his decision. But after that there was nothing, only silence.

Ranji did not stay long in Simla. He accompanied the Maharaja down to Patiala and the magnificent palaces in the Baradari Gardens and at Moti Bagh. This was his first taste of a proper court environment since his childhood days at Jasdan and Dhrangadhara, and they hardly compared with the splendours Rajinder possessed. He spent several weeks at Patiala, punctuated by a journey south to Jodhpur, luxuriating in his host's munificence. Among other things, he enjoyed Patiala's magnificent facilities for shooting big game and, on the isolated lakes of the plains, duck.

He had not, though, come to India to enjoy himself, and he still had Lt.-Col. Kennedy's proposal in his possession awaiting a reply. But he must have noted carefully the sympathetic tone of the Administrator's earlier communications and, when the time was right, he made his move.

Rajkot, 21 July 1898

My dear Col. Kennedy,

I must apologize for not writing to you before this from Rajkot but as my plans were not settled I waited to do so until they were. I am leaving Rajkot for Sarodar to visit my mother who is there now, and will stop there only a short time after which I return to Rajkot. I fully intended to write to you when I came to Kathiawar to let me know if I care to visit you after your very kind invitation. But after my arrival here so many things were pointed out to me that I refrained from carrying out my intention. I can only explain these personally when I have the pleasure of seeing you in Jamnagar. However I am glad to say that the prejudices of my people have been overcome by my persuasions and now for other reasons I write to ask you if my coming will in any way disturb or annoy any one so as to inconvenience you? If so of course it will not be right for me to put you to any trouble and cause any unpleasantness in Nawanagar. I have been so many years out of Kathiawar that I must take your advice fully on this matter.

I don't know if the Agency have any objection to my visiting and being your guest. I personally have no desire to intrigue as you may well imagine; for any steps that I may take will be first made known to the Agency. I am going to dine with Col. Hunter this evening and I shall know more fully his views on the point. I personally suggest if there be no harm in it that I visit you by the morning train and return if necessary by the afternoon the same day. I don't think I can intrigue much during this time with yourself. At any rate I shall have the opportunity of explaining some matters and the further pleasure of renewing our old acquaintance. If you will kindly reply by Tuesday to Rajkot I will know what your views are and what you wish me to do. I am grievously disappointed I am not in a position through these extraordinary Kathiawar ways to be able to take advantage of your very kind invitation as I could do without much consideration say in England.

I have heard that your good self has made all arrangements for me in your bungalow. Please accept my hearty thanks and convey them to Mrs Kennedy for your kindness.

I trust Mrs Kennedy and yourself are very well. The weather here has lately been cool but damp. I have had good games of racquet and cricket practice at the college. I played for Rajkot against Wadhwan the other day. We got badly beaten thanks to a bad batting performance.

I shall be back in Rajkot by Tuesday. I hope you will find it convenient to be able to reply by then here unless you do so kindly at Sarodar before.

With kind regards,
Believe me,
Yours sincerely,
[signed] RANJITSINHJI

It is clear that Ranjitsinhji had been advised by friends against going to Kathiawar after what Kennedy had written to him and that even he stalled at going unannounced to Jamnagar. Equally transparent was his injured pride at the thought that the British authorities regarded him as a possibly dangerous influence and wished to keep him away from the region. Although he still made no reference to it, he was obviously not prepared to agree to Kennedy's offer made eleven weeks earlier and was anxious to discuss the matter in private with both him and Hunter. But the letter is far from straightforward; it is muddled and embarrassed in tone. Had the Administrator really invited him to come and stay? Had they in fact ever met?

Jamnagar, 25 July 1898

My dear Ranjitsinhji,

Yours of 21st is somewhat mysterious.

As to your coming here doubtless it will cause a sensation locally and there will be any amount of wild gossip knocking about afterwards as to what is going to happen. The people here are adepts at this game and that sort of thing does not affect or inconvenience me.

It is natural that being so near you should wish to see Jamnagar and as I am here it will give me a great deal of pleasure to extend hospitality to you in my private capacity as I would to any other friend of mine in that way. I ask you to put up with me during your stay in Nawanagar and on my side I shall be very glad to renew our acquaintance and friendship.

You will of course recognize that I can make no official fuss over you and I feel sure you don't want anything of the sort. I shall treat you exactly as I would a personal guest and friend of mine.

If you do come let me know your day. By the way you are out about the trains, there is only one a day and it *arrives* 11.18 a.m.

If you care to do so you can show this to Col. Hunter if you wish to take his advice.

We shall hope to see you.

Yours very sincerely,
[signed] W. P. KENNEDY

It is fairly safe to say that Kennedy, who could barely conceal his alarm at the prospect of a man believed to have designs on the Nawanagar throne staying with him, a representative of the minor Jam Sahib Jassaji, had not extended the invitation that Ranjitsinhji claimed, while his reply does not definitely resolve the question of whether the two men had met before: his stated desire to 'renew our acquaintance and friendship' may be no more than a brave attempt to go along with Ranjitsinhji's 'mysterious' missive.

There can be little doubt that the two of them did meet in Jamnagar, in which case it must be possible that their discussions touched on some delicate matters of state. Certainly, Ranji was subsequently able to display a knowledge of, for example, the details of Nawanagar's financial arrangements for Lakhuba. But after their meeting Kennedy was no nearer getting Ranji to agree to any of the conditions he was supposedly endeavouring to impose on him. The fact was that Ranji did not want a final settlement of his case – unless it included the Nawanagar throne – and now that he had the support of Jodhpur and Patiala he was financially in a position to hold out for it, something the British had not anticipated.

Convinced that he could benefit from continued contact with local officials, Ranjitsinhji made Rajkot his base for the next two months. He visited his relations in Dhrangadhara; was a guest of Lord Sandhurst, the Governor of Bombay; was garlanded and escorted by torchlit processions; and was, seemingly, acclaimed everywhere. In Rajkot itself, he revisited the Rajkumar College and mixed with the town's British occupants, impressing young and old alike, who were all only too eager to have a hero in their midst, though perhaps their enthusiasm was not shared by Hunter, the Resident.

One of Rajkot's British contingent was Charles Kincaid, then Hunter's judicial assistant and later author of *The Land of Ranji and Duleep*, who described what it was like having Ranjitsinhji in town in 1898: 'All the Agency officials were anxious to meet the famous cricketer; but the situation was rather delicate. The King Emperor's [*sic*] representative at Rajkot was pledged to the support of the young Jam Jassaji. Fortunately as a judicial officer I was not so bound. I invited "Ranji" to my house, and he cordially accepted the invitation. I expected to find a young man embittered by the decision of the Government of India and his head turned by his cricket successes. I found, on the contrary, a charming youth, who treated the Viceroy's decision as a blow of fate to be endured rather than to be railed against, and who spoke of his prodigious cricket scores with the most becoming modesty. I took him as a guest to the officers' mess at Rajkot, and everyone was delighted with him. The Colonel afterwards remarked to me bluntly that he wished all his English guests had as good manners as "Ranji".'

Understandably, great interest was aroused whenever he took part in a cricket match. Large crowds of both Indians and Europeans gathered to watch in wonderment and would depart when he was out. The game at Wadhwan which Ranji referred to in his letter to Kennedy, was his first for seven weeks but, although his side lost because of a 'bad batting performance', his own contribution was a score of 54 and 11 wickets for 94. For the Rest of Kathiawar against Jhalawar he made 31 and 39, top score in both innings, and claimed 9 wickets. Then, during a four-match tour of the Bombay region with a Kathiawar team of mixed nationalities, he took 68 off Lord Sandhurst's XI and 78 (plus 11 wickets for 56) off Bombay Gymkhana, but all else was overshadowed by the ignominy awaiting him in the fixture against Poona Gymkhana.

On the same day, on a pitch soaked by heavy rain, Ranjitsinhji was out third ball for 0 in each innings to the same bowler, one Lt. Lionel Maury Ross Deas. As he walked off after his second dismissal, Ranji said with a rueful grin to one of the fieldsmen, 'It's the only time in my life I have ever made a pair of spectacles' (and it was to stay that way). He missed the last match of the tour because of a fever brought on by too much sun, the first reference to any adverse health since he had left Australia. By his own high standards, his performances in general were disappointing and Ranjitsinhji himself put his poor form down to being out of practice, to the inferior quality of the pitches and to his heavy social duties.

Meanwhile, he was continuing to gather an impressive rank of support throughout the Rajput states. On 28 September 1898, he finally made his intentions plain by addressing, through the Government of Bombay, a written application to Lord Hamilton, the Secretary of State for India. In it, titling himself Kumar Shri Ranjitsinhji Vibhaji, he stated his claim to the Nawanagar throne. He said he had been raised by Vibhaji as heir and successor in accordance with Rajput custom, and with the knowledge and approval of the Government of India, before being set aside from the succession without an inquiry. He also repeated the Rajput accusation that Jassaji was the son of one of Vibhaji's Muslim concubines. Naturally, he conveniently overlooked the fact that his adoption had never been officially carried out.

The appeal was rejected by Bombay, although on what grounds is not known.

To wait for the verdict, Ranji left Rajkot and returned to Patiala. He filled some of what must have been many tense hours playing several further cricket matches for the Maharaja's team, some of them on the ruler's own beautiful ground, where the pitch was verdant and unlike any other Ranjitsinhji came across in India. For these games, Rajinder raised some of his strongest sides, sometimes including three English county players, Brockwell, Hearne and Ranjitsinhji. Ranji failed twice in the match against the powerful Parsees, the best native cricketers in India, but in one match at Umballa against a military team, Patiala's XI amassed 633 for 4 declared, Ranji helping himself to 257 not out. He put on over 450 with Mistry, another Parsee, who scored 255. For that innings, the Maharaja presented him with a set of jewelled shirt studs; after an earlier match, in which he had scored 133, he had been given a fine pair of shooting guns.

The rejection of his appeal must have been a disappointment, but it did not signal defeat. While he was at Patiala, Lord Elgin, the Viceroy, paid an official visit there and, in order that Ranji could be in close attendance on the influential guest, Rajinder appointed him an officer in his lancers. Ranjitsinhji used the opportunity to make a personal appeal to the Viceroy and clearly he had more success with him than he had had with Lord Sandhurst: during November, when he spent a fortnight in Calcutta, Bombay received a request that the Government of India would like to see any representation submitted by K. S. Ranjitsinhji regarding a claim to the Nawanagar throne. Reluctantly, Bombay released his application, stressing that all the arguments advanced in it were known to the Government of India when they made their decision of 1884 and that 'but for the understanding' the Governor would have withheld it.

However, before the matter could be considered further, Elgin's term of office ended and, in January 1899, he was replaced as Viceroy by Lord Curzon. Curzon, who was a keen cricket follower and occasionally involved himself in the affairs of Derbyshire, his county club, seemed to be prepared to look on Ranjitsinhji favourably. On 2 February, he and his Council considered Ranji's case and while they did not feel it was sufficiently strong to warrant a reconsideration of the Nawanagar succession, they agreed to send his application to London for Lord Hamilton, the Secretary of State for India, to see.

At this, Ranji felt there was nothing further to be gained by him staying any longer in India and he set out for Britain in March 1899.

When he returned to England he showed no signs of surrendering his claim to the throne. Rather, he renewed the struggle with added zeal. He was anxious for a response from Lord Hamilton, and when one was not forthcoming he managed to get questions raised in the House of Commons on two successive weeks towards the end of July. The enquiries were put to Lord Hamilton by Sir Seymour King, a Conservative MP, who asked why, 'contrary to the legal settlement of 1878', the Government of India refused to acknowledge 'Kumar Shri Ranjitsinhji Vibhaji' as the successor to the Nawanagar throne and why there had been no response to the application of the previous year on this issue.

In all probability, King did not make these appeals because he believed particularly strongly in the legitimacy of Ranjitsinhji's claim, if indeed he had any detailed knowledge of the case. His primary interest in the young Indian was a business one: he was the head of the bankers Messrs King and Co. of London, with branches in Bombay, Delhi, Simla and Calcutta, his firm had handled many of Ranji's transactions in recent years and was almost certainly owed money by him. Although King was probably acting on a personal request from his client, his own firm stood to gain if the affair could be resolved in Ranji's favour, either through the recovery of past debts or the fruits of future business.

But his words fell on stony ground. Hamilton replied that he was not aware of any legal settlement under which Ranjitsinhji had any claim to the state of Nawanagar; his selection as an adopted son had been conditional upon no further boy being born to one of the Jam's recognized wives, an event which had subsequently happened. The Government of India had ruled on the matter in 1884 and he concurred with its decision. He had, he said, received an application from Ranji in March and had sent his reply via the Government of Bombay, but as Ranji had by then left India he would not have received it. Hamilton assured King that Ranji would be informed of his reply now.

Although his application had been rejected for a second time, Ranji still did not give up. Overtly, he was to let the matter rest for the next few years, but the princedom that had once almost been his was never far from his thoughts. He must have been encouraged by the support he had managed to gather among some of the princes and British officials he had met in India and by the fact that no one had made reference to the most important flaw in his claim, his incomplete adoption. It was this oversight that enabled his case to take on a fundamentally serious appearance, which he might rightly have interpreted as a minor triumph in itself. In the meantime, he simply resolved to set his teeth once more and show them all that they were wrong.

7

THE GOLDEN YEARS

RANJI HAD BEEN away from England some eighteen months when he went back to his rooms in Cambridge. As his absence, which was in some quarters mistakenly thought to have been on grounds of health, had gone on, fears were expressed that he might not come back at all but settle in India (a Brighton music hall song had a lament to this effect), and it was rumoured that the best chance of seeing him on the cricket field again was as captain of a team of native Indian players rumoured to be making a tour in 1900. Further, since the British public had last set eyes on their idol, he had changed physically. He had thickened out and put on weight, and one thing seemed certain: lost forever were his most sinuous movements at the crease.

Although he missed Sussex's opening match with MCC at Lord's (he never again troubled to play in this fixture, traditionally the county's first of the season), he was on the field by 8 May at the Crystal Palace, playing for the South of England v. the Australians, against whom he was naturally eager to practice. Batting lower in the order than usual and confronted with a strong attack, he was leg-before to Trumble for 8 on the first day, but on the last he and Grace added 78 in under an hour to effectively save the match before he was caught off Jones for 63. This was an encouraging start, which suggested he was not completely out of condition. Directly afterwards he played for A. J. Webbe's XI against Cambridge University at Fenner's, where rain in the night left the pitch in a treacherous state on the final day and he let his opinion be known that no one would make twenty on it. With the exception of E. R. Wilson, who was making his first-class début and who scored 70 (having hit 117 not out in the first innings),

111

he was proved correct, in no case more so than his own: he was out for 0.

At a time when he was understandably cautious, and his form uncertain, he was unfortunate in finding himself playing throughout May on mainly wet or damp pitches. He made a subdued 34, out of a stand of 102 with Fry, against Worcestershire and although he produced a composed 44 not out in one and three-quarter hours in the second innings to steer Sussex to victory, he had to work hard for modest reward in low-scoring games with Essex and Gloucestershire. When he finally did encounter reliable conditions, for the match with Somerset at Brighton, Sussex scored 479 but he missed out. Unhappy with the way he was batting, he informed the selectors he did not wish to be considered for the first Test against Australia at Trent Bridge starting on 1 June. His decision may also have been influenced by an anxiety to concentrate on furthering his claim to the Nawanagar throne and, as he himself probably recognized after his experience towards the end of the 1897 season, his form suffered at the hands of such distractions. Perhaps he felt he would be able to turn his attention fully to cricket only when he had satisfied himself that questions were to be asked in the House of Commons on his behalf.

However, the newly created three-man selection committee chose to ignore his request and named him in the England party. It proved a wise decision for, in a rather peculiar manner, he played one of his most important innings and emerged as England's saviour. In the first innings, going in at number five in a powerful batting side, he struggled to contain Jones and put together a scratchy 42, which was even so the second top score as England failed to realize their potential and, all out for 193, fell 59 runs behind.

They were eventually asked to bat out a little over two sessions of play to draw the match but were in a disastrous position at 10 for 3 when Ranji went in again. He was dropped on 29, and when he was 30 the Australians were convinced he was run out but the umpire thought otherwise. Technically he batted extremely well, particularly the longer he was in, but tactically very strangely. He seemed to take the view that if England were to save the game he personally must succeed. While this attitude may have contained a good deal of truth, it was also the case that after the score reached 19 for 4 he was partnered successively by Hayward and Tyldesley for all but the last few minutes of the game. But despite the company of two such eminent batsmen, he went to extraordinary lengths to retain the strike, on a number of occasions almost at the cost of a wicket. *Wisden* was at a loss to explain his behaviour: 'What should have possessed him to attempt short runs when there was nothing to gain and everything to lose one cannot pretend to explain.' But there were no mishaps and Ranji held out for two and three-quarter hours, batting towards the end with increasing freedom, to ensure England drew the match. They finished on 155 for 7, of which his share was 93 not out.

Ranji, always stung by murmurings that he had no business playing in the national side, undoubtedly relished the newspaper placards that trumpeted: RANJI SAVES ENGLAND. More important, his confidence had finally returned.

During the 1899 season Ranjitsinhji succeeded to the Sussex captaincy. It was one of his most singular achievements, and his selection, and the mood in which it was generally received, implies that he had become largely accepted and integrated into English society.

Murdoch, whose batting had deteriorated with increasing years, resigned in mid-June, but the transition to Ranji's appointment was not straightforward and was carried out rather discreetly, suggesting that the club committee was aware of the magnitude of bestowing such a post, usually reserved only for the most English of gentlemen, on an Indian, however lofty his supposed background. Perhaps he was assisted in the process by the fact that he was successor not to an Englishman but to an Australian.

He was chosen ahead of Sussex's two other leading amateurs, George Brann and Charles Fry. Brann, at thirty-four, was the oldest of three, while Fry was the least experienced. Ranji, aged twenty-six, had missed the 1898 season but had otherwise been faithful to the team.

At first, it was not immediately obvious, publicly, that Murdoch had stood down. On the morning of Sussex's first match after his decision, against Cambridge University at Eastbourne, the *Sussex*

Daily News was still naming him as captain, but when Sussex took the field they were led out by Brann. Brann's first decision as captain, to put his opponents in, was thoroughly vindicated when the students were bowled out for 78, and although he himself made only 5, a masterful century by the 'Indian Prince' ensured the county won comfortably. But then for the next match, against Oxford University at Brighton, Ranji took over the captaincy. The explanation given in *The Field* (24 June) was that, 'At Eastbourne Brann had acted as captain, but, not enjoying the responsibilities of that post, he gave way at Brighton to Ranjitsinhji', while the *Sussex Daily News* hinted that this second change of captain would be more permanent when it said, in its report of the first day's play in the Oxford match, that 'K. S. Ranjitsinhji is acting as captain of the county team in the absence of Mr Murdoch'.

Whether Brann was ever a serious candidate for the captaincy, or whether the committee, having learnt of Murdoch's intention to drop out of the side, always intended Ranji to succeed him, is not clear, but there can be no doubt about the relative playing abilities of the two men or who had the popular vote for the job.

Ranji's leadership skills were in fact severely tested when Oxford batted stubbornly to hold out for a draw after Bland, one of his main bowlers, had fallen ill. He retained the captaincy for the championship game against Surrey at the Oval, and although his decision there to bat was mistaken, Sussex avoided defeat when Ranji himself and Brann shared a partnership of 325 in over four hours. After that, he led the side for the rest of the season, although, naturally enough, he was often to seek Brann's advice.

Sussex did not actually win a match under Ranji's captaincy in 1899 until late July but, with two further victories under him in August during a twelve-match unbeaten run in the championship, they finished fifth in the table, the highest placing they had achieved until then, and the *Sussex Daily News* was prepared to declare that 'The Prince's captaincy has been a complete success'. In both 1900 and 1901 he was to lead them to fourth place. In each of these three seasons, Sussex won more matches than they lost, something they had only rarely achieved before. From being one of the weakest county sides, they had become one of the strongest, and for this Ranji, through his prolific batting and keen leadership, must take a large part of the credit.

Ranji brought to his captaincy the same zealous enthusiasm he applied to his batting. He played hard and to win, and it is revealing that the one time he had an opportunity to select his own side, the all-amateur team he took to the United States and Canada at the invitation of the Associated Clubs of Philadelphia, for a six-week tour in September and October of 1899, he not only saw to it that his players were lavishly fitted out with a full set of equipment and clothing, he ensured the party was a strong one; so strong in fact that the five matches were robbed of any excitement. The two important matches, against the Gentlemen of Philadelphia, were won easily, Ranji hitting 57 out of a stand of 121 in eighty minutes with MacLaren at Haverford, and 68 at Germantown. As a result, the touring party was able to regard the visit as something of a holiday and concentrate on enjoying a formidable round of social functions, at which the captain was regularly the star attraction.

As captain of Sussex he took pains over everything, going so far as to carry an aneroid barometer to get an indication of what the weather might do. But as a leader he did not always meet with the success that regularly accompanied his batting. In his first season as captain, in an effort to make the Sussex attack more penetrative, he struck on the idea of rotating his bowlers regularly during an innings but, according to *Wisden*, did so with such frequency that he only upset them and reduced their effectiveness. (It was however as a result of this that Ranji, who took 31 wickets at an average of 28.19 for Sussex, established himself as a useful change bowler for the side.)

He attempted another innovation, as he was to recall in his *Cricket Guide and How to Play Cricket* (1906): 'It is a great pity that this idea of fielding practice is not carried out to any extent . . . I once tried it with my own eleven at Sussex when I was captain of that county, and they thought I had taken leave of my senses!' He also believed captains ought to have a greater say in the composition of their sides because selection committees rarely took fielding ability into account and did not always appreciate what was taking place out in the middle.

Ranji, himself an exceptionally good fielder either in the slips or at point, must have looked on enviously as Yorkshire, with their excellent all-round fielding, ran away with the championship in 1900 and 1901.

It cannot always have been easy to play under Ranjitsinhji, who could be as autocratic as any other amateur captain. When things were going well, he undoubtedly seemed to have a special gift for the timely, inspiring gesture – such as when he presented all the regular members of the Sussex team with inscribed medallions prior to his departure for Australia – but when they were running against him, it could be a different story. On one occasion, during Surrey's innings of 489 at the Oval in 1900, he got into a heated dispute with Barlow, the umpire, who complained to MCC about the language the Sussex captain used after he had ruled a ball had gone for 4. MCC supported Ranji but Barlow refused to apologize and Ranji, probably without caring for the irony of the comment, protested to the newspapers: 'The persistence with which Barlow tries in the press to prejudice the public against myself, and attributes to me, either mistakenly or wilfully, the use of violent language towards him, almost makes it impossible for me to adopt a generous attitude.'

One of the difficulties Ranji encountered was that his ambitions often outstripped the resources of his side. Sussex, with their unprecedentedly powerful batting, were a hard team to beat, but they could not themselves count on dismissing the opposition twice. While he was captain, improved pitches meant that matches were being dominated by the batsmen of both sides and were ending in draws; in this respect, Sussex, who played nearly half their fixtures on the true, dry pitches of the Brighton ground, found themselves particularly handicapped. Their bowling simply was not strong enough for them to mount a serious challenge for the championship. During 1896, when Murdoch was captain, there had been an attempt to sign Ernest Jones but negotiations had fallen through, and for five seasons from 1897 the attack centred on the medium-paced bowling of Fred Tate, who had been playing for Sussex since 1887, and the fast bowling of Cyril Bland. If either of these professionals was off form, the side usually struggled to take wickets.

Of course, another thing Ranji discovered was that the game came much more easily to him than it did to the men under him. He was able to keep late hours the evening before a match with little detriment to his play, and in the days of Murdoch's captaincy this had been the cause of some gentle cautions about the harm that might be done, if not to his own performance then to those of his less versatile colleagues whom he encouraged to join him in these late-night entertainments.

It is likely that it was the attempts of the Sussex players to issue their captain with a similar reminder (plus his own extreme sensitivity to criticism) that led indirectly to the myths that have since built up around the circumstances of the highest score of his career, against Somerset at Taunton in 1901.

Somerset had built up a huge first-innings lead of 324, leaving Sussex no option but to attempt to bat out what remained of the match, which was over six hours. Ranji, who had scored 45 on the first day, promoted himself to go in first, one of the few instances of him doing this for Sussex, although he did so in similar circumstances at Taunton in 1899, when he opened in the follow-on, scored 42 and helped Sussex to a draw. Now in 1901 he and Vine made 40 in thirty minutes before stumps on the second day. He then batted throughout the next day (the first time he had done this), which was curtailed fifty minutes by showers, sharing a first-wicket stand with Vine of 174 before taking the total with Fry on to 466 when the game was abandoned as a draw. Ranjitsinhji carried his own score that day from 29 to 285 not out, a monumental feat of concentration as he did not give a chance in five hours twenty minutes at the crease. Two hundred of his runs came in boundaries: forty-six 4s, two 5s and one 6. It was the highest innings he was to play.

C. H. B. Pridham, author of *The Charm of Cricket Past and Present* (1949), watched the match and recollected: 'All day long Ranjitsinhji did exactly as he pleased with the bowling, and never for a moment looked like getting out. Moreover the ball only touched his pads two or three times during the whole of his innings . . . One can recall sitting for a while in the front row of seats, in the vicinity of deep square-leg. This was positively a danger zone in the front line under fire! Time after time Ranji's famous leg-glances came flashing to the rails to right and left of us, the ball spinning furiously – almost humming – from the flick imparted to it by those flexible wrists. So viciously did these strokes travel, so pronounced was the curve caused by the spin, that instinctively we withdrew our legs out of the way; whilst they were so perfectly placed through the field that there was little or no chance of intercepting them.'

Two years after the match, the following passage appeared in Standing's biography: 'The "charge" was brought against Ranjitsinhji that he had recently been keeping late hours, billiard-playing in the London hotel at Taunton and night-fishing, thus jeopardising his chances of a big score. Whereupon he deliberately spent *the whole of the night*, previous to scoring his 285, in fishing the river near Taunton, and *did not go to bed at all*. His boots were carefully deposited outside his bedroom-door, and he did not tell his comrades he had not been to bed until he was about to start his innings.' (Standing's italics.)

The story that Ranji stayed up fishing before continuing his great innings has been regularly and dutifully repeated but, in full, the original version sounds like a rather too convenient refutation of the 'charge' brought against him by his players. Significantly perhaps, Fry was reported in the following year's *Wisden* to have recounted how it had been agreed among the Sussex players on the second evening that Ranjitsinhji should bat all the next day for 300 without playing the ball with his legs (Pridham's account confirms that he did so only two or three times), but there is no reference to what would have been the far more interesting fact that Ranji had told his players he had not slept the previous night.

Although the first month of the 1899 season hardly suggested it, that summer and those of 1900 and 1901 were to see Ranji at the height of his cricketing powers. The many brilliant displays and the sheer volume of runs that came from his bat during this period excited wonderment at the time and have continued to do so since, when to simply recite the bare facts of what he did is eloquent testimony enough. It was then that his superb technique was most ideally matched with the maturity of his approach.

During his absence, he had changed in his mental outlook as well as physically. Once he rediscovered his touch, there emerged in his play a fresh determination, an added edge of steel. It may have been part of the natural development of his game, or it could have been that this development was enhanced by him seeing continued sporting achievement as the soundest, if not now the only, available means of promoting himself in the eyes of the English and thus advancing his princely ambitions.

There were of course other, more practical factors that contributed to his success. There was the quality of pitches, which improved to such an extent during the 1890s that by 1901 limits were being imposed on groundsmen as to how they could prepare them. Ranji was also particularly fortunate to play regularly at Brighton, one of the smaller first-class grounds in England and regarded, along with Fenner's, as the easiest, with pitches that were nearly always true and easy paced.

More important, he had recently received for the first time what might prove to be regular financial support from Patiala and Jodhpur. This meant that, although no longer getting his allowance from Nawanagar, he was able to continue devoting almost as much time as he wished to playing cricket for Sussex. During these three seasons, when he was consistently performing at the highest level of excellence, often in fixtures unseparated by rest days in which to make sometimes lengthy connecting journeys, he was absent from only seven championship matches, two through injury (one in July 1899, the other in May–June 1900) and two through illness (Sussex's first championship matches of 1901). If he was continuing to suffer from asthma, nothing was heard of it. The only fixtures he chose to miss were those against Hampshire at Brighton in July 1899, when he had accepted an invitation to appear against the Players at Lord's; at Worcester in August 1900, because of an unspecified last-minute business engagement; and against Nottinghamshire at Brighton in June 1901, when he preferred instead to play for London County.

After the Trent Bridge Test of 1899, Ranji's form for his county underwent a transformation. His first hundred of the season arrived on 10 June, against Middlesex at Lord's, and was promptly followed by another, 178 against Nottinghamshire at Brighton, an innings which lasted four and three-quarter hours, the longest of his career to date. The friendly bowling of the university sides was not now the problem that it had been at the beginning of the season. One and a half hours at the crease against Cambridge realized 107 runs on an awkward pitch (during which he showed further signs of greater driving powers), and in two hours and fifty-five minutes against Oxford he made 85 and 58 not out. Jessop was possibly thinking of the first of these innings, at Eastbourne, when he wrote of Ranji: 'I have seen him make centuries on wickets that other men would regard as impossible.' It was his nineteenth hundred for Sussex, which established a record, Newham then having eighteen to his credit. Towards the end of June he played another long innings, of 197, with thirty-two 4s and two 5s, to help save the match at the Oval with Surrey, the team that were to win the championship, although early on he received a superb ball from Lockwood which cut back sharply and would have had him leg-before under the modern interpretation of the law. The most remarkable thing about this innings was that he struck the first ball he faced over square-leg for 5, a very uncharacteristic opening. In one calendar month, he had accumulated over a 1,000 runs in first-class matches, a feat that only Grace, on three occasions, had previously performed.

He was at the height of confidence, and during Sussex's northern tour reeled off brilliant half-centuries against Lancashire, when circumstances were far from easy, and Yorkshire, when he and Fry batted freely on the last day, Ranji's 62 included ten 4s and one 5. Then a wrist injury kept him out of the return match with Nottinghamshire and, although he again scored heavily (174 and 83 not out) against Surrey, on a lifeless pitch at Brighton, his rhythm was once more interrupted by a crumbling Hastings pitch, on which he batted two and a quarter hours against Middlesex for a tortured 36. It was the second top score of the match for his side, but he was well and truly overshadowed in a second-wicket partnership of 126 with Fry, who struck a brilliant 94.

It was August before he found his best touch. On the excellent pitches Sussex encountered during their West Country tour, he made 80 and 78 at Worcester, a chanceless 154 in two hours forty minutes at Bristol, and 86 not out and 42 at Taunton. This was the start of a remarkable sequence of twelve first-class innings of which 42 was the lowest and his only other score under fifty one of 48 against Essex, made while he was carrying a thumb injury sustained during the fifth Test. The injury was to restrict for a while his strokes on the leg-side but, even so, in the second innings of the Essex match he managed to hit 161, including 135 before lunch. He also scored with his usual freedom off Yorkshire's attack, his 57 and 70 at Brighton including eleven and twelve 4s respectively. On 22 August, during his 102 against Lancashire at Brighton, he beat his own record run aggregate of 2,780, and a week later, in making 72 not out against Hampshire at Portsmouth, he became the first batsman to score 3,000 runs in a season (he finished with 3,159). Later in the same innings he passed 1,000 runs in August and was thus the first batsman to reach this figure for a month twice in the same year.

All this was in strange contrast to the mixed performances he continued to give in the important matches with the Australians. Against their powerful bowling, he struggled to repeat the significant contribution he had made in the first Test. The application that he found so easy to summon when playing for Sussex was less forthcoming in the Tests, although he was not helped by regularly being required to go in first wicket down only shortly after the innings had begun, because either Jones or Trumble had made an early strike.

Jones's hostile pace was instrumental in Australia gaining the only victory of the series, by 10 wickets, in the second Test at Lord's, the match in which MacLaren succeeded Grace as England captain. Jones accounted for seven batsmen in the first innings, including Ranji, who had scored only 8 when he gave a return catch trying to turn a ball to leg. When England went in again, the Indian completed a miserable game by being caught at point off the medium pace of Howell for his first duck in Test cricket.

With things going so well for him in county matches, possibly his chief problem was simply one of impatience or over-anxiety to be equally successful in the internationals. This certainly seemed to be the case both in the third Test at Headingley, where he attempted to hit out against Noble and gave a straightforward catch to mid-off when he had made only 11, and in the fourth Test at Old Trafford, where he tried a similar stroke against Jones when 21, lobbing the ball tamely to mid-on after having executed some fine leg-side strokes in conditions that were giving the bowlers pronounced movement. Both of these matches, though, offered their consolations. At Headingley, where rain washed out the final day with England needing only a further 158 to win with all their wickets in hand, he held the slip catch that enabled J. T. Hearne to complete the rare feat of a Test hat-trick; while at Old Trafford, where England gained a first-innings lead of 176 and arguably would have won had they not been obliged under the rules then in force to make Australia follow-on, he had the opportunity at the end of the match to bat for fifty minutes in trying conditions and scored 49 not out, although he was twice dropped off Trumble.

Between the fourth and fifth Tests there was an interval of a month, during which he played against the touring team twice, once at Brighton for Sussex, for whom he endured an embarrassing double failure in a high-scoring match, and once for MCC, for whom he scored 92 in two hours forty minutes on the first day, a performance which *Wisden* rated as the finest against the Australians that year after his own 93 not out in the Trent Bridge Test, although he was subdued for some time after giving a chance in the slips when only 9.

For the fifth Test at the Oval, it was originally decided that Ranji should bat lower in the order than number three, but when Jackson and Hayward made 185 for the first wicket on a perfect pitch England's best chance to level the series was to score quick runs, and it became necessary for him to revert to his usual position. This time he did not fail expectations. He put on 131 with Hayward in one hour twenty-five minutes, of which he hit 54, many of his runs coming from leg-glances or strokes behind the wicket that on the fast outfield even the Australians could not cut off. England totalled 576 and were able to leave themselves ten and a half hours to bowl their opponents out twice, but the pitch ultimately proved too good.

Ranji's run aggregate in the series was only 278 but apart from the game at the Oval they were not high-scoring matches and his average of 46.33 was England's second best. During the summer as a whole, Jones undoubtedly had the advantage of him, claiming his wicket four times in the Tests and seven times in all, but Ranji, in the spirit for which his batting is best remembered, went for his shots against him, which sometimes meant the ball being regularly dispatched to the boundary with little less speed than when it left the bowler's hand. In his last match of the season against the Australians, for the South of England at the Hastings festival, he cut, glanced and pulled Jones for five 4s, three of them in one over, in a brief but spectacular 30. Earlier, shortly before stumps on the first day, during an innings of only 15, Ranjitsinhji on-drove a ball from Trumble out of the ground and into South Terrace, which was, according to Jephson, the Surrey player, the first such hit of his career. Hastings was certainly one of the more likely venues for him to record this first hit, for it was a small ground where a carry of only 100 yards would achieve the desired result, but while a want of strength was definitely a factor, Ranjitsinhji, like Bradman, was always reluctant to attempt over-the-boundary shots because of the dangers of giving a catch; it is possible that he made less than twenty such hits in his entire first-class career.

In 1900, when he had the advantage of not having to cope with the Australians, Ranji exploited other opponents' weaknesses even more ruthlessly than before. It became almost impossible to bowl to him, and equally hard to set him a field. And once he got set, which was often, he was not easily removed. He was rarely content to stop after reaching three figures, but would bat on and on remorselessly. At the height of his season, his runs were coming at an average of one a minute – a phenomenal rate for a sequence that included several large innings – and more than twice as fast as his partners were scoring. His thirst for runs appeared insatiable (in one game, against Lancashire at Hastings, he was run out from slip trying to take a quick single to retain the strike), his powers of concentration were marvelled at, and people idly speculated whether he might not one day make a score of a thousand.

He began the season at Fenner's, where he captained A. J. Webbe's XI against Cambridge University and took 158 off a weak attack, although it took him three hours forty minutes and he was very cautious in reaching his hundred. Frustrated by cold weather and soon carrying a leg injury that severely hampered him in the match at

Christ Church, Oxford and forced him to miss the next match at Leyton, he failed to reach 40 in any of his six subsequent innings before June.

But when the runs started to come, they came in abundance. Within nine days for Sussex he scored 97 (at number seven) and 127 against Gloucestershire, 222 against Somerset, and 215 not out as he once again put his former university to the sword. The first of these innings was chanceless, while each of the double centuries contained only one let-off. These matches, two of which were played at Brighton, the other at Fenner's, well illustrate how, when Ranji was in his best form, some grounds were simply not large enough to give the fielding side a realistic opportunity to contain him. A week later he demonstrated this again on another small ground, at Tonbridge, where, dropped twice early on, he ran up 192 not out in the second innings against Kent, 133 of them in boundaries.

Proof that he was not quite infallible, however, came either side of the Kent match, when two exponents of the leg-break, A. O. Jones, of Nottinghamshire, and Mead, of Essex, found the measure of him, each dismissing him cheaply twice, once each for 0.

Perhaps suspecting that he was becoming jaded by all his run-scoring, and certainly not in need of any practice, Ranji stood down from Sussex's return fixtures with the two universities and spent a few restful days in Cambridge. Refreshed, he returned for the match with Nottinghamshire at Trent Bridge early in July, and in the second innings batted three and a quarter hours for 158, having been dropped on 27 and 84, and shared a seventh-wicket partnership of 146 with Butt, the wicket-keeper, to save Sussex from what had looked certain defeat. Although he failed twice in the next match, against Lancashire at Old Trafford, he then struck form so rich that it ran until the end of the season. He accumulated over 1,000 runs in July, the third time he had done so in one month (equalling Grace's record) and during his last nineteen innings of the summer he was dismissed for under 40 only three times – by one of Lockwood's devilish early balls at the Oval, by Mold on an over-watered Hastings pitch, and again at Hastings by Albert Trott during the festival, in his last innings of the year.

He seemed able to make runs in any situation. Whether it was in a crisis against the might of Yorkshire, the winners of the championship, or when he was looking to capitalize on the more modest resources of lowly Leicestershire, he always found the necessary inspiration. In both matches with Yorkshire he made a score of 87; at Sheffield, where he had never played before and where a crowd of 15,000 turned up to see him, he batted only two hours ten minutes for his runs, even though he went in at 8 for 3; at Brighton, going in at 15 for 2, he batted just one and a half hours. At Leicester, when he had no more to play for than a draw and to see Sussex eclipse Leicestershire's 609 for 8 declared, he batted over five hours for 275, then the highest score of his career, to ensure that both were achieved (Sussex made 686 for 8); while in the return at Brighton, going in at the comfortable score of 217 for 2, he rattled up 73 out of 84 in just fifty minutes.

The zenith of this sequence was a two-week spell from late July, which contained innings of 202 out of 262 in three hours against Middlesex at Brighton; 109 out of 169 in one and a half hours against Gloucestershire at Bristol; and 89 out of 110 in one hour ten minutes against Somerset at Taunton. The Somerset performance was on a pitch made spiteful by rain, when his tactics were to hit his way out of trouble (he was eventually caught on the long-on boundary attempting another lofted drive), but the innings against Middlesex was an even more astonishing display and is rightly remembered as one of the finest he ever gave. Joining Fry at 122 for 2 in reply to 401, he had scored 29 in twenty minutes by lunch on the second day when a thunderstorm saturated the playing area, delaying a resumption until six o'clock. The pitch, which had already given the bowlers help, especially Albert Trott, was now at its worst and in the remaining thirty-five minutes Fry and Ranji, who added only nine runs, struggled to survive. The next morning, after a further delay of forty-five minutes, Fry was out immediately for 110 and wickets continued to fall steadily at the other end, but Ranji almost single-handed kept the total moving, past the follow-on target and beyond. He actually scored 164 out of 185 added in just over two hours before being eighth out, the match safe. Apart from Fry, of those who batted for Sussex that day, the highest score after his own was 17. His last

76 came out of the 78 he put on with Bland for the eighth wicket in thirty minutes.

P. F. Warner, the Middlesex captain, had recently expressed doubts as to Ranji's ability to cope on rain-affected pitches, perhaps as a result of having witnessed him flounder for runs at Hastings the previous year. Warner was not alone in this opinion. As Iredale, who had played against him in England in 1896 and in Australia in 1897–98, said, 'He was not a great batsman on sticky wickets . . . he was not forceful enough to be a good player on these kind of wickets, and was, moreover, timid when facing bumpy ones.' But his 202 against Middlesex provided emphatic evidence that this was no longer the case and that his greater strength in front of the wicket was reaping its rewards: it is noticeable that among his thirty-five 4s in the innings were few leg-strokes but many drives. Warner was completely won over by this brilliant exhibition: not only did he say that he would never forget it, but he also defended Ranji from critics who continued to claim he could not play on fiery pitches. (It is interesting to note, however, that both Standing and Wild used this innings to refute Warner's original charge, which suggests that Ranji did not forget the slight.)

During August a well-publicized race developed between Abel, the Surrey professional, Hayward and Ranji to break the individual record for the number of centuries in a season. At one point all three stood on ten, equalling Grace in 1871 and Ranji in 1896, but on 30 August, against Kent at Brighton, Ranji made his first hundred for over three weeks to establish a new record. He achieved it in spectacular fashion, too, hitting 220 out of 293 in only three and a quarter hours on a slow pitch against bowling and fielding that was always keen. Against Blythe, whose slow left-arm bowling he rated perhaps higher than any other's (he thought it superior to Rhodes's), he took 20 runs off one over as his second hundred took just seventy minutes. He not only intimidated the Kent attack but also dominated his batting partners; of the 246 he and Collins put on for the fifth wicket, Collins's contribution was a mere 33. The next day Abel scored his eleventh century and added a twelfth in the second fixture of the Hastings festival under the captaincy of Ranji, who had turned down the opportunity to appear in the first match. However, Ranji's tally of five double centuries in the season was quite without precedent (only Bradman, with six in 1930, has equalled or beaten it since), and during the festival he took his run total past 3,000 to 3,065, at the phenomenal average of 87.57, which meant that the three highest aggregates then made stood in his name. In case it is thought that he had lost his appetite for the game by then, he was to be found batting in a minor match on Parker's Piece in Cambridge as late as 29 September, and scoring 122 not out.

This welter of runs had to reap a response, and sure enough it did. Opponents, inspired by the Australians in general and Harry Trott in particular, sought to stem the torrent of boundaries from his bat by exploiting his weaknesses and ensuring they did not feed his strengths. Of course, captains had tried to do this in the past (as early as July 1896 Ranji had been dismissed against Kent by a fieldsman placed on the leg-side specifically for his benefit), but now, more than ever, they protected the field behind square and forced him to look for his runs in front of the wicket. It was the opinion of Framjee Patel, the Indian cricketer, that Ranji, in his early years, had always been rather timid in his forward play and that it had usually consisted of him stepping forward and patting the ball rather than driving it hard. Although Ranjitsinhji had begun to show signs of adopting the straighter, more orthodox strokes, as a matter of necessity this process was accelerated dramatically during the next season, 1901.

In that season, *Wisden* reported, he 'became more and more a driving player. The opposition endeavoured to cramp his game by putting on additional short-legs but without abandoning his delightful leg-side strokes, or beautifully timed cuts, he probably got the majority of his runs by drives – a notable change from his early years as a great cricketer.' Fry was to observe a distinct difference between his colleague's driving to the on and to the off: 'When he was hitting he was an expert placer of drives to the on (forcing the direction) but always played off-drives, high or low, in the *natural* direction.' Nevertheless, while often dazzlingly successful, Ranji's revised methods of 1901 failed to reproduce the level of consistency that had characterized his two previous seasons. He never put together more than three successive scores of over 40 and there emerged in his game the first signs of a new vulnerability.

The season got off to an inauspicious start for him when influenza kept him out of Sussex's first two championship matches, against Essex and Worcestershire. He had been anxious to begin playing before then, promising to appear for London County in a match starting at Edgbaston on 9 May, but doctors advised him against turning out for the next three weeks. He was still not completely recovered when he made 65, going in at number six, against Gloucestershire at Brighton and, two days later on the same ground, 133 in two hours against Somerset. The strenuous exertion these two innings must have involved may have led to some reaction, for he struggled for runs throughout most of June. At Lord's, for MCC against the South Africans, he was out for 3 to Kotze, who was among the fastest bowlers of the period, and at Trent Bridge, though he scored 85 to help Sussex record their first victory over Nottinghamshire in forty years, in his other innings A. O. Jones's leg-breaks claimed him for 0 for the second successive year. It may have been a desire for undemanding practice that led him to miss the return with Nottinghamshire and opt instead to play for London County against Cambridge University. If so, the match at Crystal Palace had an ironic outcome, for while his side totalled almost 600 he achieved little with the bat, only to be put on to bowl when the university was sliding to defeat on the last afternoon and take 6 wickets for 53, which were to remain the best figures of his career.

It was Sussex's matches with the universities that proved to be the ones that saw him rediscover his form. Against Cambridge, going in at number six with over 400 on the board, he ran up 70 not out; against Oxford, 84 in one hour twenty-five minutes in a partnership of 167 with Fry, before being run out in his enthusiasm to get the strike, a sure sign that he was feeling happier with the world. These were the last times, as a regular county player, that he would appear in these fixtures.

In the tougher environment of Sussex's northern tour, he made a brilliant 57 at Bradford, the only half-century of the match (Sussex were bowled out for 52 in under one and a half hours on the first day), and 69 and a chanceless 170 not out at Old Trafford. Though he made only modest scores for the Gentlemen at Lord's, the Players' attack was a formidable one, Braund, bowling leg-breaks, taking his wicket for the first but not the last time. Leicestershire were treated to 55 in less than an hour before he was bowled by a ball from Geeson, another leg-break bowler, that he did not attempt to play, and Essex to 219 in four and a quarter hours, but he seemed destined to come up against players in inspired form. On the last day against Essex, his second innings, and effectively Sussex's chance of victory, were ended by a brilliant catch by a substitute; while at Lord's, Albert Trott, in the course of taking 15 wickets in the match, bowled him twice in the twenties. His consolation was to take some easy runs towards an unbeaten century against Surrey, after a draw had been guaranteed.

In the match at Worcester, he again ran himself out, as he had against Oxford University, though this time for 0, and once more he seemed to become anxious about his form. In the second innings, he began cautiously to build himself a big score before blossoming out to reach his hundred out of 129 in two hours. Batting on until he was out for 139, he delayed the Sussex declaration and Worcestershire, who finished with 9 wickets down, managed to escape with a draw. Although he failed at Bristol, Sussex's West Country tour was to finish on a high note for him at Taunton, where he was to score that career-best innings of 285 not out.

The heroics did not end there. After a journey back to the south coast and only a day's rest, he was soon out in the middle at Brighton, surviving some early movement from the Lancashire bowlers and a chance offered when 6, but went on to bat all day for an unbeaten 200. He was out next morning for 204.

There had not been a result in a match on the friendly pitches at Brighton since June, and that record was maintained until the end of the season as Sussex amassed totals of over 500 in each of their last three matches there. Ranji, who went in at number four, was now seemingly content to let others play the major roles, satisfying himself with flogging the tired bowlers of Yorkshire for 86 not out and of Middlesex for 74, but lost his wicket for 30 trying to force the pace against Kent. He subsequently had the opportunity to play a more substantial innings at the Hastings festival, where he took 115 off Yorkshire, who dropped him twice. Though this innings, his last of the season, took his average over 70, and his aggregate was impressive (2,468), he had accumulated significantly fewer runs than in the two previous years.

The amateur batsman who came nearest to approaching Ranji's feats during the three seasons from 1899 to 1901 was Charles Fry. They were unrivalled as run-makers among amateurs, and few of the professionals could keep touch with them either (in 1901, Abel broke Ranjitsinhji's aggregate record for a season with 3,309 runs but batted ten more times than the Indian did in 1899). Despite his ungainly methods, Fry's potential had been apparent since his years at Oxford; indeed before leaving for Australia, Ranji had declared him the most promising batsman in England. He knew that Fry was as dedicated to the theory and practice of the game as himself. After June 1898, following a rather unorthodox marriage settlement, Fry was able to play regularly, and his application had its reward that year when, with a predominantly on-side technique, he totalled twice as many runs as he had achieved previously in a season. Then, in 1899 and 1900 he accumulated over 2,300 runs, and in 1901 over 3,000, more even than Ranji, though in none of these years did Fry have the better average.

The remarkable thing was that they were both able to score so heavily while playing for the same club. They were, between them, astonishingly consistent. Of the seventy-eight Sussex matches during the three seasons in which one or both of them appeared – it was generally both – forty-three included at least one century and a further twenty-four at least one fifty by either Fry or Ranji. In only three matches (one in 1899, two in 1900) did both fail in either innings to make at least a half-century. But spectators were lucky to see the two great batsmen spend so long together at the crease. They were to share twenty-five century stands together in all first-class cricket (twenty-three for Sussex), but were often both scoring so quickly that they rarely stayed together longer than one and a half hours; comfortably the longest partnership they had at this time was the one of two hours fifty minutes when they added 292 unbroken at Taunton in 1901. Cardus's intuitive grasp of the truth about things of which he had little or no first-hand experience let him down when he wrote, apparently full of nostalgia (though he actually never saw Ranji bat at Brighton), in *English Cricket* (1945): 'Who will ever forget the cricket ground at Hove in those days, salt tang in the air, and the deck-chairs full, and a stand in progress between Ranji and Fry? East and West twain for hours, the occult and the rational.' Although Cardus may have witnessed as a young man Fry and Ranjitsinhji share century stands in three successive matches in Manchester (his home town) between 1901 and 1904, they hardly ever batted together 'for hours'.

All this was no coincidence. After 1899, their first full season together, Ranji and Fry made deliberate efforts to avoid, when practicable, batting with each other. While Fry remained an opener, Ranji, a regular number three since the start of his Sussex career, dropped to number four for most of 1900. He reverted to number three many times in 1901, but after that he was rarely to be found higher than four – and often as low as six. This increased the possibility of one of them getting settled in and then being able to monopolize the strike over the other less gifted and less productive Sussex batsmen (who were, if they were professionals, in any case usually expected to play a more junior role to the amateur stars), while also reducing the necessity for them both to succeed on the same occasion. It seems, in fact, that they did not especially like being partners, for their gladiatorial rivalry would have been diminished by direct competition. Fry certainly felt that Ranji was the more adept at keeping the strike, although he would occasionally dominate their stands, usually because he was already set when Ranji came to the wicket. But it did him little good. According to Cardus, Fry was later to admit: 'There were no eyes for me. I played in Ranji's shadow.'

There were times when their rivalry could not help surfacing. One such occasion was during 1900, when Fry unexpectedly chose to extend a week's fishing holiday in Scotland by a further seven days, deliberately missing the fixtures in Nottinghamshire and Lancashire. For Fry to be absent from a county championship game was as unusual as it was for Ranjitsinhji; from 1899 to 1901 he missed only five, and these were two of them. An explanation for his curious behaviour was mooted, and, perhaps significantly, denied by Standing: 'Fry's brief absence from the team was said, by certain newspapers, to be due to "dissensions" with his friend and captain – a sample of the usual Press "yarns".' But only a few days before he took his holiday Fry may have felt he had been given just cause for a show of dissent, following some strange tactics by Ranji in the match with Kent at Tonbridge. Fry's own first-innings century had been instrumental in Sussex gaining a lead of 157, but Ranji chose not to enforce the follow-on and, delaying his declaration beyond everybody's expectations, set his opponents the absurdly remote target of 469 in five hours. With the help of a thunderstorm, Kent had escaped with a draw. It was only too easy to surmise an ulterior motive for Ranji's actions: in Sussex's second innings, scoring rapidly except for forty minutes going through the nineties, he had helped himself to 192 not out. The Kent side had been reminding him that he had never scored a century against them (in seventeen first-class innings), after which, as even Standing admitted: 'Ranji thereupon tried to make a hundred and succeeded.'

Interestingly, when Fry rejoined Sussex, for the fixture with Yorkshire at Sheffield, he and Ranji shared a middle-order stand of 104 in one hour twenty-five minutes in a desperate but futile attempt to avert defeat. Then, sensationally, they both scored centuries in the same innings during each of the next four matches they played together, against Leicestershire at Leicester (putting on 194), Surrey at Brighton (a truly remarkable 197 in one hour forty minutes), Middlesex at Brighton (77 in fifty-five minutes) and Gloucestershire at Bristol (a breathtaking 169 in one and a half hours). This jousting with Fry coincided with the start of Ranji's purple patch in the second half of the 1900 season, and the two events may not have been totally unconnected.

Few county bowlers could have claimed to have had any command over Fry and Ranji between 1899 and 1901. One who did was Walter Mead, the Essex right-arm slow-medium bowler, who had turned thirty in 1898 but who retained exceptional powers of spin, able to

1. Ranji at the height of his fame: England, c 1896.

2–5. The master batsman in action. Ranji demonstrates his celebrated leg-glance (*top left*), a turn to leg (*bottom left*), the finish to an off-drive (*top right*) and preparing to drive (*bottom right*). It is interesting to note (*top right*) that, although Ranji has played the stroke, his front foot has yet to reach the ground, an indication of how late he sometimes played his shots.

6. The England team that played Australia at the Oval in 1896. Several played prominent parts in Ranji's career (*back row, from left to right*): Hayward, Lilley, Richardson, Hearne (J. T.); (*front row, from left to right*): A. C. MacLaren, K. S. Ranjitsinhji, W. G. Grace, F. S. Jackson, Capt E. G. Wynyard; (*in front*) Abel, Peel.

7. In less happy times, Ranji leaves the Old Trafford pavilion during the disastrous 1902 Test to take the field with Braund (*left*), MacLaren (*centre*) and Palairet (*right*).

8. A golden combination for Sussex and England at the turn of the century:
Ranji and Fry, each the scourge of bowlers.

9. Vibhaji, the Jam Sahib of Nawanagar from 1852 until 1895, who was popularly but mistakenly believed to have formally adopted Ranji as his heir.

10. Ranji in regal dress during the early years of his reign.

JOHN BULL: "Look here! old man. Remember. my friend there has to live and has to pay his way."

11. *John Bull*, of 14 November 1908, shows another side to Ranji's princely qualities.

Khachar that Ranjit Singh had filed a written answer in the Bombay High Court stating that part of the loan had been spent in Mansur Khachar's own interest, and that the rest was a free gift.

It strikes me from the above that there is a good deal below the surface which has not come to light. It seems incredible that Mansur Khachar, a man of intelligence and education, and well acquainted with Ranjit Singh could really believe that Ranjit Singh who was in low water and discredited (except as a cricketer) could possibly have any strong influence with Lord Curzon, which could be worked to his (Mansur Khachar's) advantage.

At the time of the alleged loan of £10,000, both men were in the same position with claims in Native States, which they could have had very little hope of making good. It also seems extraordinary that Mansur Khachar, when he found Ranjit Singh was playing him false, should nevertheless have been persuaded to withdraw his suit in the High Court, and also to give a letter stating that he had no legal claim against him.

W.H.C. Wyllie —

5/2/08

12. An extract from Sir Curzon Wyllie's confidential report of Mansur Khachar's accusations made against Ranjitsinhji in 1908.

13. Lt-Col Henry Berthon, who effectively administered Nawanagar for many years during Ranji's reign.

14. The bust in Vibha Villas palace in Jamnagar, understood to depict Edith Borissow.

15. Ranji, in his garden at Staines in 1932, only a few months before his death.

make the ball break either way even on the best of pitches. He always seemed to reserve his best for the arrival of the two Sussex maestros, Ranji in particular rarely being at ease against him early in an innings. Mead was deadly on pitches affected by rain and two of the three matches in which Fry and Ranji both fell in each innings for under fifty were against Essex in just such conditions. At Leyton in May 1899, Mead took 10 for 94, dismissing Ranji (27 and 17) once and Fry (1 and 47) twice. Then, at Eastbourne in June 1900, he claimed 13 for 69, again twice capturing the wicket of Fry (16 and 43). In the first innings, having been hit by him for three 4s, Mead bowled Ranji for 14 with a fine ball which broke across the wicket and just removed the off bail; in the second, during a devastating spell of 5 wickets in five overs, he bowled him first ball.

In the two other county fixtures in which he faced Mead at this time, at Brighton in 1899 and 1901, Ranji gave magnificent displays to score 161 and 219, but even then it was far from plain sailing. On the first occasion, when 10 not out and with Mead bowling with venom at the other end, there was an appeal for a catch at slip by Ayres off Young; the fieldsman insisted he had got his hand well under the ball but the umpire said 'Not out'. On the second occasion, although Ranji gave no chance, on 91 he had to survive a very confident appeal for leg-before by Mead.

Ranji's cricket career, and his fortunes in general, would not have been the same if he had been a white man playing the game. The colour of his skin was both a weakness and a strength. Many British people, noting what seemed to them his strange appearance and witnessing his phenomenal performances, suspected he possessed unnatural powers – in many ways that was the basis of his popularity – but for them the mystery went no deeper. Others were more hostile.

An indication of the prejudice Ranji had to contend with can be gained from the fact that, as late as the 1870s, the Prince of Wales, during a visit to India, had cause to protest in a letter to his mother, Queen Victoria: 'Because a man has a black face and a different religion from our own, there is no reason why he should be treated as a brute.' Things, as we have seen, were not much better by the last decade of the century; a Prime Minister attempting to denigrate an Indian parliamentary candidate by referring to his colour, Ranji's treatment at Cambridge and the reaction of some MCC members to his successful Test début, were all testimony to this, as was the assumption implicit in the comment of Kincaid's Rajkot colonel that an Englishman ought to have better manners than an Indian, even one who was an educated and a well-known public figure.

This attitude extended to the way Ranjitsinhji played his cricket. Those used to the trusted principles of batting which had served well for generations, were offended by his horizontal bat and ingenious strokeplay and considered him to be no more than juggling with the ball. The remark that Cardus ascribed to Wainwright, the Yorkshire player, that Ranji never played a Christian stroke in his life, expressed what was for some a heartfelt sentiment, hence the description of him once as a 'faddling hedonist'. Fry, too, in 1897, reported how someone had said to him of Ranjitsinhji: 'Yes, he can play, but he must have a lot of Satan in him.'

The same people were quick to find limitations in his play. R. H. Lyttelton, writing about 1899 in an essay in *Giants of the Game*, was strident in his criticism: 'The English public is a curious one, and one of its peculiarities is a readiness to deify a cricketer all the more because he is not an Englishman and is of a different colour. They would have admired Ranjitsinhji as a white batsman, but they worship him because he is black. Many critics are too apt to admire the latest performer, and some have gone so far as to couple the Indian with Grace as equal in merit . . . The Indian has yet to show himself to be a really great bat on wickets that favour the bowler.' Doubts were also raised not only about him playing for England but, more unreasonably, about his right to appear for the Gentlemen, although strictly the only qualification required was to be an amateur.

Perhaps the real objection was that, as A. G. Gardiner said: 'Here was what the late Lord Salisbury would have called "a black man" playing cricket for all the world as if he were a white man. Then they realized that he did not play it as a white man, but as an artist of another and a superior strain.'

Part of Ranjitsinhji's genius, of course, was that he understood this situation perfectly and learnt to use it to his advantage. He once told D. J. Knight, of Surrey, perhaps not entirely seriously but certainly with relish, that his own skill as a batsman was largely attributable to eyesight: 'It is just a gift of the people of my race. The message from the eye to the brain, and from thence to the muscles, is flashed with a rapidity that has no equal amongst Englishmen.'

8

A DESERTED SHRINE

'THE FALL OF the leaf brought sadness with it. I allude to a family bereavement sustained by Ranjitsinhji, which caused his thoughts to turn Indiawards while most people were preparing for the Christmas festivities . . . His friend, the Maharaja of Patiala, had gone to the silent land, and this revisiting of the old sights and sounds touched with a peculiar poignancy the memory of one whose love for Ranjitsinhji had been reciprocated with all the strength of a warmly affectionate nature.'

This is the explanation given in Standing's biography for Ranji's visit to India from December 1901. While not doubting the sentiments expressed, Ranji's reason for going was tinged with more practical considerations than simply the loss of a close friend. The truth was that Rajinder Singh's sudden death from gastritis at the age of only twenty-eight had occurred thirteen months earlier, in November 1900, and had brought an unexpected halt to a valuable source of income for Ranji. He had been receiving substantial funds from Patiala and Jodhpur for over two and a half years, but financing his trip to India and his generally extravagant life style (Wild said he was the first owner of a motor car in Cambridge) meant that he had spent the money as quickly as he got it. Thus, it cannot have been long after Rajinder's death before Ranjitsinhji began to feel severely his reduction in income, and this may partly explain the note of uncertainty that entered his cricket the following season. By the autumn of 1901, he was teetering on the edge of bankruptcy.

That October, his solicitors, Messrs Redfern and Hunt, had written to Lord Hamilton, the Secretary of State for India, with an urgent request for an increase in their client's Nawanagar allowance (perhaps for fear of leaving himself open to the charge of agitating his claim to the throne, Ranji had begun to make his communications with British officials through other parties). He must have suspected it would be a futile errand. In the spring of 1900, when his financial position was not yet desperate, Messrs King and Co, his agents in Bombay, had made a speculative enquiry on his behalf to Lt.-Col. Kennedy as to why he had not received any funds from Nawanagar for well over two years. Kennedy had replied firmly that Ranji 'has before him an official offer which will give him an enhanced rate from 1 May 1898 of double the sum of Rs5,714 per annum . . . So far the Kumar has not thought fit to take any action.' But nothing was going to make him agree to the conditions attached to that offer, however much money he might need.

Redfern and Hunt's letter to Hamilton in October 1901 was accompanied by a personal appeal from Ranjitsinhji, who threw in another copy of his written claim to the Nawanagour succession for good measure. 'I respectfully submit that the allowance made to me [of Rs5,714] is inadequate and insufficient and I humbly pray your Lordship to take into your kindly consideration all the facts mentioned in my memorial of September 1898 and to render me the needed assistance to obtain an allowance sufficient to maintain my position with propriety and credit to my family and relations and I respectfully suggest the annual sum of Rs40,000 payable quarterly or half yearly.' Needless to say, Hamilton's office turned down flat this outrageous demand which, if met, would have meant a fourteen-fold increase in the original allowance awarded to Ranjitsinhji as a child.

It was obviously a move born out of desperation, for, on Saturday 30 November 1901, a petition in bankruptcy filed against Ranjitsinhji was due to come for hearing in London. The creditor was apparently an Indian from whom he had purchased goods while last in India, during 1898. A few days before the hearing his solicitors again wrote to the India Office, explaining the urgency of the matter. They pleaded that Ranji had only bought the goods at the request of Pratap Singh and that Pratap and Sardar Singh, the Maharaja of Jodhpur, had promised they would provide him with funds (a reference to his Jodhpur allowance, arranged by Pratap, as Regent, in March 1898).

They said that the Maharaja, while recently in England, had given a letter to Ranji consenting to abide by the arrangement. That seemed to do the trick. The secretary of the Political and Secret Department at the India Office wrote to a superior on Thursday 28 November, only two days before the scheduled hearing: 'It seems to us that it will be rather unfortunate if all this has to come out in the Bankruptcy Court and be reported in the newspapers.' Redfern and Hunt were informed that provided they could produce the letter in which the Maharaja gave his financial undertaking to Ranjitsinhji, the India Office would give the petitioning creditor their assurance that the Maharaja would remit the funds due to him. Redfern and Hunt were able to produce a typed letter, dated 28 September 1901, addressed 'To My Relative' and signed 'the Maharaja of Jodhpur', agreeing to Ranjitsinhji being appointed a sirdar of his state and receiving an allowance of Rs30,000 a year. It was sufficient to prevent Ranjitsinhji being declared a bankrupt, for the time being at least.

Within a matter of days of his escape, Ranji had left for India on the journey Standing was to attribute to Rajinder's death. His main purpose was to go to Patiala and Jodhpur and extract assurances that past guarantees would be adhered to in the future. Presumably he had no difficulty at Jodhpur but at Patiala it is doubtful if he could find an accessible face at court with which to negotiate: Rajinder Singh's son was but ten years old and a Regency in Council was ruling in his stead. The Council's primary concern was with putting back on a firm footing the finances and administration of the state, which had slipped into confusion during the extravagances of Rajinder's reign, and many a supplicant's appeal must have fallen on deaf ears.

One other possibility presented itself to Ranji while he was in India. Around April 1902 Devisinhji, his half-brother, was for about a month the guest of the Maharao of Kutch, who had shown some sympathy for Ranji's cause. According to the Resident in Bhuj, during the visit Devisinhji asked the Maharao for a loan of money, saying Ranji was in debt, and offered to deposit some jewellery as security. The Maharao declined to help and was very annoyed when on 1 May he received a telegram from Ranji asking for Rs30,000, which he asserted had been promised him through Devisinhji. It was the parting shot of a desperate man.

The Bhuj Resident was to report another event during Devisinhji's stay in Kutch: a rumour began to circulate that a plot was being laid against the life of Jam Sahib Jassaji. The plan 'looked on the face of it to be the project of a madman. The Jam was to have been murdered in open day when playing at tennis with Captain Hancock [his tutor] and other British officers.' Enquiries were made but the story was discounted when it transpired the informant was a man at enmity with the Kutch court.

Although Standing says Ranji returned to England in time for Sussex's opening match of 1902, in fact his business in India kept him so long he missed the start of the season, and in his absence Fry took over the captaincy. During this time, Ranji's whereabouts continued to be something of a mystery, though it was presumed he was not yet back in the country. As far as the general public were concerned, when he could have spent the winter with MacLaren's team on a tour of Australia, for some reason he had chosen to stay in England, only suddenly and inexplicably to leave for India.

A week before Sussex's first fixture, Fry, writing in the *Daily Express*, in an article assessing the club's prospects for the new season, speculated that Ranji was either in the wilds of Jamnagar or on the high seas, and said the last he had heard of him he had shot eight black buck somewhere in India and was heading for the massive Gir Forest in Kathiawar to shoot panthers. Fry expressed fears for his safety: 'our prospects depend a great deal on panthers and the P&O . . .'

Ranjitsinhji's boat reached England on Friday 16 May, and by Sunday afternoon he was in Brighton. Sussex had a match there starting the next day, against Gloucestershire, but he had not been selected and it seemed scarcely probable he would play. On Monday morning though, to the delight of the spectators, he was at the ground. After a few hits in the nets, he decided to play and resume the captaincy, one of the professionals being left out on full pay to make room for him.

It was agreed he would bat down the order but Sussex collapsed late on the first day and he batted for twenty-five minutes before the close. In that time he made only 6 runs, having been dropped off Jessop before he had scored. He was out first ball the following morning. When his side batted again he hit 23 in half an hour before being bowled by a yorker. He also missed a catch as Sussex suffered a heavy defeat.

That he was scarcely fit for cricket – mentally or physically – was borne out not only in that game but by what happened over the next two months, when, despite all endeavours, he was unable to apply himself fully to the game. The threat of bankruptcy and the failure of his mission to India left him once more feeling acutely the pressure of his situation.

A championship match with Somerset followed immediately on the same ground. It began in very cold weather and early on Ranji put down another catch. In a low-scoring match won by Sussex, he batted only fifteen minutes in the first innings and twenty in the second, when he hit out at almost every ball. Both times he gave catches on the off-side from the leg-break bowling of Braund.

Sussex did not then have a fixture, but with the opening Test of a five-match series against Australia only three days away, Ranji, no doubt anxious for match practice, turned out for MCC against the touring team at Lord's. Still he could not find his touch. In his first innings he was at the crease for nearly two hours for 67, but it was littered with uncharacteristic errors; apart from being dropped twice, he made risky, uppish strokes. In the second, he gave a catch to mid-off after thirty minutes.

When the players arrived at Edgbaston, where a Test was being staged for the first time, the pitch looked to be perfect for batting. MacLaren won the toss and opened the batting with Fry, who was out to Jones in the third over. This brought in Ranji, plainly very nervous. Eager to get off the mark, he started for a hopeless single and but for an inaccurate throw would have been run out. That fright only increased his anxiety and he seemed unable to establish any kind of rapport with MacLaren. They had added 8 runs when MacLaren stepped down the pitch and played the ball out on the off-side behind the wicket. A fielder was virtually on the ball; MacLaren began to recover his ground but as it was his partner's call turned to check, only to find Ranji advancing towards him, considering the possibility of a run. MacLaren shouted to him to get back, but the throw came in at his end, where he had not yet regained his crease, and Ranji's shout of warning was too late to prevent him being run out. For several further overs Ranjitsinhji wrestled to concentrate, before finally being clean bowled by a straightforward leg-break.

England made an impressive recovery but Ranji, in his despair at having brought about his captain's downfall, was oblivious; as one of the team, Jessop, recorded, 'He was upset for a whole day'. The press castigated him for his ineptitude and although *Wisden* said he 'considered himself somewhat unjustly blamed' for MacLaren's dismissal, it is probable that what he objected to most was the public censure. Perhaps he felt he was starting to be hunted as relentlessly for his mistakes on the field as for those off it; perhaps he began to think he should have stayed in India.

In his next match, against Nottinghamshire at Trent Bridge, he was out for 0, having lasted less than an over. Nothing was going right for him, but, as Jessop again observed, he was not a lucky batsman: if he was out of touch, he rarely survived.

Of course, it was inevitable that eventually his terrible loss of form would come to an end, even if only temporarily. It happened against Surrey at the Oval on 10 June, amid rumours in the press that he did not wish to play in the second Test at Lord's later the same week. He scored a chanceless 135 in three hours twenty minutes to ensure Sussex avoided the follow-on and, ultimately, defeat. Possibly unable to contemplate facing Richardson and Lockwood, who were bowling finely in overcast conditions, while they were still fresh, he had gone in at number seven (he scarcely ventured higher than number five for Sussex during this traumatic year), with the score 70 for 5. For one and a half hours he struggled to make 44 but towards the end was hitting out with all the brilliancy once so commonplace to him. Cordingley, who scored 24 not out, helped him add 115 in ninety-five minutes for the ninth wicket.

Jephson, captaining Surrey in this match, described what it was like to witness the transformation. 'Sussex are in, and seven are out for 107, but Ranjitsinhji is there. Playing at first with the feeling that he had not made runs – playing with the knowledge that he wanted practice – he was the acme of caution, a prototype of prudence. After fifty minutes he had made 14! – and then? Why, only those who were at the Oval on Tuesday could say how he played. There was every stroke that was known to *man*, and the variety of strokes that belong to *himself alone*! He never plays forward – he occasionally walks to the ball, and every one played back is met in the centre of the bat. And when he hits there is no wild motion of effort, no swinging the bat round the head; a short step, and Richardson is driven straight as a die on to the "first floor front" of the pavilion.'

After that Ranjitsinhji decided to play in the second Test, taking up his customary England position at number three. Rain delayed the start until mid-afternoon, when he went out to bat in the second over of the innings. He was to last less than two overs, falling for 0 to Hopkins, a bowler of little reputation who would probably not have been opening the attack had not the Australian side been depleted by influenza. The ball turned into him from the off-side on pitching, and was deflected by his pad into the stumps. As Fry, the other great run-maker of recent seasons, had also been dismissed by Hopkins for a duck, England's score of 0 for 2 was not without its irony. Although MacLaren and Jackson then began to recover the situation, when the score had reached 102 rain again intervened, and was to prevent any further play on the two subsequent days.

Ranji missed the match with Nottinghamshire at Brighton because of unspecified business in London, but during the next month he continued to make fundamental errors of a sort normally foreign to him. Against Middlesex, he pulled a ball from Hearne hard into his wicket; against the Players at Lord's he succumbed twice again to Braund, whose bowling he must now have anticipated with dread; and against Yorkshire, after being well set, he ran himself out going for a risky single, a folly he repeated in the match with Kent, against whom he collected a duck – his third of the season – in the second innings, caught off Blythe.

It is not surprising, therefore, that on the two occasions he managed to pass a hundred he made sure he gorged himself with runs. At Leyton, after giving a stumping chance in the 20s and being dropped when 176, he scored 230 in five hours twenty minutes against Essex; at one point Sussex were 92 for 6, but he and Newham shared a partnership of 344 (which stood for fifty-two years as a world record for the seventh wicket). And on the small Hastings ground, on a pitch ideal for batting and coming in at 331 for 3, he made 234 not out without giving a chance in just three hours twenty-five minutes against Surrey; 180 of his runs were scored in two and a half hours during the second morning session, when he placed the ball unerringly all round the wicket, most of his runs coming in boundaries. This remains the individual record for runs scored in a morning session in a first-class match in England. After a quiet spell in which he took his score from 124 to 147 by means of ones and twos, his last 87 runs included twenty 4s, his only other scoring strokes in the period being seven singles. He hit thirty-nine 4s in all and shared two spectacular partnerships, 192 in a hundred minutes for the seventh wicket with George Cox and 160 unbroken in only seventy minutes for the ninth wicket with Fred Tate. In both matches Sussex batted first, for totals of 520 and 705 for 8 declared respectively, but in neither did they have enough time to force a win.

For much of the time that he was at the crease during these innings, it must have seemed as if he had never known what it was like to be out of form. E. H. D. Sewell, who was playing for Essex in the first match, testified in his *Cricket Up-To-Date* (1931) what an almost faultless display it was: '. . . the only things that troubled him were Mead's leg-breaks. But that ball was the only one at which this player – and Tom Hayward also – had the semblance of a weakness. Early in "Ranji's" innings there was an appeal for stumped that would have done credit to the Surrey 2nd XI – who were the best appellants in the history of cricket – off one of Mead's leg-breaks. I have always blessed the umpire who disagreed with those of Essex who were in a position to see, since the sequel was a batting treat. Indeed, until "Ranji", in trying to drive straight one of McGahey's make-believe leg-breaks, which were never known to turn, skied the ball to the on, I cannot recall him hitting a ball anywhere near a fielder.'

The two performances had differing consequences for Ranji. The first took place directly before the third Test in Sheffield, the second ten days before the fourth in Manchester. During the match at Leyton he strained his right calf and finished the innings using a runner. It was not believed to be a bad injury, and although he fielded on the second day he did not on the third, when he cabled MacLaren to tell him he would not be able to appear in the Test starting the next day. It is just possible that, still lacking confidence, he was looking for an excuse not to play, for five days later he managed to turn out for the Gentlemen. The innings at Hastings, on the other hand, gave him such satisfaction, according to Framjee Patel in 1905 and S. J. Southerton in 1934, that he talked of it as the greatest of his career. It also persuaded him that he might not fail totally if he played in the Test at Old Trafford – the scene, six years earlier, of his most famous triumph.

Having lost the third Test by 143 runs, England had to win the Old Trafford match if they were to retain hopes of winning the series and, although the summer's dismal weather showed few signs of changing, large crowds watched each of the three days of play: 20,000 on the first, 25,000 on the second and another 20,000 on the third.

Australia gained an important advantage by winning the toss; there had been heavy rain in the early hours of Thursday, making conditions almost impossible for the fielding side before lunch. Lockwood, now England's senior professional bowler, did not go on for over an hour for fear of slipping on the greasy run-ups; in the meantime all the other bowlers struggled, including Fred Tate, who, on his thirty-fifth birthday, was playing in his first Test. Tate had been called up on the eve of the match because of his ability to exploit wet pitches, but he could do nothing while the field remained saturated. By the time Lockwood went on, the score was already 129 for no wicket, but the sun came out, transforming the soft, slow pitch into a spiteful one, and eventually he brought about a collapse, Australia sliding from 256 for 4 to 299 all out. However, England themselves collapsed to 70 for 5 by the close of play and Australia looked to have the game won.

On the Friday, however, England dramatically turned things

around in their favour. A heavy dew allowed the pitch to play more easily than on the Thursday evening – as did subsequent rainfalls – and Jackson and Braund stayed together for two hours. Jackson, who finished with 128, shared in small but valuable stands with each of the tailenders and in the end England's first-innings deficit was only 37. After that, Lockwood was instrumental in seeing Australia reduced to 85 for 8. The last two wickets fell for one run on Saturday morning.

Rain in the night delayed the start on the final day by an hour and MacLaren's tactics, when England began batting in search of 124 to win, made perfect sense. During the morning session the Australian bowling was tight but MacLaren, who had reverted to his usual role of opening the innings, after batting at number four on the first day, looked for runs at every opportunity and England did not lose a wicket in making 36 in fifty minutes. Throughout the three days, both he and Joe Darling, the Australian captain, were vindicated in their advocacy of forceful strokeplay; the turf never had a chance to dry sufficiently for runs to come by stealth. By lunch, the skies over Manchester were again threatening and the atmosphere around the boundary tense. With England needing only 88 for victory, the crowd, anxiously aware of the part the weather might yet play, sensed the game's climax was near.

But what of Ranjitsinhji? How was he faring in this important game? Unfortunately, for him the match could not have been more different from his brilliant Test début on the same ground in 1896. He was, in fact, managing to focus his mind on the unfolding drama only with the greatest difficulty, for what he had feared since returning to England had happened: he was being pursued once more by his creditors. Sometime during the days leading up to the match, or during the match itself, he was issued with a demand for payment by their solicitors, who described him as 'somewhat largely indebted'. What Ranji had told them, according to a letter from the solicitors to the India Office on 30 July, four days after the Test finished, was that Pratap Singh was willing to pay on his behalf but was unable to do so until he had gained the permission of the India Office, which he was in the process of seeking. This, in fact, was not true; no such application was being made, but it had bought valuable time. But how much time? Ranjitsinhji played out the Old Trafford Test fearing that any day another petition in bankruptcy would be filed against him and that this time it would be even harder, perhaps impossible, to avert financial ruin and public humiliation than it had been eight months earlier.

It was scarcely surprising that he was having such an undistinguished match, although his preparations had been in any case hardly ideal, he and Fry having chosen to miss the preceding championship match at Worcester. In England's first innings, going in down the order at number five, he had arrived at the crease with the score 14 for 3 and never seemed at ease. He scored only 2 before he was leg-before to Trumble trying to turn the ball off his leg-stump. There had also been an expensive error on the Friday which might not have happened had he been his normal self. The mistake involved Darling being missed early in his innings of 37 by Tate at backward square-leg, just in from the boundary, off the bowling of Braund. Tate had initially judged the ball well – it was not a difficult chance – but he was in an unfamiliar position (he normally fielded at either slip or mid-on and never in the deep) and the flight of the fiercely-spinning ball deceived him. He was fielding there because Braund did not have a slip, and mid-on, unusually, was occupied by the troubled Ranjitsinhji. MacLaren, who was probably privy to his friend's dilemma, may have felt that with Ranji in his present frame of mind he could not risk him in an important catching position and had therefore placed him where he had, mid-on and mid-off being the customary places to shield unreliable players. In Standing's account, shortly before Tate dropped the catch, Ranji had suggested to MacLaren that he, rather than Tate, should fall back to the leg boundary, which Braund was defending with six men, but his captain had refused. MacLaren had told him: 'I must have you near the wicket.'

Knowing that he was almost certainly about to be needed to play a part in the decisive phase of the match, Ranji spent the lunch interval on the final day sitting in the amateurs' dressing-room, pale with nerves. At a time when a heavy rainfall would have suited him well, the weather held and the afternoon session began on time. MacLaren had promoted him one place in the order, although the Australians said later that, after noticing the way Ranji looked during the lunch interval, he had momentarily thought of putting him in last. At all events, within twenty-five minutes MacLaren lost two partners and Ranji found himself having to go in to bat. The score was 68 for 2; 56 more needed for victory. As he emerged from the pavilion a great cheer greeted him from the expectant crowd. Perhaps he and his captain would make the runs between them and share the glory?

Darling was setting attacking fields for each of the batsmen, while the bowlers were continuing to pitch on a length and get plenty of work on the ball. Ranji had not been in long when MacLaren was ensnared, caught at long-on trying to hit over the top. Abel, the new batsman, was not an aggressive player and the responsibility lay with Ranji to assume command. But it was becoming obvious that he had lost all confidence in himself. He was crippled by uncertainty; in Cardus's phrase, 'a deserted shrine'. He could neither adjust to the pace of the pitch nor gauge the spin. Shortly, a shower of rain interrupted play. When a resumption was made after fifteen minutes it was evident Abel had been instructed to hit out. Ranji continued to struggle; the Australians had never seen him play so badly. Trumble, the supreme exponent of medium-paced bowling, had a deceptively straight delivery which he released as though he was screwing the cover off the ball, and Ranji had to survive several appeals for leg-before. Abel rose to his task well: Darling was trying to trap him as he had MacLaren, but twice Abel drove clear of long-on to the boundary. Then there was another appeal by Trumble for leg-before against Ranji, and this one was upheld. He had scored only 4.

From that point, everything changed for England. Ranji had played as though the pitch once more had a devil in it, and the subsequent batsmen became apprehensive; even Abel remembered himself. The Australians, who began to bowl and field like men possessed, grasped the initiative and during the next fifty minutes 5 more wickets fell for the addition of only 24 runs.

When Tate, the last man, went in to join Rhodes, the young Yorkshire all-rounder, England still needed eight runs for victory, but before he could reach the middle a heavy shower brought the players off. The Australians, who knew they would have to use a

147

greasy ball, thought their opponents would still win but determined
to get Tate to the striker's end. England, probably aware they should
not have allowed the situation to get so desperate, were not so
confident of their own chances; they decided Rhodes should go for
the runs and Tate concentrate on survival. Around the ground the
spectators waited in suspense.

After a forty-five minute delay play resumed. Rhodes faced Trumble but was unable to score from the four balls that remained of the
interrupted over. Tate was thus left with the strike. The first ball he
edged fortuitously to the fine-leg boundary, the second he stopped,
the third passed harmlessly by. The next ball kept low and beat the
bat; the leg- and middle-stumps, and their bail, were left undisturbed
but the off-stump was plucked from its socket. It was left lying on
the ground, turf clinging to its base. Australia had won by three runs.

Shortly before five o'clock the crowds began to leave, thrilled at
the climactic moments they had just witnessed but anguishing at the
way England had thrown the game away. Meanwhile, in the home
dressing-rooms, amateurs and professionals alike must have sat in
numbed disbelief. Tate, in particular, was beside himself with disappointment, conscious that his colleagues felt he had let them down.
Braund eventually attempted to console him, saying: 'There now, it
is only a game, go upstairs and collect your pay.' Tate, it was said,
took a hansom cab and rode to the railway station alone, with the
blinds drawn down.

This remarkable match is one of the most famous in Test history,
and Tate, as is now widely recognized, was wrongly blamed as the
man who lost for England a game they should have won. For many
years regrets were regularly expressed about the selection of the
England XI, particularly the choice of Tate, but the fact was that
several other members of the team failed to play their part, notably
Ranji, whose abject performance was in marked contrast to his former
days of splendour. The real reason for his poor performance has
remained the knowledge of only a very few. At the time, a polite veil
was drawn over his failure but he was never to play for England
again.

MacLaren was to reveal the guilt and responsibility he felt for the defeat. In a letter to *The Times* in July 1919, he maintained he had given the selectors a list of the players he wanted for the match, but that neither at their original meeting nor when a wet-pitch specialist was called up did they give him the players he wanted. He also went to great lengths to justify his field-setting at the time Tate dropped Darling, explaining that Ranjitsinhji was fielding at mid-on because he was 'dead lame', though there is no evidence to support this claim.

Meanwhile, in Standing's work, published the following year, Ranji, who may have suspected his reputation had been irreparably damaged in the match, was to give his opinion that not only was Tate, his Sussex colleague, an uncertain catcher, he was also not a good enough bowler to have been picked for a Test. Standing was also to contend that Ranji's dismissal in the second innings was 'largely due to the remarkably reckless and irresponsible manner in which the colonial bowlers kept appealing for lbw'.

After the humiliating defeat in the Old Trafford Test, Ranji played in two frustrating matches for Sussex, against Middlesex at Eastbourne and the Australians at Brighton. Apart from the fact he failed in each with the bat, both games might have followed very different courses had Sussex not dropped a number of catches. This contributed to their failure to achieve victory over Middlesex, while the Australians, after being 152 for 5, were allowed to run up a total of 580 for 6 declared. Noble, the touring team's leading all-rounder, was missed more than once as he flogged the weary bowlers for 284, the highest innings of the season, comfortably surpassing both of Ranji's double centuries.

In the Middlesex match Ranji partly brought troubles down on his own head. In the first innings he put himself on to bowl, having not previously done so during the season, and stayed on for almost two hours, picking up 5 wickets. Encouraged by this, he used himself early on in the second innings and called upon Tate only as his fifth-choice bowler. Tate finished with 8 wickets but by then Middlesex had scored 401.

After that, Ranji missed Sussex's fixtures in Gloucestershire and Somerset, and at Brighton with Lancashire and Leicestershire.

Initially, his absence seemed innocent enough. He must have known very well that after his recent performances he would be dropped for the final Test at the Oval but, by making himself unavailable for county matches, he to some extent pre-empted the selectors' decision, perhaps a reflection of how hard he took his impending omission, the first time he had been left out of the national side. Possibly he also realized that it would mark the end of what for some had been an embarrassing association. He attended the Test as a spectator and was accompanied by Fry, already dropped by England after the third Test and now covering the match for the *Daily Express*.

Darling, the Australian captain and a man who had inherited Harry Trott's tactical acumen, later claimed some of the credit for Ranji being dropped from the England side, although even if his claim was correct it must be said that there was at least an element of sharp practice in his strategy. He wrote: 'To block this juggler, a past-master at playing the ball to beat short-leg and mid-on, I placed five fieldsmen on the leg-side. I moved our finest fieldsman, Syd Gregory, from cover to close fine-leg and went to close short-leg myself. After "Ranji" looked to see where we stood we would move as the bowler delivered the ball, sometimes drifting one way, sometimes another. Once it resulted in a glance a few inches above the ground being caught by Syd Gregory. From that day "Ranji" was never the same batsman, as he never knew where we were actually fielding. This worried him and eventually led to England leaving him out.'

Darling does not specify when this dramatic collapse of Ranji's confidence took place, and unfortunately his account is flawed in more than one respect. Ranjitsinhji, who played in two series against Australia in which Darling was captain, in 1899 and 1902, only once gave a catch either square or backward of square on the on-side and that was to Duff at short-leg in a match for MCC after he had already been left out by England. The only time Gregory caught him in this period was at mid-off in an earlier match against MCC, in May 1902. It is certainly true that after that game Ranjitsinhji scored few runs against the Australians, and none of those with any confidence, and it may have been that occasion which Darling was inaccurately recollecting, although as we have seen external factors contributed to the loss of form. The only other incident that might have provided justification for Darling's comments occurred during the third Test at Headingley in 1899, when, shortly before he was out, Ranji narrowly escaped being caught at short-leg. In eighteen subsequent innings against Darling's men he passed 30 only five times, and four of those displays were scrappy and contained let-offs. The exception was his 54 in the Oval Test in 1899, when he went in at 185 for 1, a very rare instance against the Australians after 1897–98 of him going to the wicket without his side being in difficulties, a burden that Ranjitsinhji recognized and which may have had as much to do with his modest sequence of scores as any of Darling's tactics.

It was only when Fry returned to the Sussex side for the match with Leicestershire, while his companion did not, that speculation began to mount that Ranji had walked out on his club. Instead of appearing for the county at Brighton, he preferred instead to take a last fling at the Australians, for MCC at Lord's, where he made an undistinguished 60 and 10. *The Times* reported that, 'Ranjitsinhji was not in his best form. He mistimed the bowling at both ends and seemed always scraping for his runs', but added generously, 'Of course he made many fine hits, and while he was in the batting was the best of the day.' Talk circulated that he was disappointed at his county's performances. It was not difficult to surmise that he had not always seen eye to eye with the Sussex committee, while his own efforts to improve fielding and find a new good fast bowler were well known; he had had the club engage a trainer, while, earlier in the season, he had recommended to Sussex one fast-medium bowler from Scotland, Charles Clarke, who had not proved a success, taking only one wicket in three matches. The conclusive argument seemed to be the recent, exasperating matches with Middlesex and the Australians.

These were taken as the reasons for him standing down but he received little sympathy from the local press, chiefly because Sussex, despite everything, were clearly going to finish near the top of the championship table and it was felt to be an ill-chosen time to make a show of dissent: the *Sussex County Cricket Annual* described it as coming at 'the most critical stage of their programme'. At the end of the season and with the county having finished as runners-up, the

Sussex Daily News made a point of saying that Brann, very much a pro-committee man, had been a popular captain during the absence of Ranji and Fry. During this period the accusations of thoughtlessness and irresponsibility, which Standing admits were frequently levelled at Ranji, perhaps reached their height, although his recent fragile batting escaped censure, largely because, by virtue of his three centuries, which contributed over half his season's tally of 1,106 runs, he finished second in the national averages with 46.08.

Although there were elements of truth in many of the criticisms made of Ranji, they were, ironically, hiding the true cause of his walk-out. *Wisden* hinted at this in its report of Sussex's season: 'For some reason which was not allowed to become public Ranjitsinhji dropped out of the team altogether during the last few weeks of the county season, finishing up with the Australian match at the beginning of August. Rumours were freely circulated as to his having had differences with one or more of the professionals, but on this point, in the absence of definite information, one can say nothing.'

The reason that was not allowed to become public was, of course, the haunting spectre of his creditors, which was sufficiently disturbing for him to decide that it would be best if he temporarily gave up his cricket. It was a timely move because on 6 August, four days after his last appearance for Sussex, the India Office told his creditors' solicitors that they had no information about an application by Pratap Singh to pay off Ranji's debts, and, after some debate, the private decision was also taken inside Whitehall that if Pratap should ask leave to borrow in the London money markets, he should be refused.

What happened next is uncertain but as there is no evidence of Ranji being presented with another bankruptcy petition it seems he must, somehow, have managed to raise the money himself, unless Pratap discreetly raised it for him. The most likely explanation is that Ranji succeeded in obtaining a loan from the one firm that might have entertained the idea, Messrs King and Co., with whom he had dealt in the past and with whom he had a personal contact in its head, Sir Seymour King. This theory is supported by the fact that King was one of the first people Ranji cabled after receiving confirmation that he was to be made Jam Sahib, an event which ensured his financial security.

For a fortnight Ranji stayed in London with Pratap Singh, who, like dignitaries from all over the Empire, had come to Britain for the coronation of Edward VII. When Pratap left to return to India, Ranji, during the third week in August, travelled north to Gilling East and the rectory he had stayed in as an unknown and unworldly youth thirteen summers earlier. The rectory was now the home of the Reverend Borissow, who, after thirty years as chaplain of Trinity College, Cambridge, had accepted the living of the village's church the previous year.

Ranji was to spend the entire winter in the house of his old guardian, and it was almost certainly during this time that his relationship with one of Borissow's daughters, Edith, red-headed and now twenty-nine years of age, blossomed. He had paid several visits to the Borissow household in Cambridge during his most recent winter in England, in 1900–01, and had taken Edith and her younger sister, Beatrice, to London to watch the funeral procession of Queen Victoria. Ranji, whose princely image had made him such an attractive figure to women not only in Britain but particularly in Australia and the United States, ended up falling for one of the first white girls he can have met.

According to E. H. D. Sewell, who got to know Ranji well late in life, Ranji and Edith were actually engaged to be married. Sewell, in his *Cricket Wallah* (1945), did not refer to her by name, but clearly identified the woman he was talking about as the Reverend Borissow's elder daughter. Sewell's account was a little vague; at one point he said he thought they had got engaged while Ranji was in his late teens or early twenties and still at Trinity, but at another implied the engagement dated from 1902. The latter seems the more likely option, coinciding as it does with a time when Ranji spent several months staying at her family home. Sewell wrote: 'The father of the lady was, I believe, very doubtful about a mixed marriage, as well as about "Ranji's" future . . . . But the father was very fond of "Ranji" and I believe made some sort of very fair compromise about waiting for a few years. The girl naturally liked being engaged to a possible future prince, and was fond of "Ranji" in a sisterly way, but whether she really, knowing all the difficulties, ever gave her hand to marry him, cannot be said.' The engagement, while it lasted, would have been a well-kept secret.

Sewell also emphasized something that Wild confirmed, that Ranji was, throughout his life, shy, distant and courteous towards women. It was an attitude that was reflected in his reverential regard for his mother. It was also illustrated by an episode during the voyage to Australia, when the heat drove many passengers to sleep either on or near the deck. Standing described what happened one night when it began to rain. Ranji 'left the deck, and went to sleep, as he supposed, in company with the other men – but, horror upon horrors! . . . he discovered, when morning broke, that certain recumbent *female* forms lay around him, and that in the dark he must have wandered into the music-saloon dedicated to the ladies! By almost smothering himself with a blanket he contrived to remain concealed until they had all gone.' (Standing's italics.) Through the circumstances of his upbringing, Ranji had had little early contact with the opposite sex, to the extent that even as an adult he would still rather nearly smother himself than see a woman half-dressed, and this possibly meant that, in the early stages of their engagement at least, Edith was hardly encouraged by him to show anything more than a sisterly fondness.

Ranji's decision to holiday in Yorkshire, once it became known, only added to the gossip then surrounding him. It was being said by some that he had accepted a post with the London County club based at the Crystal Palace where Grace and Murdoch were playing out their days, though was quick to deny it. Many of his hours in Gilling were spent fishing, and, no doubt, in contemplation about his future.

In September, a few days after Sussex's last match of the season and while the Hastings festival, which he usually played in, was going on, Ranji invited four of his county's leading professionals to join him for a week of fishing and shooting. Tate was personally received at the station. During their stay Ranji arranged two matches in which they and other county cricketers took part, much to the delight of the local inhabitants. It was a skilful piece of diplomacy on his part and did much to end rumours of differences between himself and his players before any serious damage was done.

9

PLAYING THE GAME

O N 11 APRIL 1903, Chandrakhunt, the superintendent of police
in Rajkot, filed an urgent report to the Resident. Near its
head, he underlined the words: 'Conspiracy to take away the life of
the present Jam Sahib'.

The superintendent was clearly excited at his discovery: he had just
learnt of the news while in the Baroda area, from a colleague who
told him the plan had been to murder Jassaji before he formally
inherited the administration of Nawanagar from the British. Although
the transfer of power, which had been marked by several days of
celebration and a public ceremony involving the exchange of the seal
of state and the keys to the treasury, had gone ahead successfully on
19 March, there was always the possibility that the treacherous scheme
had not yet been abandoned.

Apparently, the assassination was to have been carried out by a
gang based at Shikarpur in Kutch. The accomplices, Chandrakhunt
reported, were to have spent five or six days in Jamnagar before
carrying out the killing when Jassaji made one of his frequent visits
to a Hindu temple at Rozi Island, six miles north of the capital and
connected to the mainland by desolate mud flats. It was understood
the gang were in the capital, making their preliminary arrangements,
on 10 March. Why, at virtually the last moment, they had not carried
out their task remained a mystery. Perhaps their resolve had weakened;
perhaps they had heard the police knew of their mission (it was in the
week leading up to 19 March that the police official in Baroda first
got word of the plot).

The Resident's office, however, had already heard reports of the
plot and dismissed it as a story got up to discredit those supposedly

involved; it was, in any case, constantly being assailed with tales of intrigue, few of which proved to have any substance. The office was more concerned that Jassaji, now twenty years of age, should waste no more time producing an heir. Though it regarded him as frank and honest, it felt him to be inexperienced in the ways of the world (unfortunately a proposed year-long tour of Europe to broaden his education had had to be replaced by a less instructive three-month trip to Southern India and Ceylon when a severe drought plunged the state into debt), and it was afraid that hostile factions at court might be trying to take advantage of this. In February 1901 Jassaji had taken five wives, chosen for him by his father several years earlier, and an heir, the British had felt for some time, would be the best means of increasing 'the likelihood of other aspirants [to the throne] resigning themselves to their present lot'.

Who those aspirants were thought to be was revealed in the superintendent's report on the planned assassination: 'The venture is undertaken in the interest of two pretenders to the claim of the gadi, Ranjitsinhji and Lakhuba son of Kalubha.'

Although the British in Rajkot had been quick to reject the idea of a plan to murder Jassaji, there was, intriguingly, once more evidence to suggest the involvement of Ranjitsinhji's faction in such a scheme, as there had been in the case of the supposed plot to kill Jassaji in April 1902, which the Resident in Bhuj had linked with Devisinhji. The instigator of the Rozi Island project, Chandrakhunt had reported, was a father-in-law to the Maharao of Kutch and a relative of the Raj Sahib of Dhrangadhara (who was, of course, a relative himself of Ranjitsinhji), while one of his fellow conspirators was the chief minister of Dhrangadhara.

Although the conspiracy to assassinate Jassaji was not taken completely seriously, the Rajkot Resident nevertheless informed the Jam Sahib of it. As a result, the youthful and ill-starred prince became rather nervous about attempts on his life and began to keep close company with his European superintendent of police.

On the face of it, Ranji put all his problems on the cricket field behind him in 1903 when, on pitches often as treacherous and rain-affected as those of the previous year, he enjoyed a far more productive season, scoring 1,924 runs at an average of 56.58. But in fact things were still far from right with him. Although still capable of scoring runs in all sorts of situations with the facility that had always marked his play, he was again not as consistent as of old. Ranjitsinhji's frustration at playing at anything less than his own outstanding best was often clear, as though such near-perfection was itself a failure. And, although he adhered to a promise to play regularly for Sussex, missing only two championship matches, his form hinted at a reduced commitment to the club, which was confirmed when, in December, he resigned the captaincy in favour of Fry.

In his first four matches, his highest score was just 28. A change came with his first visit to Old Trafford since the Test the previous season, as he treated Lancashire to a faultless 105 out of a stand of 196 with Fry. He followed this with a great defensive innings against Gloucestershire at Brighton, of which the opposing captain, Jessop, would write: 'A sounder innings I never saw, nor one in which the ball met the middle of the bat with such frequency.' After being out for 0 in the first innings and going in at 10 for 2 in the follow-on, Ranji exercised great restraint over four hours to score 162 not out and save the game.

There can be little doubt that by this match he had recaptured his appetite for the game. Shortly afterwards he studiously compiled 93 in two hours against Yorkshire and 99 in two and three-quarter hours against Middlesex, Sussex's two chief rivals for the championship. These two games, in which he shared stands of 174 and 107 with Fry, were separated by a fixture at Leyton, where Mead dismissed him for 6 and Sussex for 77 on a spiteful pitch.

In the last week in June, Ranji had the misfortune, while captaining MCC against Cambridge University at Lord's, to pull a muscle so seriously that he was not to regain full fitness until August. Having scored 83 when the incident happened, he retired hurt, but perhaps unwisely resumed his innings the next day, adding only 5 before he was out. Persevering, he played at Eastbourne, but only succeeded in aggravating the tear and was obliged to miss the fixture with Surrey at Brighton. Returning, he struggled manfully to make 60 in a partnership of 142 in one hour fifty minutes with Fry as the Gentlemen amassed 500 for 2 declared in the follow-on against the Players at Lord's, but for the first fifty minutes his injury rendered him virtually scoreless.

During the next month, in six championship innings, he made just one score of fifty, at Trent Bridge. When he faced Lancashire at Brighton on 10 August, it had been a long time since he had taken runs off a strong attack. Although Sussex got off to a good start, he had still not scored after thirty-five minutes at the crease, possibly an unprecedented occurrence for him. Generously but rather foolishly MacLaren then put himself on, Ranji took two runs for a shot the fieldsman should have stopped and over the next three and a quarter hours went on to make 144 not out. This episode embarrassed Ranji and, although he incorrectly identified the ground as Old Trafford, it was almost certainly the incident Wild was referring to when he inaccurately wrote: 'He was barracked for refusing to hit out while still playing himself in. Ranji was quite unmoved by the demonstration, and when he had settled himself to his own satisfaction and was sent some leg balls to punish, he refused to hit them . . .'

In the following match at Portsmouth he was again jeered by the crowd, along with Fry, as he batted about three hours for 95, but neither of them later hurried in making unbeaten half-centuries in a rain-ruined match against Middlesex at Lord's. Part of the problem was that pitches generally had become badly affected by persistent rain and were so slow as to make strokeplay an unfamiliar and dangerous exercise. Towards the end of August, Ranji took himself off to find form in a country house match at Warnham Lodge, near Horsham, and after scoring 84 came back to take 72 not out off Kent and 204 off Surrey. His innings at the Oval was a chanceless and impressive exhibition of batsmanship, but *Cricket* did not hesitate to criticize him for declaring (at tea on the second day at 600 for 7) only after he had got his own double century. He finished with three festival matches, two at Hastings and one at the Oval for the Rest of England against Middlesex, the county champions (Sussex were runners-up again). In these games he showed glimpses of his best form, but during a Gentlemen v. Players match ruined by the weather

– at one point it was so cold the players had to leave the field – Braund, who had taken his wicket on each their three previous encounters during the season, dismissed him cheaply, bowled off the pad offering no stroke.

The following season, 1904, saw Ranji produce a series of brilliant performances that would have graced any of his earlier years. During the central part of the summer, in a ten-week period between 14 June and 23 August, and despite an eleven-day break, he scored eight hundreds and five fifties, and finished top of the national averages for the fourth time. However, unburdened of the captaincy, he showed a continuing decline in the time he was prepared to give to playing for Sussex, missing eight championship fixtures, more than in any previous year except 1902, and a large number of his runs came in matches that were not for his county and were often devoid of the usual pressures.

It was the match with Yorkshire at Sheffield that saw the start of his run of glorious form. Joining Fry at 86 for 2, he gave an easy chance to Jackson when 33 but the two great batsmen stayed together for three hours fifty minutes, the longest partnership they were to have. The pitch was too slow for either to be at his best, but they added 255 runs, Ranji's share being 148. He followed this by picking up an unbeaten fifty at the end of a drawn match with Lancashire (when he and Fry added 118 unbroken, the last century stand they were to share), and although he then missed Sussex's next four fixtures, with the two universities, Leicestershire and Essex, he did play in games elsewhere. Only days after his own county had played them, he turned out against the two student sides for MCC at Lord's. On each occasion he had no difficulty making runs. Opening the batting against Cambridge, he scored 59 and 166 not out; against Oxford, in a match lasting two days but recognized as first-class, he made 142. His first century occupied him three hours, his second ten minutes less, and both were chanceless.

Meanwhile, a controversy had been developing over MCC's failure to invite him to play for the Gentlemen against the Players at Lord's in early July, the first time he had been overlooked during his Sussex career. Warner, in *Lord's 1787–1945* (1946), stated that Ranji was not selected because of the mistaken theory that he could not bat on a fiery pitch. A few days before the match, however, A. J. Turner, the Essex amateur, dropped out and Ranji was brought in, only to end up, rather bemusingly, being asked to captain the team. On the first two days the ball kicked up and in the first innings Ranji was out for only 5 (to Braund) but in the second, when the pitch had rolled out better and the Gentlemen were chasing 412 to win, he produced one of his greatest displays – Jessop called it 'absolutely perfect'. Against a powerful bowling side he scored 121 and his partnership of 194 in two hours thirty-five minutes with Jackson took the Gentlemen a long way towards a remarkable triumph by two wickets.

He then accepted an invitation to lead the Gentlemen at the Oval, the first time he had appeared against the Players there since 1893. His side won by an innings, partly because Murdoch, at the age of forty-nine and in borrowed clothing, scored 140 after being allowed to substitute for one of two sick players, an action on the part of Ranji and Lilley, the two captains, which MCC later ruled to be against the laws of the game.

Rejoining Sussex for his first championship match in almost a month, Ranji made a superb 135, containing twenty-five 4s, against Kent at Tunbridge Wells, after which he coped better than most of his side with Schwarz's unfamiliar mix of googlies and top-spinners when he played for an England XI against the South Africans. Against Surrey at Brighton he made 152 with ease, confining his scoring almost entirely to the leg-side, and in Sussex's first match in Derbyshire for twenty years, he struck an imperious 82 not out in as many minutes. He then decided to miss Sussex's next three matches – at Bath (where he disappointed an expectant crowd), Bristol and Brighton, to stay in the north and visit the Borissows in Gilling. However, while there his extraordinary talents were given a fresh challenge, when he batted against a local side fielding not 11 but 22. He managed 87.

Preparing to play in Sussex's last seven matches, he went back to Brighton and almost single-handed saved his county from defeat against Lancashire. He scored 99 in two and a half hours in Sussex's first innings of 203, and in the second, when they were 180 behind, 207 not out in five and a quarter hours. Except for the final two hours, when Albert Relf stayed with him and the draw was ensured, he was uncharacteristically content to wait for scoring opportunities and concentrate instead on defence. He batted unwaveringly throughout the final day.

It was his last major championship performance of the summer. He took a quick 80 off Hampshire and a hard-fought 52 off Middlesex, in his last match of the season at Brighton, but failed against Surrey, Yorkshire and Kent. He did play one further big innings for Sussex, late in August against the South Africans at Brighton, batting faultlessly for three hours for 178 not out against an attack including Kotze. He actually slowed up after reaching his hundred but the reason was not far to seek: when Fry declared, his colleague had just passed 2,000 runs for the season (he finished with 2,077 at the impressively high average of 74.17). Ranji's final first-class match of 1904 was a festival game at Bournemouth. Although no one knew it at the time, it was to be his last first-class game in England for several years, and an inglorious exit it proved – bowled in each innings for single figures by Albert Trott. Perhaps, as we shall see, his mind was already elsewhere.

There was one last game: towards the end of September on Parker's Piece, he played for a Cambridge XVII against Tom Hayward's XI, and scored 68, with five 5s and eight 4s.

Thus, his career as a regular cricketer ended in the place where it had effectively begun.

Ranjitsinhji's rather fitful approach to his cricket during 1903 and 1904 was a reflection of his changing priorities. He had been galvanized by reports that the young Jassaji had taken full control of his state, an event which can have served only to heighten his awareness of his own declining fortunes. Wild described the transfer of power in Nawanagar in March 1903 as the 'shattering of his dreams', although Ranjitsinhji ought to have known it was no more than a formality, though just possibly he was surprised to hear that Jassaji was still alive. Once he was reconciled to the transfer having taken place, he had to contend with the fact that he himself was now over thirty years of age and that if he was to realize his princely ambitions, time was no longer on his side.

In an attempt to avert a repetition of the traumatic affairs of 1902, he was driven to finding means of supplementing his income. During his winter in Gilling he worked on a revised edition of *The Jubilee Book of Cricket*, and when he returned to playing he followed the example of Fry and tried his hand at newspaper journalism. He wrote columns with first the *Sun* and then the *Daily Mail*, giving characteristically free rein to his frank opinions about the game, although he aroused most debate over a letter he sent to *The Times* early in 1903 criticizing attempts, led by Lord Harris, to defend a widely recognized decline in fielding standards as the cause for the great increase in drawn matches. He also contributed a chapter on batting to a book of technical instruction edited by Jessop and published by C. Arthur Pearson in April 1903, while later the same year the first biography of him appeared. Written by Percy Cross Standing and published in paperback by J. W. Arrowsmith of Bristol, *Ranjitsinhji Prince of Cricket* was designed for popular consumption and, except to say, incorrectly, that the subject was the adopted son of the late ruler of the state, the book passed over the question of the Nawanagar succession, concentrating instead on eulogizing his deeds on the cricket field. ·

Although financially successful enough in his writing, Ranji was less easily able to restore the reputation he had tarnished during his most recent, disastrous Test series. Some people seemed to have already decided that his international career was at an end. When, in July 1903, MCC issued invitations for a tour of Australia it was to make the following winter, he was not among those to receive one, nor was he when several other leading amateurs made themselves unavailable.

Ranji, in any case, had other plans. During the winter, he went back to India. His intentions, according to Wild, were to sound out his chances of acquiring the Nawanagar throne – although even Ranjitsinhji must have acknowledged that these were now practically nil – and to make further attempts to raise money. Naturally, in his first aim he achieved only limited success, although it was claimed that he received much sympathy for his position. He travelled out by the same steamer as Lord Lamington, the new Governor of Bombay, whom he had previously met in Australia, where Lamington had been Governor of Queensland, and subsequently renewed his acquaintance with the local British officers in Kathiawar. Without suggesting that any of these officials failed in their duty to the reigning Jam Sahib, some were obviously guilty of the most absurd prejudices. One, Charles Kincaid, was to write, nearly thirty years later, of Jassaji: 'He was an unattractive figure. He had had every advantage . . . Yet he never learnt to play any game properly. Nor did he ever show the least interest in sport. I, as an Agency official, attended the ceremony of installation. I well remember my disgust when I saw this loutish bastard of a lowborn concubine seated on the throne . . . while my unfortunate friend, the rightful heir, had not even been invited to the investiture.'

Ranji may also have taken heart from the recent example of his 'uncle', Pratap Singh. Pratap had laid a rather speculative claim to the vacant throne of Idar, a neighbouring fifteen-gun state whose ruling family was closely related to the Jodhpur House. Maharajkumar Rajendrasingh of Idar remembered, in Charles Allen's *Lives of the Indian Princes* (1984), that: 'While the other claimants were fighting it out and trying to make good their claims in India with the Viceroy, my great-great-grandfather went over his head and appealed straightaway to the Queen. He sent her a cable saying simply, "Idar is mine" – and somehow it worked, because we got it.' Pratap had succeeded to the Idar throne in January 1903.

More tangible success came to Ranji in his other aim, to raise funds. First of all, he further developed the friendship of the Nawab of Junagadh (a state on the southern tip of the Kathiawar peninsula), whom he had first met during his previous visit in 1901–02. Although he possibly did not immediately benefit financially from the relationship, the Nawab was to become, according to Nawanagar's present court historian, the greatest of all Ranji's benefactors, greater even than Jodhpur. In the meantime Ranjitsinhji achieved a significant financial coup when he persuaded his old schoolfriend Mansur Khachar, on about 28 April 1904, to lend him the huge sum of £10,000 in return for a promise to help him with his claim to the Jasdan throne. Two days later, Ranjitsinhji was on his way back to England on the same

ship as Lord Curzon, who was returning home for several months'
leave and with whom he later claimed to Mansur to have had a
conversation about the Jasdan succession during the voyage.

It must be probable that, but for Mansur Khachar's loan, Ranjitsinhji
would not have returned to England at all for the 1904 cricket season.
Even as it was, he was unable to arrive in time for the start of Sussex's
season, reaching Dover on 14 May, the final day of their first match,
against MCC at Lord's. During the season, when Sussex played at
Derby in late July, he met Curzon again, *Cricket* reporting that
Ranjitsinhji, 'who recently wrote a review of Lord Curzon's work in
India', was seen to have had a long conversation with the Viceroy. It
was directly after this game that Ranji made a fairly sudden decision
to miss three successive championship fixtures and spend ten days
with Edith Borissow and her family in Gilling, suggesting that he had
by then resolved to return to India once the season was over. On 9
October he departed Britain again.

On his previous visit to the subcontinent he had gone alone,
although while there he was joined briefly by Percy Standing, his
biographer. This time he was accompanied by MacLaren, the Lancashire and England captain. Their first destination was Marseilles,
where the P&O steamship *Marmora* was bound for India. Ranji had
with him a rather unusual consignment, a motor car. Publicly, he had
let it be believed he was taking the car to compete in the Baroda Cup
race the following January; in fact, he had promised to act as an agent
to the Lanchester Company, selling their vehicles to Indian princes.

MacLaren, who was said to be going to India 'on business', had
recently privately agreed to act as Ranjitsinhji's personal secretary.
The two men had first formed a friendship during the 1897–98 tour
of Australia, when they began to acclaim one another as the greatest
batsman of the day. Ranji wrote of MacLaren in *With Stoddart's Team
in Australia*: 'Archie, as he is called by his friends, is, indeed, a most
amusing and agreeable companion. He affords much amusement to
us all by his queer sayings and witty remarks. He is always cheerful
and full of "go". He imagines he is unlucky with everything, but
Archie without his grumbling, as someone remarked the other day,
would be like curry without chutney . . . In short, he is a thorough

sportsman and a grand fellow.' MacLaren was undoubtedly an exceptionally fine batsman, much admired for the correct public school style which he paraded with some panache, but he was another amateur who had problems financing himself. He had done so with a succession of jobs, although his county club had given him quite lucrative assistance for three years by making him their assistant secretary. He was, by many accounts, an arrogant, high-handed and often extremely rude man, who was notoriously unreliable with money; he could also be quite charming and on the infrequent occasions he came into funds would invariably spend all of it on himself and his friends in extravagant haste. The position, therefore, that Ranji (who had recently acted as godfather to his child) offered him in 1904 must have been very welcome and readily accepted.

On arriving in India, they travelled to Calcutta, Ranjitsinhji's immediate purpose seemingly being to gain an official audience with Curzon in an attempt to have his claim to the Nawanagar throne reviewed. By the time they got there, they had been joined by Lord Hawke, the Yorkshire captain, who was on a four-month shooting trip, and Mansur Khachar, who was accompanying them in the belief that Ranji planned to use his influence with Curzon for Mansur's benefit as well as his own, though it is probable that Ranji did nothing for him.

Over New Year a three-day cricket match was staged in the capital British India between the Calcutta club and I Zingari, the English wandering side, and Ranji, MacLaren and Hawke all took part. Curzon watched some of the match and saw Ranji score a century, but the attempt to gain an interview failed. Thus, if Ranji's informal meeting with the Viceroy at Derby six months earlier had been an encouragement to him, it led to no immediately tangible results.

After that, it is difficult to see what of significance Ranji could have hoped to achieve by staying in India at a stage when, in the words of a prominent member of the India Office in London, Sir Curzon Wyllie, he 'could have had very little hope of making good' his claim to the succession. But stay he did, apparently content to bide his time and continue cultivating his friendships with a variety of British officials. This was probably one of the periods Anthony de Mello had in mind when he wrote, in *Portrait of Indian Sport* (1959), that before Ranjitsinhji became Jam Sahib he 'wandered, virtually homeless, for many years'. At some point, Ranji and his party went on a shooting trip, possibly to Junagadh, where he could have combined an expedition to the Gir Forest, where there were the only lions in India, with a visit to the Nawab.

On 24 March 1905 MacLaren returned to England. It is likely that, had things gone according to plan, Ranji would have followed him in time for the start of the new cricket season. But he tried to mislead Mansur again, perhaps with a view to then promptly departing for Britain; for once, however, he miscalculated the liberties he could successfully take with the same person. Attempting to sell Mansur his post as a car agent, he produced a list of sales he claimed to have made, but Mansur chanced to discover that one of them was bogus and he began to suspect that his friend had been playing him false all along. In about May 1905, Mansur filed a suit against Ranjitsinhji in the Bombay High Court to recover the £10,000 he had lent him the previous year.

In the months that followed, while MacLaren played in the Test series against Australia, the British press speculated on why Ranji had not also returned. In July, the newspapers reported that he had had an attack of malaria and would not reach England before the end of the season; later they said he was not expected until the following May (Fry wrote in 1939 that Ranji almost died of asthma at about this time, but he may have been thinking of the serious illness that afflicted him shortly after he became Jam Sahib). Meanwhile, Ranji stayed on in Rajkot, from where possibly he wrote his modestly sized *Cricket Guide and How to Play Cricket*, published in London in June 1906 as part of Spalding's Athletic Library series. Whatever else he was doing, he was not endearing himself to Jassaji, who, on hearing of the imminent arrival of Ranjitsinhji during Lt.-Col. Kennedy's retirement party at the Resident's house in February 1906, left immediately. This may have been the inspiration for the incident described in Wild, when Ranjitsinhji, 'saw Jam Jassaji drive through Rajkot. The carriage clattered past with its escort, and the dust rose in a cloud. Ranji gazed at the departing cavalcade. "That's where I should be . . ." he said gently.'

When he did not return for the 1906 cricket season either, people in England must have suspected him of having abandoned for good Sussex, his cricket career, his rooms in Cambridge and many of his friends. But he was unable to return even if he had wished to. The shadow cast by Mansur Khachar's suit in the Bombay courts, far more menacing than had been the spectre of bankruptcy in Britain, was committing him to numerous desperate but fruitless attempts to prevent an action that threatened to result in the destruction of any hopes he still clung to of one day succeeding to the Nawanagar throne.

On 3 August 1906, a British surgeon was summoned to Jamnagar to attend to Jassaji, who had a severe fever. It was feared, as ever, to be typhoid. He had contracted typhoid before, four years earlier while in Ceylon, and on that occasion had shaken it off after a week. This time he showed distinct signs of being better after four days and, as there no longer seemed cause for alarm, the surgeon returned home and was replaced by an Indian doctor. If the subsequent account of his wives is to be believed, Jassaji's illness returned with a vengeance three days later, on 10 August, and he lost consciousness. But it was not for another two days that Merwanji, the chief minister, wired Percy Seymour Fitzgerald, the new Resident, to say the Jam Sahib was in a serious condition. An English doctor was sent by special train, while a surgeon was brought from Bombay, but Jassaji's decline was rapid. On 14 August, at twenty minutes past eleven in the evening, he died.

He was twenty-four years and four days old, had no son by any of his wives, and had not adopted an heir, even as a temporary measure.

Fitzgerald, who had seen Jassaji alive and in good health only three weeks earlier, did not speak to the surgeon during the following few days but understood the cause of death to be 'a particularly insidious form of typhoid fever'. Nothing more seems to have been heard of the matter.

There is, of course, every possibility that the cause of death was a perfectly natural one. None of the Resident's surviving papers suggests anything to the contrary (though few of these exist, a fact not in itself particularly strange: many sensitive documents concerning the princes were destroyed before independence to protect them from Congress). There is, however, some circumstantial evidence of foul play, which was not at all uncommon in the numerous courts of princely India, where many people often stood to benefit by a change of ruler. This was certainly the case in Nawanagar at that time: the following year Fitzgerald admitted that 'Jamnagar has been the prey of intrigue and scheming ever since the [British] Administration ceased', while, as we have seen, rumours of plots against Jassaji's life date back at least to April 1902. Moreover, Fitzgerald's annual report for 1906–07 confirmed earlier British fears that Jassaji was taken advantage of during his minority by 'unscrupulous and undesirable' people, particularly one Merubha of Sayla, who had become 'virtually ruler of the state' and 'adverse and disloyal' to the government. With such an environment at court, it would not have been impossible to orchestrate the young Jam Sahib's death, even from outside.

Those who stood to gain most by the death of Jassaji were the two men who had already formally contested his right to have succeeded to the throne ahead of them, Lakhuba and Ranjitsinhji. It was on their behalf that the March 1903 plot against Jassaji's life was said to have been planned. When Jassaji died, Lakhuba was in England, where he had completed his education, and was apparently taken unawares, but Ranjitsinhji was in Kathiawar, where he had been for the past two years, having at first given up his cricket career in England once more actively to dispute the succession, only then to be detained by an imminent law suit that threatened to ruin his prospects once and for all. Even if Jassaji's death was not arranged by him or his faction, Ranji would have had to admit that it could not have happened at a better time for him.

The most concrete evidence for believing Jassaji was murdered comes from that inveterate gossip, E. H. D. Sewell, who became a close friend of Ranjitsinhji. In *Cricket Wallah*, he wrote of Ranji: 'He had some bitter enemies dating, some of them, back to the time of his struggle for the gadi . . . It is possible that "Ranji's" predecessor, the half-bred, was poisoned (I know something was told me in later years about a state subject who seemed to have a hand in it!) but this is "suspect". "Ranji" told me himself he thought he was slightly poisoned soon after achieving the gadi, and nearly died. These are not mere surmises. There is little doubt that things of a most tortuous kind did happen. But direct evidence about them is, of course, impossible to obtain. "Ranji" was really rather secretive. He seemed to me to possess a double personality.'

It is such details as these that have led Satrusalyasinhji, the present Jam Sahib, to the opinion that Jassaji did not die of typhoid but of poison, at the hands of those who supported his great-uncle.

Over the months that followed British officials both in London and India were to display a peculiar sense of that fair play for which they were supposedly famous.

First of all, they failed to install a successor within thirteen days of the death of the previous ruler, as was the usual procedure. Although initially the delay may have been because of a need to establish that none of Jassaji's widows was carrying his child, a final decision, incredibly, was not taken for over six months.

Several parties showed an interest in the succession. Of the applications submitted to the Government of India, only three merited serious consideration. They were from Ranji on 11 September, Lakhuba on 26 September, and Jassaji's widows on 7 November. Ranji and Lakhuba each claimed to be heir to the throne, while the widows argued there was no heir and that according to custom they had the right to adopt the new ruler.

Ranji's case was based on the claim that he had at one time been the adoptive heir to Vibhaji; Lakhuba's on the fact that he was Vibhaji's grandson. Both were at pains to point out why they believed they had the superior claim, but in fact their positions were remarkably similar. First, both of them had forfeited a place in the succession because their families had incurred Vibhaji's displeasure by agitating for their rights to succeed. Second, both had refused to sign declarations that they would have no further personal interest in the Nawanagar throne. And third, both, of course, had then submitted applications staking their claims to the succession which had been rejected, since when neither's circumstances had materially altered.

The difference in their cases was that Ranjitsinhji had never been in the succession, because his adoption had never been carried out.

All this would appear to have led fairly naturally to the conclusions of the third application, from the widows. They said that Jassaji's death had been so sudden he had not had a chance to nominate an heir, and cited a number of precedents in support of their claim that with the throne vacant the right to adopt a successor devolved on them. These included some recent instances and two in Nawanagar itself, one in the 17th century and another involving the adoption of Vibhaji's father, Ranmalji, in 1820. They asked for the assistance of the Government of India in making a suitable choice, but it was unthinkable that they would have agreed to a recommendation of either Lakhuba or Ranjitsinhji, both of whose actions had displayed an animosity towards their dead husband.

Ranji, with the advantage over Lakhuba in England, moved fast once he learnt of Jassaji's death. The first thing he did was to appeal successfully to Mansur Khachar to withdraw his suit in the Bombay High Court on the understanding that once he had succeeded to the Nawanagar throne he would repay the debt with interest. He then orchestrated declarations of support on his behalf from Jodhpur, Idar, Dhrangadhara and, importantly, Kutch. Other influential states in Rajputana, while not advocating one candidate in particular, demanded that the new ruler be a pure Rajput, which was also likely to have been helpful to him, even if the Jadejas were not high in the Rajput hierarchy.

In Britain the assumption was being made that Ranji had already come into his own. Not long after Jassaji's death, several newspapers stated this as a categorical fact, the *Daily Mail* of 4 September, for example, carrying the headline RANJI'S THRONE: THE STORY OF HIS SUCCESSION. Ranji's popularity was largely responsible for this, just as it had earlier accounted for the credulous way in which it was accepted that he was a prince and, later, that he was in a justifiable dispute over the succession with Jassaji. Now, realizing the continuing importance of public opinon in Britain, he called the press to his assistance. On 13 November an unsigned article appeared in *The Times* which argued at length his claim to the Nawanagar throne.

Three days later the same newspaper was obliged to publish a letter from Lakhuba's London solicitors objecting to the article, taking issue with some of its statements and protesting that their client had 'consistently refrained from inspiring any press comments or from giving out his petition to the press'.

Once Ranji felt he could do nothing more, he went to Sarodar to stay with his mother and await events. He made no secret of his confidence over the outcome of the succession. He may even have been completely sincere when he wrote, in a letter to Newton Digby, a Cambridge journalist, in October 1906: 'There are several claimants to the throne, some possessing some shadow of right, others none at all. I honestly believe my claim to be just and right, as I did even during the life-time of the late possessor.' As far as he was concerned, he was about to restore his family's good name.

In Rajkot, Fitzgerald, the Resident, began to compile a report on the relative merits of the various claimants. On the face of it, this task could not have been given to a better qualified man. Fitzgerald had spent over twenty-five years with the Bombay government and had acted as an assistant to the Resident in Kathiawar between 1878 and 1884, a period that had witnessed Vibhaji's struggle to have his infant son recognized as his heir. Now, as chance would have it, only a few months earlier in March 1906, he had been asked to return as Resident himself. It was to be the last post he would hold before retiring in 1908.

He completed his confidential report on 20 October. His conclusions were endorsed by the Government of Bombay on 7 December and, after a long delay which seemed unnecessary but which may have been due to some delicate negotiation, ratified and formally made public by the Government of India on 20 February 1907. They were that the British should make the choice of successor themselves and find in favour of Ranjitsinhji.

Fitzgerald accepted Ranji's reasoning that the situation was as it had been before Jassaji was born, and that then it had been Vibhaji's intention that Ranji should be the successor. Fitzgerald said he had read every document on the subject and could find nothing to contradict this argument, but if that was so he should have known Vibhaji never carried out Ranji's adoption ceremony in four years prior to Jassaji's birth and subsequently made it perfectly clear he wished to have nothing more to do with the Sarodar family. Fitzgerald dismissed the widows' case by saying that only a ruling chief could select an heir, though their appeal had provided evidence to suggest that this was not so. But his report raised no eyebrows with any of his superiors.

Of course, Ranji was significantly assisted in his claim by his immense popularity as a cricketer and also by his friendship with the British, perhaps particularly his personal acquaintance with Lord Lamington, the Governor of Bombay. Also, according to Wild, while the matter was under consideration, Pratap Singh paid a visit to the new Viceroy, Lord Minto. Minto had succeeded Lord Curzon, whose inflammatory attempts at reform in India had resulted in his resignation, in January 1906. Minto was an affable figure, appropriate to the conciliatory policy the newly elected Liberal government sought to adopt in India. Pratap apparently gained an audience with him and declared that his future loyalty to the British crown depended on the outcome of the Nawanagar succession.

Further considerations were perhaps that Ranji was thoroughly westernized, a rare and attractive claim for a prospective Indian ruler to be able to make, and also that, if spurned, he might still pursue a political career, a dangerously uncertain possibility.

Ranji had to wait until 25 February before being able formally to communicate his great news to England, with telegrams to Redfern and Hunt, his solicitors, and Sir Seymour King; but Archie MacLaren, who had come out to India with Arthur Priestley (now an MP) to join him, had been writing to the Lancashire club as early as 27 January to tell them he would no longer be able to play for them regularly. Clearly, enough was known by then to anticipate that MacLaren's position as Ranji's private secretary would be taking up much more of his time.

It was only when he read the press reports in the week following the announcement of Ranjitsinhji's selection that Lakhuba, in England, knew his case had failed. The first thing his solicitors did was to demand from the India Office a reply to his application, as they wished to exercise their client's right to appeal.

No allowance had been made for this awkward eventuality, which would necessitate a further delay. The Government of Bombay wanted Ranji's installation ceremony to take place before 10 March, as Lamington was then leaving for the hill districts. After telegrams had passed between Lord Morley, the Secretary of State for India, in London and Minto in Simla, Lakhuba received his reply on 8 March (it is doubtful if Jassaji's widows ever got theirs) and was told that Ranjitsinhji's installation would not prejudice consideration of any appeal he might wish to make. That cleared the way for the installation to take place three days later, although without Lamington.

Fitzgerald's subsequent behaviour was revealing. Although Lakhuba's appeal had no realistic chance of success, Fitzgerald nevertheless did nothing with it for nearly three months. The reason was that he had been sent only one copy and was afraid to release it for extra copies to be printed: 'I have kept the whole thing secret, my office even know nothing about it . . . once it became public property in Kathiawar there would be a renewal of intrigue and uncertainty.'

The only passages which could have caused controversy were those pointing out that the new ruler had never been adopted as heir.

The idea of becoming Jam Sahib had consumed much of Ranji's thoughts during his adult life. In his moments of triumph, when anything seemed possible, he must have imagined what it would be like; in times of disappointment, he must have felt it was destined to remain nothing more than a dream. Yet when it actually did happen, it can hardly have been equal to his expectation.

First of all, the circumstances that surrounded his succession meant that, though Jam Sahib–elect and said to be a descendant of a 17th-century ruler of the state, he was virtually a complete stranger to his people. The British, even after dropping their idea of barring him forever from Jamnagar nine years earlier, had strongly discouraged his presence there since, while his selection had been far from straightforward, coming only after considerable debate, when a lengthy period was allowed to elapse since the death of Jassaji. All this can only have helped create a mood of uncertainty, particularly in the mind of Ranjitsinhji as he arrived in the capital on the eve of his installation.

The element of danger that surrounded his arrival was not lessened by the natural desire of the population to get a glimpse of their new ruler. He came in at 6.30 a.m. on a special steam train from neighbouring Porbandar, where he had been given a farewell party the previous night. Despite the early hour, large numbers of people had long been gathering and some gained access to the crowded station platform, where they jostled around waiting delegations.

When he stepped down from the railway carriage, the throng managed to wait fairly patiently while photographs were taken and a band completed the British national anthem, but as he was presented to Merwanji, who was to be retained as chief minister, a commotion broke out. People began rushing forward and throwing garlands and there was no possibility of Ranji being introduced to other officials. Only with the greatest difficulty was a passage made for him out into the square. Accompanied by Fitzgerald and Devisinhji, he was then driven in a procession of carriages and elephants on an hour-long cavalcade to the Lal bungalow, where he was met by his mother and where initially he and his family were to live, rather than enter the palace, which was still occupied by Jassaji's relatives and courtiers. Along the way, buildings had been decorated with flags and banners of welcome and as Ranjitsinhji passed beneath, flowers were thrown down onto him by well-wishers. (These scenes encouraged some news reports to hail him as 'undoubtedly the most popular Jam who has ever ruled in Jamnagar'.)

The following afternoon, when he rode on an elephant to the civic ceremony to mark his installation, it was a similar story. Crowds several rows deep congregated from an early hour on the approaches to the palace square and in the square itself, where the ceremony was held. They took up vantage points in the roads, at some places impeding the procession, and on the roofs of houses, while on the balconies of the palace zenana women peered out through the lattice screens.

All this only emphasized the need for the greatest degree of security for Ranji's person, and one thing that emerges from the account in the *Times of India* on 16 March 1907 is the elaborateness of these arrangements. When his carriage arrived at the station on the first morning, it stood at the platform for thirty minutes, as outside the sun climbed higher. The reason given for the delay was that within rites were being performed and astrologers consulted, but equally likely final checks were being made on preparations for his entrance into his new capital. Drawn up inside the station, and around three sides of the square outside, were ranks of state troops, supplemented by Kathiawar Imperial Service Lancers. For his journey to the bungalow, a circuitous route, lined with further armed guards, was taken, probably another security measure although again passed off as the instruction of the astrologers. Once more, on the next afternoon, troops lined the route to the palace square and formed a guard outside the large shamiana where the main ceremony took place. As an additional precaution, the Nawab of Junagadh provided Ranji with a large Arab bodyguard plus servants to supervise his food.

Circumstances apart, there was another respect in which the succession cannot have met Ranji's expectations. He may long have imagined that as Jam Sahib he would possess unimaginable wealth and complete freedom to do with it as he wished; if so, he was sadly mistaken.

The state he inherited was very poor. It had not recovered from a crippling three-year drought at the turn of the century and was stricken not only with poverty but with disease. At about the time of Ranji's succession, the capital alone had a death toll in the region of thirty a day. Wild records that Ranji's overwhelming impression during his first ride through Jamnagar as Jam Sahib was its all-pervading squalor: 'an evil slum'. Even the ancient palace, where he attended religious ceremonies during the morning of his installation, was enveloped in tawdry dwellings.

Ranji also discovered to his alarm that practically all the state's jewellery had been sold off. He wore the best of what was left, robes brocaded with gold, a jewelled belt, a pearl necklace and a sword

175

inlaid wih gems (though this may have been the sword presented to him as a gift by the Maharao of Kutch, as head of the Jadeja Rajputs), but it is probable that he had to endure the embarrassment of being outshone in splendour by the variegated finery of his guests.

Even before the installation, he had received clear indications that his transition to ruling prince was not going to be as smooth as he would have wished. From the start, his financial difficulties, for a man about to be placed in charge of the management of an entire state, had caused anxiety, and shortly before the Government of India gave its consent to his selection he had had to submit a petition answering the allegation that he was in debt. And, although he was about to become nominal master of nearly 3,800 square miles, 350,000 people, an army of 2,700, and an annual revenue of about £140,000, the British had not been slow to impose their conditions. Most seriously, they proposed a nazarana, or levy equivalent to one's year revenue, as a token of Nawanagar's allegiance. They also stressed the need for the strictest economies: the state owed about £80,000, apart from a sizeable loan for the construction of the Jamnagar–Rajkot railway which would not be repaid until 1910. Ranjitsinhji's personal income, they said, was to be limited to £2,000 per month.

There was no possibility of a lavish installation. Seven days before it was to take place, Ranji had been obliged to publish an announcement in *The Times* that said: 'I have abandoned the idea of celebrating my installation on a large scale, to enable English friends to join later.' In fact, although he was to receive hundreds of telegrams of congratulation, the only visitors he had from England were MacLaren and Priestley, who had already been with him for several weeks. It was in some sort of attempt to accord with the popular conception of a coronation that many of the ceremonial trappings – shamianas, landaus, railway carriages, musical bands, even bedding – were borrowed from neighbouring states. But there was no place to lodge the entourage of attendant princes from Rajputana and Kathiawar; instead they had to be housed in a town of tents built on the maidan facing the main guest house.

Clearly, having fought so long for the hour to arrive, Ranji cannot have liked the restrictions the British placed on him, but he had little choice. It is interesting to note that the civic ceremony, which was due to begin at three o'clock in the afternoon with the arrival of Fitzgerald, standing in for the absent Lord Lamington, was delayed two hours until almost sunset because Ranjitsinhji refused to go on (despite protests from Fitzgerald) until the seal of state and the keys to the treasury were delivered up to him.

When the ceremony eventually got under way, Fitzgerald made it quite clear in his speech of welcome who was the senior partner in the new relationship. He was complimentary enough to Ranjitsinhji, saying that no Jam Sahib had been better equipped to rule than he was and tactfully praising his father as 'the beau ideal of a Rajput gentleman', but he stated quite openly that it was due to Pratap Singh that Ranjitsinhji now sat on the throne. And he went on to issue some very specific pieces of advice.

'I feel that there is no need to warn you against flatterers, intriguers, and sycophants', he said. 'Your antecedents give me no reason to fear that you will be idle, luxurious or indifferent . . . It will behove you in the present financial circumstances of the state to proceed with caution at first, but as your means permit it you should extend your railway towards Dwarka; irrigation, forestry and the development of the magnificent harbour which you have at Salaya should claim your attention and you should be strong to maintain and lose no opportunity of extending the reforms which were inaugurated during the period that the state was under the direct administration of the British government. Be always careful of the various departments of your administration, employ the best men, pay them adequately, insist on efficiency, and do not be led by any mistaken feelings of kindness into retaining a bad man . . . Mix freely with your subjects, give ready audience to the humblest, ascertain the truth for yourself, and watch over everything.'

The new Jam Sahib of Nawanagar gave a reply that was appropriately humble: 'I can only say I shall endeavour to play the game so as not to lose whatever credit I have gained in another field . . . I hope to abide loyally by the traditions of this state, in its deep unswerving loyalty to the British throne.' And he promised not to be idle, luxurious or indifferent.

Within a few days, little remained to remind Ranji of his installation. There was no week-long celebration, as when Jassaji assumed power; the main ceremony took place less than thirty-six hours after his arrival in the capital and many of his guests stayed less than twenty-four. He and his family, so long of Sarodar, may have reflected delightedly on their changed circumstances, but they were in a largely unfamiliar and possibly dangerous city. One of the first steps Ranjitsinhji took was to nominate, secretly, a nephew as heir.

His life had undergone a sudden transformation and it would only have been natural if he suffered some difficulty adjusting. For a start, his responsibilities, in theory at any rate, were no longer only to himself but also to many other people. However, after four months, his only major step had been to appoint an officer to inquire into improving means of collecting land revenue. Several important matters awaited his decision: just two examples were the Dwarka railway extension, which he asked for more time to consider, and the nazarana, about which he planned to make a representation. He had, though, begun the process of getting a cricket pitch prepared and a pavilion built – he was, he declared, going to produce a team of Rajputs to beat even the Parsees. He had made a donation to the Sussex club and had ordered the drains in the old palace to be uprooted and work to begin on a magnificent new palace. Quite quickly, his new situation must have begun to frustrate him. He took off for a fortnight's shooting in Ratlam and invited MacLaren, who had returned to England only two months earlier, and Lilley to come out in October to see him.

Then, in August, shortly after returning from a shooting expedition with Fitzgerald and his family, he became dangerously ill with typhoid, although, as we have seen, Ranji himself believed he had been 'slightly poisoned'. He was taken to a hospital in Bombay. After six weeks he was three stones lighter and barely had the strength to stand upright. But, gradually, he got over the worst of it and there was talk of him being moved to Poona to complete his recuperation.

Fitzgerald was therefore surprised to receive from Ranji's doctor a report, of 17 September, recommending that His Highness should be sent for one year to Europe fully to restore his health. When Fitzgerald got word from Ranji, he was not actually presented with a request to go away but supposed it to be Ranji's wish. Fitzgerald, remembering the intrigues of recent years, was anxious about what might happen in his absence, but in the face of official medical opinion he found it difficult to object. But he was adamant that a suitable Administrator would have to be found, as he considered Merwanji too weak.

Ranji departed his capital on 26 October, bound for England. As Fitzgerald observed ruefully, 'H. H.'s expenses in Europe will not be small'.

10

IDLE, LUXURIOUS AND INDIFFERENT?

IN HIS AUTHORIZED biography, Wild wrote of Ranji's first stay in Britain as a ruling prince: 'There was more in his return, however, than a recuperative visit. For he was now paramount in his own land, and he wished to repay all the hospitality he had received in England. His chance had come to show gratitude, and he did so right royally . . . He determined to resume his old life on a new level of lavish hospitality. He contemplated with delight the parties he would give, the friends who would stay with him for a whole season's cricket.'

And certainly it seemed to be that way. Shortly after Ranjitsinhji, or H. H. the Jam Sahib of Nawanagar as he was now known, had arrived, he gave a splendid reunion dinner in London for many of his old friends, and once he had settled in to the beautiful country residence he was renting at Shillinglee Park, between the Sussex Downs and the Surrey hills, the magnificent house parties began. Despite his announcement in *The Times* abandoning plans for a large celebration, it had been reported in England that his installation was an event on the grandest scale and so expectations of opulence must have been high. In such matters, Ranji had never been one to disappoint: with a large staff of servants, hospitality was lavished on a host of the aristocracy and leading cricketers, some of whom stayed with him for weeks on end. It was the idyllic life: privilege and prosperity, elegance and extravagance; all a well-bred party.

Naturally, there was sport in abundance. Trout-fishing and duck and pheasant shoots were arranged for visitors as a matter of course, while Ranji, having had a pitch prepared on the grounds at the side of the house, organized cricket matches for himself and his guests. For a three-day match in mid-May his opposing captain was Grace, for a two-day game in early June, Stoddart; and several other notable players were invited to take part. On the first occasion, it appears everyone was entertained possibly too well, for it was an unusually low-scoring game. Lilley, one of the participants in these matches, recalled that the general public, who were allowed to view play from the path, could not have been altogether satisfied at the late starts and lengthy intervals, though their feelings may have been assuaged when, on one occasion, they were afterwards invited to take tea in a marquee themselves.

Yet the impression of benevolence was not quite what it seemed. During the first nine months of his stay in England, it is not certain that Ranji paid any of his bills satisfactorily. He ran up sizeable accounts with a number of tradesmen, including a supplier of large quantities of pheasant, a Birmingham wine merchant (from whom he also got supplies of port shipped back to Jamnagar); a York bookseller and stationer; a laundry firm; and a firm of millers. In addition, he did not meet the costs for Shillinglee, nor is it even certain whether he paid for the five Lanchester motor cars he was then running. Having had for years a natural desire for extravagance curbed by regular reminders that his resources were sadly limited, Ranji apparently interpreted his new-found wealth as a signal to feed that extravagance to excess, and all other thoughts of money went from his mind. It never seemed to occur to him that his failure to pay might stick in the minds of others. As far as he was concerned, the acts of extravagance were what atoned for all the generous hospitality he had received in the past; actually paying for them had no significance whatsoever. He simply ignored the repeated applications for payment from people who found it difficult to get hold of a man who was always playing cricket.

Nor, of course, were his English creditors alone. Mansur Khachar, who had attended the installation ceremony in Jamnagar the previous year, was also in Britain during 1908, anxious to recover his £10,000 from the new Jam Sahib.

Mansur Khachar called on Sir Curzon Wyllie, the political aide-de-camp to Lord Morley, the Secretary of State for India, on 5 March at his room in the India Office. Wyllie had asked to see Mansur after seeing the previous day a letter from Mansur to the Secretary of State, dated 29 February, consisting of five large sheets of typed paper. The letter bristled with implications. Not only did it detail events involving perhaps India's best-known prince but also Lord Curzon, until two years previously the Viceroy, and Lord Hugh Cecil, the fifth and youngest son of the late Prime Minister, Lord Salisbury. The letter suggested that the Jam Sahib of Nawanagar, who in the eyes of the public could do no wrong, was not in fact playing with a straight bat – if, indeed, he ever had!

Wyllie and Mansur went through the letter together, Wyllie taking notes throughout the interview. The letter began:

I have the honour to submit the following facts to Your Excellency and I would beg you to advise and assist me . . . I am the third son of the late chief of Jasdan in Kathiawar [who] died on 29 January 1904 and I became a claimant to a quarter share of the state . . . While my claim was being dealt with I was approached by H. H. the Jam of Nawanagar (then Kumar Shri Ranjitsinhji) with offers of assistance. H. H. informed me that he was heavily in debt, that the various allowances made to him by the Maharajas of Jodhpur, Patiala and Idar were in arrears, and that if I would advance him £10,000 he would be able to clear himself from his liabilities, proceed to England and support my claim.

The loan of £10,000 asked for was made on or about 28 April 1904, H. H. assigning to me as security the alleged arrears of the allowances mentioned above and also handing to me IOUs for the amount of my advance, the receipt of Messrs King and Co., of Bombay, to whom the money was paid and who remitted it to England to H. H.'s solicitors, and a letter authorizing them to pay to me any arrears of the yearly allowances that might be paid into His Highness's account by the Maharajas of Jodhpur, Patiala and Idar or from any other source.

On the following day H. H. informed me the £10,000 had been duly transmitted to England to enable his debts to be paid and he obtained from me a further loan of Rs10,000 [about £580] on his statement that he was without money; for this loan I obtained no acknowledgment.

On 30 April 1904 H. H. left for England and I received various letters from him in which he wrote that he was doing his utmost to further my claims and that he had had a conversation with Lord Curzon, who was travelling to England by the same vessel, about me. Subsequently H. H. cabled to me for £10,000 which sum he informed me by letter was to be given to Lord Hugh Cecil who would thereby be induced to advance my interests. I fully believed that the statements made to me by H. H. were true, but I was unable to make the loan. I had further communications from H. H. who informed me that owing to the non-receipt of the £10,000 he had been unable to do anything for me with Lord Hugh Cecil The original correspondence is in my possession . . .

Mansur first of all explained that he was induced to give Ranji the £10,000 (which, at modern prices, would be worth well over £350,000), because Ranji had been his great friend for the five years they had attended the Rajkumar College in Rajkot together. He emphasized that he was under the impression that Ranji would be able to assist him through his alleged friendship with Lord Curzon. The exchange of money had clearly centred on the fact that Lord Curzon, who had agreed to accept a second term in office as Viceroy, was due within days to sail for England for several months' leave and if Ranji, who was to share his voyage, was to use his influence with him, Mansur Khachar had to act quickly and entrust his money to his old friend.

Mansur believed that Lord Hugh Cecil, for whom Ranji had requested a further sum of £10,000, was a member of the legal profession and possessed great personal influence, as his father, Lord Salisbury, although no longer Prime Minister, remained a prominent figure in the Conservative government. But of course, as Wyllie was possibly aware, Cecil was not a legal man at all. After leaving Oxford in 1891 he had been preparing to take holy orders when he was persuaded to become assistant private secretary to his father, who was then both Prime Minister and foreign secretary. This had provided him with his introduction to politics; from 1895 until 1906 he had been MP for Greenwich. Whether Ranjitsinhji had intended the money as a legal fee or for the purchase of personal favours (or 'for *anything*', Wyllie noted), Mansur did not know.

That Ranjitsinhji may have been contemplating bribing the son of a former Prime Minister for the advancement of a friend, was certainly Mansur's most astonishing claim. Even if Ranjitsinhji was simply trying to deceive Mansur into giving him money, how daring a story! The letter went on:

On his return to India in 1905, H. H. requested me to go with him to Calcutta when he would, so he stated, use his influence with Lord Curzon. The journey was made but no interview with Lord Curzon was accorded us.

At about this date on H. H. representing to me he was in serious financial difficulties I advanced him a sum of Rs5,000, H. H. stating that this money was to enable him to pay for certain things he had ordered and that he would return it within a week as he was expecting to receive a cheque from Messrs Geo. Newnes for whom he had undertaken to write a book.

In about February 1905 H. H. went to England and entered into communication with me regarding the agency in India of a certain make of motor car. H. H. subsequently brought one of these cars to India and while there furnished me with a list of sales effected by him. I subsequently met one of the alleged purchasers (H. H. the Maharaja of Kapurthala) who denied any knowledge of such a purchase. I at once asked H. H. the Jam Sahib of Nawanagar (then Kumar Shri Ranjitsinhji) for an explanation but could receive no satisfactory reply. Becoming suspicious I applied to him for repayment of the moneys advanced but failed to recover any portion, and accordingly commenced a suit against him for the sum of £11,000 advanced.

Mansur said that Ranji, on his return to India (which in fact was probably as early as November 1904), had claimed he was acting as an agent for the Lanchester Company, selling vehicles to Indian princes. Mansur had a pecuniary interest in the Eastern Trading Company in Bombay, an import agency firm, and Ranjitsinhji had said he could secure for him the post of agent for Rs10,000 through a Mr Barnsley or a Mr Bardsley, the university cricketer (Mansur could not recall the exact name, but Gerald Bardswell, an Oxford University and Lancashire amateur cricketer, who died in the United States in December 1906, may be the name Ranji gave, though Bardswell's only known business connection was with the wine trade). Ranji told him he had already made six sales and, in the end, Mansur had made him an offer, which was accepted, of £200. The six sales had proved to be bogus. Ranji, he said, was in partnership with a Mr Esdaile, a man of various means and a blackguard. (There is some independent, if tenuous, evidence to suggest that Ranji did, indeed, act as an agent for Lanchester: shortly after becoming Jam Sahib he purchased for himself several cars through the company, while MacLaren was once to include car salesman in a list of jobs he had undertaken to finance his cricket.)

Mansur added that he had filed his suit in the Bombay High Court in about May 1905:

Attempts were made amicably to settle the case and among other things I was offered as further security the assignment of H. H.'s share in a book called *Rulers and Princes of India* to which he informed me he had already obtained 2,000 subscribers at ten guineas each. Ultimately he could only produce a list of 150, and negotiations for a settlement fell through.

Before my suit could be heard H. H. the late Jam Sahib of Nawanagar died and H. H. the present Jam Sahib appealed to me to withdraw my suit, alleging that it would harm him in the eyes of Government, if, pending the decision regarding his claim to succeed to the gadi of Nawanagar, judgement in any suit such as mine was given against him. At his earnest solicitation I agreed to withdraw my case, it being understood between us that on his succession to the gadi he would repay his debt with interest. I have received letters of thanks and gratitude both from H. H. and his mother.

185

Mansur explained to Wyllie that after he had filed his suit, Ranji sent someone called Devisinhji, who described himself as Ranji's elder brother, in an attempt to persuade him to withdraw. When he refused, Ranji addressed a letter to the court claiming that part of the £11,000 had been spent in Mansur's own interests and that the rest was a free gift.

Mansur emphasized that he only withdrew his suit when Ranji pleaded that if he did not do so his chances of succeeding to the Nawanagar throne would be ruined . . .

On H. H. succeeding to the gadi of Nawanagar he continued to delay payment and ultimately sent one of his private secretaries to me asking me to give him a letter stating that I had no further legal claim against him: he informed me that this letter was necessary in order that he might prove to the authorities that he was not in any way helping me. The fact of his succession to the gadi nullified my legal claims against him and accordingly I gave him the letter asked for, he promising to pay me Rs25,000 immediately through a third person in such form as to make it appear that the actual advance came from him. The amount paid to me was in fact only Rs12,500 and with that sum I duly credited H. H.'s account.

Subsequently I came to England and, H. H. being here, I made various attempts to obtain payment from him: he refused to make any payment and ultimately sent a Mr A. C. MacLaren with a proposal that I would give him a further letter to the effect that I had no claim against him, stating that not until this was done would he think of helping me.

The amount (exclusive of interest) which H. H. owes at this date is £10,166 13s 4d.

The IOUs and other documents referred to in this letter are in my possession and can be obtained from India should you so desire it. The facts as stated can be verified by application to the various people named.

Legally I am aware that no claim can be enforced against His Highness, he being a ruling chief. The loss of the money is serious to me and my claim under ordinary circumstances could not be contested. I therefore beg of you to assist me in recovering my advances by advising me as to the right authorities to whom any application on my part should be addressed.

So the letter had ended.

Wyllie managed to establish that Mansur did not in fact have documentary evidence on all points. For example, he could provide no evidence that Ranji said he would use his influence with Lord Curzon, nor could he produce receipts for the loans of Rs10,000 or Rs5,000 (Mansur was prepared, though, to regard the Rs5,000 as defrayment of the expenses of a shooting party organized three years earlier by Ranji for some English friends and of which Mansur himself was a member). It also transpired that the letters of thanks from Ranji and his mother after he had succeeded to the Nawanagar throne were worded in only the most general terms and that subsequent communication was conducted through His Highness's private secretaries, initially a man called Jeyashankar. The letter in which Mansur declared he had no further legal claim against the Jam Sahib was actually drafted, Mansur said, by Ranji himself, who had drawn it up because he said it had better not be known that he was paying off personal debts out of state funds. But, importantly, Mansur said he did have documentary evidence of the original loan of £10,000.

Wyllie sent a minute to the secretary of the Political and Secret Department recording the conversation. He gave his own thoughts: 'It strikes me . . . that there is a good deal below the surface which has not come to light. It seems incredible that Mansur Khachar, a man of intelligence and education, and well acquainted with Ranjitsinhji, could really believe that Ranjitsinhji who was in low water and discredited (except as a cricketer) could possibly have any influence with Lord Curzon which could be worked to his (Mansur Khachar's) advantage.

'At the time of the alleged loan of £10,000, both men were in the same position with claims in Native States, which they could have had very little hope of making good. It also seems extraordinary that Mansur Khachar, when he found Ranjitsinhji was playing him false, should nevertheless have been persuaded to withdraw his suit in the

High Court, and also to give a letter stating that he had no legal claim against him.'

What it was that Wyllie thought might be 'below the surface' is not clear, but presumably he suspected either that Mansur was lying, or, as seems far more likely, that Ranji had been putting more pressure on Mansur than the latter was prepared to admit. Wyllie added: 'On my return from leave three or four weeks hence, I will ask the Jam to come and see me, and hear what he has to say in reply to these accusations.'

Ranji saw Sir Curzon Wyllie five weeks later, on the afternoon of Monday, 6 April. Wyllie read Mansur Khachar's letter to him. Although Ranjitsinhji was to reply that many of the statements were incorrect, the real state of affairs was to become transparent from the nature of his replies. The flimsy and inadequate excuses he offered revealed a casual disregard for the truth and a barely concealed contempt for the plight of his one-time friend.

According to Wyllie's account of their conversation, Ranji said it was Mansur who had appealed to him for assistance, saying that he, Ranji, was well acquainted with England and could be of great assistance to him if he would return there and help him in establishing his claim to a share of the Jasdan throne. Ranji had replied that he could not go to England unless he first came to some settlement with his English creditors. Mansur, he said, had still pressed him to go and finally it was agreed that he should do so, on the understanding that Mansur advance him £3,000 for expenses and £7,000 to satisfy his creditors; in exchange Ranji would make over to Mansur the letter from Sardar Singh, the Maharaja of Jodhpur, promising to continue an allowance of Rs30,000 a year bestowed on Ranji by his father.

Ranji stressed that Mansur gave him the £10,000 on the distinct understanding that payment was to be recovered from the arrears of his Jodhpur allowance and that at no time was Mansur to appeal to him for repayment in any other form. The allowance, he said, had been drawn by him through Pratap Singh, then chief minister of the Jodhpur state, for nearly three years up to the death in 1895 of Maharaja Jaswant Singh, Sardar Singh's father, one of whose wives was closely related to Ranjitsinhji. When Ranjitsinhji reached

England in 1904, he had engaged his solicitors, Messrs Redfern and Hunt, to handle the arrangement made with Mansur. He claimed to having acted as intermediary in England, carrying out from time to time such instructions as Mansur sent him from India.

It was at this point that Ranji's answers began to appear more flimsy. He said that, as regards the Rs10,000, he had no recollection of having obtained the loan, but it was possible he may have received the money. As for his travelling to Britain in the same steamer with Lord Curzon, that had been purely accidental, and all he had told Mansur was that one day at dinner the conversation with Lord Curzon had turned on the Jasdan succession and he had gathered that Mansur had a very poor chance. He admitted to having cabled Mansur for a further sum of £10,000, but said it was quite untrue that he had represented the money was for Lord Hugh Cecil. Lord Hugh Cecil's name had merely appeared in the cable as a code word, which Mansur himself had given to him in Bombay.

He denied having asked Mansur to accompany him to Calcutta. They did not travel there together, although they were in the city at the same time. It was also untrue that Mansur advanced him a further sum of Rs5,000, or that they entered into any agreement regarding motor cars. It was true, however, that Mansur filed a suit against him for the recovery of several loans amounting to £11,000.

Through some friends an amicable settlement had been attempted on the basis that Sardar Singh's letter, promising a continuation of the Jodhpur allowance, should be returned to Ranji and that the proceeds of the book entitled *Rulers and Princes of India* which he was then writing should go towards the liquidation of the debt of £7,000. Those negotiations, he conceded, had fallen through.

He denied that on the death of the late Jam of Nawanagar he had asked Mansur to withdraw his suit on the grounds that it would injure him in the eyes of the government. While it was true that he had thanked Mansur for withdrawing the suit, he had never asked him to do so. He said he had not sent, on succeeding to the throne, one of his private secretaries to ask Mansur to give a letter stating that he had no further legal claim against him. Mansur had voluntarily sent a letter expressing regret for misunderstandings in the past, saying

189

that he had no legal claim against him and hoping that on the strength of their long family friendship Ranji would give him any help in the future that he could. Ranji had not promised Mansur Rs25,000, nor had he paid him Rs12,500 in cash through a third person.

Finally, he explained that although they had been schoolfriends, of late Mansur Khachar had developed a bitter enmity towards him and had begun to villify him on every possible occasion and in every possible way.

Ranji did not explain (nor, it appears, was he asked to explain) what the true significance was of Lord Hugh Cecil's name in the cable; nor why the book on Indian rulers that he had been supposedly working on three years earlier had never appeared; nor why Mansur should have had a sudden change of heart and dropped the suit against him, since when, equally inexplicably, his 'bitter enmity' had returned; nor why Mansur was familiar with the name of his private secretary, A. C. MacLaren, if he had never met him.

Wyllie, having listened to Ranji's various explanations, pointed out that, setting aside other questions, the plain fact remained that Ranji had received £10,000 from Mansur Khachar for which practically no consideration had been given or repayment made. The case as it stood, he ventured, bore an ugly complexion against His Highness. Wyllie suggested that perhaps he would care to go to court in order to clear his good name. Now, both Ranji and Wyllie would have been aware that, although Mansur's case was weakened by the absence of full documentary evidence and although he was under the impression that he had no legal claim against Ranji (largely, it seems, because of what he had been told by MacLaren), if the story was to become public and filter back to India, it could be severely embarrassing to the new ruler of Nawanagar. Ranji took the hint and said that he was perfectly willing to go to court but was also ready to leave the decision in Wyllie's hands, and to repay Mansur £7,000 or even £10,000 if he thought it proper. The two men parted, agreeing that a repayment should be made.

Ranji's solicitors offered to repay Mansur £5,000 in exchange for documents and letters, an offer which Mansur accepted after being reminded that Ranji, as a ruling prince, was legally under no obligation to him. Initially he received about £1,700, but over the months that followed a draft for £500 was to be dishonoured, before he was refused any more money until he returned every last document, which, hardly surprisingly, he was unable to do.

Meanwhile, the public, aware of none of these things, was anxious to know if its idol was going to make a return to the first-class cricket field; whether indeed he was capable of making a return. Ranji's thoughts had been working along the same lines and, with the assistance of the professional bowlers among his guests at Shillinglee Park, he practised hard during May. Towards the end of the month he made his reappearance, in The Parks at Oxford for the Gentlemen of England against the University. It was, curiously, his first match on the ground and he scored 9 and 31. The change in him was immediately noticeable; despite his recent illness, he was so obviously much stouter than in 1904, and not so fleet-footed, while Ranji himself found that, although his defence was as sound as ever, he could no longer trust himself to run the risks with the unorthodox strokes. Two of his entourage played in the match: the young Thakor Sahib of Rajkot, and MacLaren, who was also playing his first match of the season and who failed abjectly.

After that, until September, Ranji was to confine himself to matches in Sussex and London, and every time he played he was fêted as though it was the last the crowds would ever see of him. Nine days after the Oxford match, he was back for his county, batting at number six against Kent on his old hunting ground at Brighton, but the crowds there saw little of his former splendour. Those at Lord's, for the next match against Middlesex, were more fortunate, as he occupied the crease for a total of five hours forty-five minutes for 153 not out and 78, giving only one chance and shoring up each innings in turn through fifth-wicket stands of 207 with Vine and 141 with Killick.

This was his first match in London for almost four years, and it aroused a great deal of interest. Ranji, as usual, knew how to rise to the occasion. C. H. B. Pridham recalled: 'Everybody had come to see "Ranji", and the large attendance was agog with excitement . . . Then, as soon as the last batsman (number five) disappeared up the

191

pavilion steps, all eyes remained fixed on the centre gate, but "Ranji" – like some great stage star – kept us on tenterhooks. It seemed as if the full two minutes allowance must have expired by the time we caught the first glimpse of him; but even before that a chorus of applause broke out all around the ground, to be maintained unceasingly until after he had taken his guard. It was an entry magnificently timed, and a grand ovation. The thought of it will remain as long as life lasts – the delight of the crowd at seeing once more that fascinating figure; the jaunty stride out to the crease – no one has ever walked to the wicket quite as "Ranji" did!'

Pridham added that this was the time when Ranji returned to the dressing-room to receive the congratulations of MacLaren and others, only to reply with typically severe self-criticism: 'No, I was not playing well; look at my pads, they are not clean.'

Shortly after this triumph, Ranji took a month off from the championship, preferring to appear in the less strenuous fixtures against the university sides and the more glamorous ones against the Players, but, although he was reported as saying there were no longer any good bowlers in England, his form was never anything other than moderate and by mid-July he had played eighteen innings in all and had failed to make another score of fifty.

Naturally the Sussex club must have been pleased to have had his services again, but his approach was far more carefree and he was available only when his hectic and distracting social life permitted. With Fry, though captain, hesitating before the end of June to play in the championship amid rumours that he was about to join Hampshire, their effect on the morale of the side was far from helpful. *Wisden* pointedly remarked: 'Playing in some matches and standing out of others, Ranjitsinhji and Fry might be compared to the stars of an opera company. They did brilliant things themselves but they did not help the ensemble.' The two of them also played in the Gentlemen's shambolic two-day defeat at the hands of the Players at Lord's, when they were unable to prevent from becoming public their disappointment that neither of them, particularly the recently ennobled Ranjitsinhji, had been made captain.

Moreover, perhaps the best-known match Ranji took part in during the season was one chiefly remembered for events that did not occur on the field. The game was against Hampshire at Priory Park, Chichester in July, and the first day's play was abandoned in early afternoon after a downpour lasting three hours. Ranji invited the rest of the Sussex side to be his guests overnight at Shillinglee, which was only twenty-two miles away, and the majority accepted. The next morning, the umpires inspected the pitch and decided that play could begin at 11.30 as planned, and sent a telegram to Shillinglee at 10.15 with the news. With the weather in Chichester fair and the prospect of seeing Fry and Ranji, who had both kept their promises to play, a large crowd had gathered for the start. The only problem was that when the time arrived, although the Hampshire team were at the ground, the Sussex XI were not.

The first Sussex players to arrive were the two who had not been staying with Ranji, and it was almost an hour after the scheduled start before Fry arrived with Vine, one of his senior professionals, to jocular cheers from the spectators. Fry's explanation was that it had been raining hard when they left Shillinglee and, believing the rain to be general in the district and the Chichester ground to be still sodden from the previous day's rain, he had come only with the intention of arranging the abandonment of the day's play. His argument was corroborated by the subsequent recollections of Albert Relf, another of the Sussex professionals: 'When we awakened in the morning the rain was coming down in sheets. We all settled down to make ourselves as comfortable as we could for the day – all except Mr Fry and Joe Vine, who motored over to Chichester, where they found the streets perfectly dry and people waiting to see the cricket.'

Two further telegrams were then sent to Shillinglee Park, but over the next three hours there was no sign of the remaining seven members of the team. From shortly before one o'clock intermittent showers fell, between two of which Fry indulged in some net practice for the benefit of the spectators, but at least one and a half hours of play had already been lost because of the absent players. Finally, at 3.30, two of Ranjitsinhji's Lanchesters (which were, incidentally, untaxed) brought him and the other Sussex men into Priory Park. It was only with their arrival that the truth of what had happened earlier emerged.

According to the *Sussex Daily News*, when Fry reached Priory Park he had stated that before he left Shillinglee the telegram telling of a proposed 11.30 start had not been received; however, the version of events garnered from other players was that it had been received but, as it was still raining at Shillinglee, His Highness had remained confident there would be no play in Chichester and they were persuaded to stay. It was only when the later telegrams arrived that they had set off on their hurried journey.

By 4.15, the Sussex players were changed and on the field, but no sooner were they there than there was another heavy rainfall which put paid to any chance of play that day. On the final day of the match, the Saturday, when there was certainly no longer the possibility of a result, quite a large crowd of spectators came to the ground, perhaps simply to see if the home team would bother to turn up. When Sussex batted, Ranji, no doubt embarrassed by what had happened (E. M. Sprot, the Hampshire captain, could have, had he wished, claimed the game by default the previous day), produced some of his best strokes in scoring 51 not out.

Ironically, that innings proved to be the start of a return to form, highlighted when against Surrey at the Oval he compiled a chanceless 200. It occupied him five hours forty-five minutes, the longest innings of his career until then – although there was yet to be one longer – and demonstrated that although he could not consistently perform at the old heights of excellence, he could still by application be as prolific.

There is evidence that during this summer Ranji was seriously considering marriage. Certainly the older members of the Borissow family and of Gilling itself well remember talk that he chiefly enjoyed visiting the village because he was in love with one of Louis Borrisow's daughters. Only a few months after he had become Jam Sahib, Fitzgerald had urged him to marry and produce an heir, or adopt one if necessary, and in August 1907 Ranjitsinhji had replied: 'As you know I hope shortly to marry. The delay is occasioned because as I intend to have one wife I want to make a good and careful choice and enquiry before I finally decide on the lady who is to be my partner for life . . . I mean to marry and have children of my own.' (His attitude to wedlock was peculiarly European. In an article in the *London Magazine* for September 1904 on princely marriage in India, he had aroused comment by giving the impression that a ruler took only one bride.) Then, several months later, in April 1908, during another stay in Gilling, Ranji had written to the Coupe Company, whom he had commissioned to design a new palace and durbar hall in Jamnagar, for copies of their architect's latest plans, explaining that he wanted to show them to his friends. He had already approved the details in principle (the cost was estimated at £36,000) but his wish to have the opinion of someone in Gilling, presumably Edith, suggests that he might have been harbouring thoughts of her one day living in the palace with him.

There was still a fundamental problem, however, for mixed marriages were then fraught with social dangers. As we have seen, Edith's father already had his doubts about such an alliance, but aside from what the British thought of the matter, Ranji would have had to take particular care that marriage between a ruling prince and a white woman did not offend the religious sensibilities of his countrymen. If he married an Englishwoman he would almost certainly have upset the same extreme Rajput allies who had earlier so vehemently objected to Vibhaji's Muslim liaisons; they surely would have wished him to marry into one of their ruling Houses (that he was never to do so was perhaps evidence itself that his affections lay elsewhere). This may explain why, when the essence of his confidential letter to Fitzgerald of August 1907 appeared in the British press a few weeks later, Ranji went to the trouble of denying the marriage rumours from Bombay. And possibly he was tacitly admitting the dilemma to Edith herself when he wrote to her shortly before his selection as Jam Sahib: 'I think I can be certain of sitting on the gadi, but I am not altogether certain that I want to . . .'

During August 1908, Ranji responded to a request to help an appeal to raise funds for Gilling's parish church, in order to restore its old bell-tower and provide it with the first clock in its ancient history, by getting together a side of first-class cricketers to play a two-day match in Gilling against a local eleven. A month after the match, Ranji returned to the village for several days. On the Monday afternoon of his visit, he joined the church congregation for a festival service at which the new clock was dedicated. It had cost between £90 and £100, and gate money from the match plus the sale of full-length photographs of Ranji had raised about £64. During the service a former rector of the church referred to Ranji and said he was connected with the parish by ties of 'the closest affection'.

One day in April of that year – eight days after his interview with Sir Curzon Wyllie at the India Office – Ranji gave a sitting to a Mrs Mary Tayler, an artist who specialized in miniature portraits of Europe's aristocracy. She went to Shillinglee and took lunch with Ranji, MacLaren, Henry Tuke (another eminent artist already in the process of painting the Jam Sahib's portrait, and whose finished picture was to be exhibited at the Royal Academy in 1909) and various other house guests. Then, for two hours, she and Tuke worked while Ranji sat, probably observed for at least part of the time by some of his friends. His jewels and decorations were produced for her to sketch and she remembered the day as a very pleasant experience.

Afterwards, according to Mrs Tayler, she and MacLaren discussed a price and agreed on 100 guineas for one ivory miniature, or 180 for a pair. When she asked for half the amount by cheque in advance, MacLaren went into another room, where Ranji was discussing building designs for his palace, and returned to say His Highness was not in a position to approve the advance but promised to send her the money by cheque by that evening's post. Before she left she did in fact see Ranji again but all he did was help her pack up, hand her a wrapped turban in cloth of gold to work from, and promise to send to her London studio later that day the robes she was to represent him as also wearing. More than once during the days that followed, Mrs Tayler had a model come to her studio, but the robes failed to arrive, as did the cheque. She began to write repeated enquiries as to why these promises had been broken, but received only a series of unsatisfactory replies from the Jam Sahib's personal secretary, MacLaren. Nevertheless, she spent fifteen days finishing and perfecting two miniatures and in June sent them to Ranji. After two weeks MacLaren returned them, saying that in Ranji's opinion they were not at all like him and that she had been told from the start not to expect payment until His Highness had seen and approved her work.

On hearing this, Mrs Tayler issued a writ for 180 guineas against the Jam Sahib in the High Court. An anxiety to recover her fee was not the only motive; her professional pride was hurt by the unfavourable opinion of the miniatures. Although able to take consolation in her generally flourishing reputation – she was even asked to paint another portrait of Ranji, by a man delighted at the Jam Sahib's century the previous day against Middlesex at Lord's – she could not rid herself of the memory of this slight. In September, Edward VII's wife, Queen Alexandra, before commissioning Mrs Tayler to paint her portrait, was shown some of her work, and on seeing one of the miniatures of Ranji had commented that it 'glorified his likeness'. The artist later confided in a letter: 'He is so marked by smallpox one would say this as the marks are not shown in my work.'

It was soon apparent, though, that Mrs Tayler was going to have to wait if she wanted her claim heard in the High Court, and her solicitor advised her to transfer it to a county court. This is what she did, though to do so it was necessary for her to reduce her claim to £100. The case was referred to Brighton and Edward Hunt, Ranjitsinhji's solicitor, later protested that the case had only been switched there to deliberately and unfairly arouse publicity: 'A number of officials and clerks in two county courts in the districts of which my client resides and is constantly playing cricket, knew of it.' Mrs Tayler's opinion, though, was that her summons had 'annoyed and astonished them all, particularly so as the Jam was already exceedingly well known in the Brighton county court'; it was her belief that Ranjitsinhji's debts ran into thousands of pounds. It may have been the adverse publicity he was receiving in the courts that accounted for his sudden and unexplained disappearance from the first-class cricket field after his double century against Surrey late in July. He was to spend the following four weeks at Gilling and Shillinglee Park, where he staged a three-day, twelve-a-side match against a Cambridge team, scoring 103 not out at number eleven in a total of 599, before going shooting in Scotland.

When Mrs Tayler's case came up for hearing, Hunt immediately entered a plea on behalf of his client that he was exempt from the jurisdiction of the courts of England because he was the ruling sovereign of an independent state. This was not the first time Hunt had made this plea in an English court that summer and it was because the magistrate had already heard a similar claim against the Jam Sahib that he decided on this occasion not to dismiss the case on the grounds cited by Hunt but to adjourn it, in order to establish whether indeed Ranjitsinhji could be regarded as in charge of an independent state and therefore entitled to claim immunity. The magistrate said that an interesting and important point had been raised, which had to be gone into sooner or later.

However, before the magistrate could complete his enquiries, the case was settled by other means. Mrs Tayler had asked Walter Long, a Conservative MP for almost thirty years, to request that Lord Morley, the Secretary of State for India, should intervene on her behalf. The India Office replied that Morley could not do so formally but that he would attempt to use his private influence with Ranjitsinhji. This seemed to do the trick because on 30 July Hunt proposed that if Mrs Tayler would withdraw her court action his client would reconsider her claim and, even if they could not agree a sum between themselves, would be willing to submit to the arbitration of a third party. Mrs Tayler agreed, and the case was dropped.

Seven weeks elapsed and still no offer of any payment was made to her. She began to suspect that Ranjitsinhji's solicitor was deliberately procrastinating. Hunt accounted for the delay by saying it was necessary to first consult MacLaren, who had been involved in the original discussions about her fee, but that MacLaren unfortunately had recently been involved in a motor accident and was recuperating in the country. This appeared to be supported by MacLaren's absence from the cricket scores in the press after early August. It was on Monday 5 October that Mrs Tayler learnt how 'astonishingly careless in their handling of the truth' (as she was to write in a letter to Wyllie) MacLaren and Hunt had been. That morning she read a newspaper report of MacLaren's appearance in Guildford county court the previous Saturday for non-payment of the rates on his house in Alford Parish, which adjoined Shillinglee. MacLaren claimed that the house had been taken for him by Ranjitsinhji, who as a ruling prince was exempt from prosecution, but the magistrate ruled that the rates were in respect of the premises and that they belonged to MacLaren. Unless they were paid by the following Tuesday, the magistrate added, a distress warrant would be issued. As this was the last that was heard of the matter, MacLaren must have paid up, although he probably had to go to Ranjitsinhji for the money.

Mrs Tayler immediately wrote to Sir Curzon Wyllie at the India Office, with whom she had recently been in correspondence:

I have this morning heard that there is not, nor has there been a single thing the matter with the Jam Sahib of Nawanagar's personal secretary, Mr A. C. MacLaren. The statement made to you therefore by the representative of Messrs Redfern and Hunt by way of excuses for not having paid my claim are absolutely false.

The enclosed cutting will show you more plainly than any words of mine what Mr MacLaren's code of honour is. He has carefully instructed the Jam Sahib of Nawanagar in the same – the result of it all will be many, many will be 'let in' for large sums, of which a penny will never be paid . . . These people are *so* insulting, and though I am quite certain in your presence they behave as they should, out of it, by a letter now before me, they say, 'What can the India Office or Colonel Sir Curzon Wyllie do?' i.e. they mean to go on making untrue excuses and untrue statements.

The people of Nawanagar are *not* very well represented by their Jam Sahib.

After this, the India Office began to heed her fears that Hunt was delaying with a view to Ranji fleeing the country. On 3 November they themselves adjudicated on her case. They said that because Mrs Tayler had been foolish enough to keep no copy of the letter in which she made her original request for a sitting (Hunt said the letter was missing, either lost or destroyed), she could not substantiate her claim. However, they retained plenty of criticism for the other party – 'the Jam Sahib and his ridiculous private secretary are to blame for keeping the miniatures so long' – and felt that, in consideration of his position and as an act of grace, Ranjitsinhji ought to pay her £75. Mrs Tayler, who was to keep the miniatures, was thought to be fairly satisfied with this, although after paying her lawyer's fee she got only £35.

The earlier case the Brighton magistrate had heard involving Ranjitsinhji was one instituted by four Misses Welch against him, Billy Murdoch and his wife, and a Mr F. W. Clements, to recover £923 5s 5d from the terms of an 1896 deed of covenant, the details of which are sadly unknown. Ranji had issued a summons asking that his name be struck out of the action and, although his claim was upheld, the plaintiffs had been given the right to appeal, which was heard in early July by the Judge in Chambers at the Royal Courts of Justice. Revealingly, the vital evidence at the hearing came from the India Office, which had been asked by the courts to confirm whether Ranjitsinhji was an independent sovereign and entitled to the privileges he claimed. The under-secretary had replied that the matter was one for the courts to decide, but added: 'The Jam has been recognized by the Government of India as a ruling chief governing his own territories under the suzerainty of His Majesty . . . The Government of India do not regard or treat His Highness's territory as being part of British India or of His Majesty's dominions, and they do not regard or treat him or his subjects as subjects of His Majesty.' Hardly surprisingly, the judge interpreted this as meaning Ranjitsinhji was indeed an independent sovereign.

In early October, the plaintiffs, convinced there must be some means by which they could recover their money, appealed again. Their solicitors wrote to the India Office for assistance, unaware that it had been the source of their earlier defeat. Their case, they said, was to show that Ranji was not an independent sovereign; to do so, they were going to argue that he had been made the ruling chief of Nawanagar by ministers of King Edward VII, who was his suzerain and to whom he owed allegiance. Could the India Office, they asked, provide any evidence of the circumstances of his accession, particularly the supervision exercised by the Resident and the Government of India and thus tacitly accepted by Ranjitsinhji?

This was a penetrating line of argument, but one to which the India Office failed to give an adequate answer. It did what it had been doing for the past several months, to most of the appeals for help made on behalf of Mrs Taylcr, the Misses Welch and Ranjitsinhji's numerous other creditors: it sent back a series of vague and unhelpful replies that threatened to ruin their case. But then the India Office's primary responsibility had never been to look after the interests of these few individuals but to ensure Britain maintained its unwritten support for the princes for India.

As Ranji's appearanccs in court diminished, so those on the field increased. After an absence of almost a month, hc turned out against Yorkshire at Brighton, where those who had been awaiting his return must have been disappointed; he lasted lcss than four overs and was bowled for 0, the first duck he had made against the most consistently strong county opponents in his career. After one more championship match, against Gloucestcrshire, he was ready for the festival crowds at Hastings and Scarborough, where he faced sides comprising members of the MCC tcam successful in Australia the previous winter. At Hastings, during an innings of 64, he passed 1,000 runs for the season (he finished with 1,138 at 45.52, placing him seventh in the averages), while at Scarborough, where hc had not played for fourteen years, he made a century for Lord Londesborough's England XI against an attack including Rhodes, Blythe and Braund. He scored runs on the leg-side in his old manner and *Wisden* described it as his most characteristic innings of the summer.

Whatever some people might have thought of him, as a cricketer Ranji was as revered as he had been for so long. The Sussex professionals presented him with a silver cigarette box as a memento of the year, while on 19 October a farewell dinner was given to him at the Cambridge Guildhall. It had been arranged since mid-May and drew comparisons with the great banquet given in his honour in 1896, although it was a smaller occasion, with only half the previous number of guests. There was another distinguished array of town and county officials and leading amateur cricketers, but there were some significant absentees, among them Lord Curzon, Lord Harris, who declined to propose the toast, and Alfred Lyttelton, a former England cricketer and more recently a Conservative cabinet minister. Harris, who had never shown much admiration for the Indian's achievements, might not have chosen to attend under any circumstances, but all their absences may have been a reflection of Ranjitsinhji's recent troubles, which were such that speculation had reached the press that he was intending to abdicate his throne in favour of a nephew. Ever-widening rumours of his unreliability with debts would certainly explain Lilley's later desire to stress the Jam's loyalty to England and that his good feelings towards the English people were fully reciprocated.

The Cambridge evening provided further evidence of Ranji's increasingly precarious position. In the end, the toast was proposed by his close friend Arthur Priestley, who, in his speech, defended the position of the ruling princes, emphasizing their importance in the Government of India, and pointing out how well suited Ranjitsinhji was to the administration of his state. When Ranji himself spoke, he reiterated Priestley's remarks, especially the sense of duty possessed by the princes, but while anxious to clarify his stance, added: 'It must not be forgotten that the Government of India owe them something . . . they must see that their authority is respected.'

Ranji, typically, was unable to accept that he was responsible for the trouble he now found himself in. Eventually, he switched his speech from a thinly veiled defence of his own behaviour to an unexpected attack on the British government: 'I think it would be wrong to jump to the conclusion that, because there are a few mischievous people in a population of 280 million, India is disloyal. When you read from day to day that there are malcontents in England, may I not make an apology for the malcontents in India? . . . I think that the British Empire ought to treat all British subjects alike. The doors to Indian peoples have unfortunately been shut in Australia, and in Canada and South Africa . . . ' Alan Ross has suggested that these comments may have been inspired by legislation in the Transvaal, but the motive was a little nearer to home than that.

For the controversy surrounding his financial affairs, Ranji had been feeling unjustly blamed for some time. In a letter in September, he had written: 'I have had a great holiday but not so much freedom as I would have liked. And there are things which simply turn one inside out, and sour our hearts. As an Indian loyal to the Crown, I regret this beyond measure.'

Unfortunately, there was more trouble in store for him. Walter Long, who had helped Mary Tayler with her case against Ranji and was angry at its outcome, had determined not to let the matter rest. He decided to leak the letter Hunt, Ranji's solicitor, had written to Lord Morley on 30 July when attempts were being made to settle Mrs Tayler's case (a copy had been sent to Long to show him how Ranji was prepared to consider her claim).

First of all, on 24 October, a small item appeared in the editorial columns of the penny weekly *John Bull*, a campaigning newspaper recently established by Horatio Bottomley. Bottomley was a Liberal MP, a former proprietor of the *Sun* for whom Ranji, ironically, had once worked, and a man whose methods did not always come above suspicion, although in this case he appears to have acted correctly enough. Sir Curzon Wyllie was later to refer to *John Bull* as 'a disreputable paper, I believe, but none the less, a paper'. Noting the farewell dinner in Cambridge, the editorial suggested that the Jam of Nawanagar should make sure all his bills were paid before he left the country. Complaints had reached the paper, it said, that his creditors had had considerable difficulty getting their money, and that if they began to show impatience they were told he was immune from legal proceedings.

This created alarm at the India Office. Until then, relatively few people were privy to knowledge of the acrimony Ranji had aroused; until then, his court cases had been discreet and little publicized. Wyllie was concerned as to exactly how much Bottomley knew and how he had come to know of it, and felt the time had come to act. On 2 November he wrote to Ranjitsinhji, warning him that the Secretary of State had heard, 'with some concern', of the enquiries coming into the office. He advised him to have more circumspection with money and asked to see him to discuss the matter. He was careful not to issue an actual reproof; he personally did not have the authority to interfere in the affairs of a ruling Indian prince. The India Office itself, though, had begun to give fairly firm indications in private as to what it wanted to see done with regard to Ranji's affairs; on 20 October, for example, it had successfully deterred a London firm from taking a contract to provide furnishings worth £70,000 for his new palace in Jamnager.

Ranji agreed to a meeting, only then, to Wyllie's great annoyance, to send Hunt in his place. A few days later, Ranji wrote to Wyllie to say he had met all his creditors in a way that made him 'very hurt and annoyed at being continually thought ill of', and added, 'Morley can examine my private affairs in any way he desires to clear my reputation'. Shortly after this, however, he agreed to arrive at a 'friendly settlement' with the four Misses Welch and thus avoided what could have been an embarrassing and difficult appeal case. As was usually the case with the many debts he ran up in the early years of his reign, Ranji's 'friendly settlement' involved him paying about half the claim. Dragging his heels over the payment of bills had become a way of life for him ever since his impecunious days as an undergraduate, and now that apparently he had the protection of the law, he used it to his advantage by paying only when he was asked by the courts or the India Office to do so as an act of grace, which invariably constituted honouring only a proportion of the original debt.

What concerned Wyllie was not the relatively minor injustice involved in each case so much as the wider implications that this steady profusion of complaints against one of the best known of Indian ruling princes might have so soon after his succession. Wyllie's greatest fear was that the matter would get into the press in India and there lead to demands for Ranjitsinhji's removal from the Nawanagar throne. Such things did happen; Jay Singh was deposed as Maharaja of Alwar in 1933 for 'gross misrule'. Rumours that Ranjitsinhji might abdicate were probably not unconnected with this possibility, and reports in August that he was about to receive a high decoration may have been instituted to counter them.

Then, on 14 November, Bottomley played his trump card. His newspaper contained a large article subtitled: HOW THE JAM DEALS WITH HIS ENGLISH DEBTS. Accompanying it was a full-page sketch depicting John Bull, with a glum English tradesman standing some way off holding a handful of bills, pleading with a regally dressed Ranjitsinhji: 'Look here! old man. Remember, my friend there has to live and has to pay *his* way.' Wyllie thought it 'a hideous and rather pointless cartoon'. Bottomley advertised his latest issue with placards in the streets of London proclaiming: RANJI FLOUTS OUR COURTS.

The backbone of the article was a passage from Hunt's letter to Lord Morley:

It is of course necessary that claims against persons in the position of His Highness should be dealt with in a far more liberal and generous way than claims against ordinary persons, but, on the other hand, the sovereign rights of persons in the position of His Highness must be guarded with the utmost care; and whilst everything possible should be done to promote good will between the Government of India and the Suzerain Rulers, it cannot extend to abandoning the Sovereign rights they possess, and which in the case of my client have been judicially recognized by the King's Privy Council and the India Office. Therefore, I cannot advise my client to allow any action to proceed against him in the English courts. To do so, would be to abandon one of his Sovereign rights.

The article declared it 'an absurd survival of the dark ages that any man of less station than a member of the Royal Family should be above the law', and asked: 'Should not English firms be made to clearly understand the risks they run?'

Apart from being an embarrassment to the government, the article also gave Ranji himself a fright. He immediately drafted a letter to *The Times*, regretting that a court ruling was being used to create ill feeling between the English people and Indian rulers. Far from flouting the English courts, he wrote, he had applied to them for protection against unfounded claims. He was advised against sending the letter.

On 17 December 1908, after spending several unusually quiet weeks at Shillinglee Park but still with almost two months of his tenancy to run, he left for India. Wild attempted to imply that he was returning to his duties there with a keen purpose ('When he left . . . he faced a greater game. There were rumours that he would never come back to England'), but the man who at his first Cambridge banquet twelve years earlier had been hailed as an ambassador between two races, left Britain after his second with a brazen disregard for the feelings of either.

11

A FADING STAR

WHEN RANJITSINHJI LEFT Britain towards the end of 1908, he took with him to his capital, as members of his staff, a party of nearly twenty people, several of them white. This, while unremarkable in itself, provided an early indication of a desire on his part to be always surrounded by European faces that was to become even more manifest over the years to come. Moreover, the group that was seen off in London by many of his old friends, among them Grace, Dr. Heasman, the former Sussex amateur, Lord Hawke and Lt.-Col. Kennedy, involved some notable inclusions and omissions.

A. C. MacLaren had relinquished his post as private secretary, his official duties since Ranjitsinhji became Jam Sahib having prevented him touring with MCC or appearing regularly in county cricket. During that period, when MacLaren had played, even in minor matches, he had seemed in poor physical condition and badly out of form, and his workload had been getting greater and more onerous as time went on. In a letter to Mary Tayler in February 1908 he had apologized, 'my writing is to blame and you are not the only one unable to read it, as the Mahraja often tells me how hopeless it is at times but I wish he had my amount of writing to get thro'. After five years in the job, the prospect of returning to his own villa in Jamnagar was clearly not enough for MacLaren, who nevertheless accompanied Ranji to India on this occasion for a holiday. He was back in England in time for the 1909 season, when he continued to struggle for form, although he nevertheless captained England throughout the disastrous Test series against Australia (chiefly because Hawke, the chairman of the selectors, refused to accept his resignation after the defeat at

Lord's). MacLaren never played for England again after that year and never really recovered his form.

MacLaren was replaced as personal secretary by Harry Simms, a young Australian-born amateur who had played occasionally for Sussex since 1905, when he was only seventeen years old. Another member of the staff was Geoffrey Foster, aged twenty-four, the stylish Oxford University and Worcestershire batsman and one of the famous cricketing family. Foster's presence, along with that of Simms, led to speculation in England that Ranji would raise a powerful Nawanagar side, but despite his enthusiastic declarations of intent, his XI played only occasional matches and failed to equal in stature the Maharaja of Patiala's team of twenty years earlier, possibly partly because of lack of good opposition in the Kathiawar region.

A number of servants were also in Ranjitsinhji's party, including a housekeeper and two English chauffeurs. In addition, he transported some of his recent purchases, among them seven carriage horses, but it would be reasonable to question the veracity of the statement in the *Sussex Daily News* that, 'It has been a busy year for the villages in the neighbourhood of Shillinglee and there is a keen sense of regret at the Jam's departure.'

The identity of the housekeeper remains unknown. At first, it was probably the woman who managed Shillinglee Park, but later the post may have been used as a guise for what probably developed into lengthy stays at the palace by someone much closer to his affections, Edith Borissow. The housekeeper had her own suite of rooms in the Vibha Villas palace in Jamnagar, a two-storey building begun by Vibhaji but not completed before his death, which Ranji originally intended to occupy only until his new palace was complete. Her suite was on the first floor to the right of the central staircase, Ranji's was to the left; the close proximity was due to the need to regularly conduct the business of the house. At some stage, according to the present Jam Sahib, a corridor passing behind the main staircase was built in rather makeshift fashion, on to the original structure of the palace. It can still be seen today, although its existence probably remained unknown to most other members of the household, for the connecting doors (one in Ranji's bedroom, one in the other suite) were concealed by hanging carpets. Revealingly perhaps, Ranji was never to move out of Vibha Villas, even when his larger palace was finished. Also, Satrusalyasinhji, the present Jam Sahib, avows that one of Ranji's most treasured objects was a marble bust of a beautiful young woman, which, less obvious than a photograph, may have depicted his great-uncle's mistress.

All this would suggest that Ranji was of the opinion during the early years of his reign that until he was securely established as ruler it would be too inflammatory an act to marry an Englishwoman, and that he might do better to continue his relationship with Edith on a discreet level. At all events he began, skilfully, to delay. About a year after his return to India, he told Claude Hill, the Resident, what he had told his predecessor, Fitzgerald, over two years earlier, that he still intended to marry, saying he realized the political import of marrying soon, but that, in Hill's word, 'he cannot marry until his palace is habitable'. He explained to Hill that in order for him to get married, large sums of money would be required for the completion of his new palace, for increased allotments for ceremonial purposes for housing for other members of his family, and for the wedding celebrations themselves. He even persuaded Hill to include these costs in the expenditure estimates submitted to the Government of India that were to lead to the nazarana payment being dropped by almost a third to £72,000 on condition that Ranji himself reduced his personal spending from £2,000 per month to £1,500. (He pleaded in vain with the government for a total remission of the nazarana, arguing, interestingly, that otherwise it would show they 'only *favoured* my selection and not because they recognized my right of succession'.) But if the extensive preparations were eventually carried out, the wedding itself was not.

The problems confronting Ranji in Jamnagar, far from diminishing during his fifteen-month absence, had, in fact, multiplied. He felt renewed frustration, and was inclined to blame Vibhaji, Jassaji and the British Administration for the run-down and insanitary condition of his state, but his feelings of despair must have been at least partly inspired by the knowledge that he himself was inadequately equipped to deal with the problems.

Nor, as Fitzgerald had feared, had he made things any easier for himself by going to Europe when he had. In his absence the management of the state appears to have become even more disorganized, the *Kathiawar News* reporting on 26 November 1908, when Ranjitsinhji was still in England, that there had been wholesale departures among his staff. He returned to find that speculation had indeed reached the Indian press that he might be about to abdicate. Moreover, a plot to murder him as he was travelling back to India was uncovered, and it transpired there had been other, aborted schemes at his installation and while he was in Britain. Lakhuba's family were thought to have been behind the plans, but the would-be assassins were never caught. Having learned of such threats, Ranji was resigned to spending the rest of his life in the very real fear of falling victim to a more successful attempt. In those early days, like the unfortunate Jassaji before him, he must have felt very alone and looked with gratitude on the support given him by the local British officials.

His inexperience as a ruler was obvious in many of his early actions. One of his most impracticable orders was that his people must remove all wild dogs either from his capital or out of his sight; another, more controversial decision, was to publicly hang a Brahmin, a member of the priestly caste, who had been brought before him accused of murder. One Premchand Keshavji, a Hindu merchant of Bombay, suspected of giving financial assistance to the plot to murder him, had his property confiscated and was sentenced to ten years' hard labour, apparently without proper trial, and was released on condition of good behaviour only after Hill, petitioned by Keshavji's wife, began to make enquiries into the handling of the affair. Meanwhile, despite the restrictions imposed on his spending, he began to vigorously accumulate the jewels, horses, carriages and furniture that had been so obviously wanting at his installation ceremony, while, although he told the Coupe Company in August 1910 that he would not be wanting their designs, work was continuing on his new palace.

His most disastrous mistakes were his efforts to increase revenue. The British had tried to encourage him to economize and develop his state, but even after four years of his reign the railway extension to Dwarka and the harbour development, though acknowledged as the key to a healthier annual income, were barely begun. Instead, in 1911, he commandeered a British officer, Lt.-Col. Henry Berthon, who had been in Rajkot nine years and was a guest of his at the Cambridge banquet of 1908, to administer the repossession of almost a quarter of the state's lands given away as gifts by previous rulers. He also reduced the revenue tax of 25 per cent by half in good years and by a third in bad, but imposed an additional annual rent of 2.5 rupees on every acre of land. That year only three inches of rain fell; the death toll in the state mounted alarmingly and the government agreed to delay the nazarana payment. But when twenty-four villages, crippled by the combined effects of the drought and the introduction of the new land rent, refused to cooperate with his changes, Ranjitsinhji, according to Nawanagar's court historian, sent the police to enforce his laws. Some of them were killed in the attempt. To exact retribution, the new Jam Sahib ordered that the rebellious villages be annihilated by his army.

Fry wrote of this episode in his *Life Worth Living*: 'Not long after Ranjitsinhji was installed on the gadi of Nawanagar, he was confronted with a rebellion, which had its origin among the piratically inclined people on the west coast. It was a serious business. Ranji took the field himself and conducted a masterly little campaign. He used to tell the story with emphasis on the fact that most of the casualties in his own troops were due to the bursting of the out-of-date rifles, which were the best he was allowed by the Government for their equipment; whereas the rebels were armed with the best modern rifles.

These events were monitored closely by the British, who from an early stage had been concerned about Ranjitsinhji's ability to fulfil his position satisfactorily. In May 1909 Hill wrote that, 'even after His Highness's return to India I was, for two or three months, very doubtful as to whether the Jam Sahib would ever be able to settle down to his work and responsibilities as a chief, and whether it would be possible to rely upon him to set to work and retrieve the fortunes of his somewhat neglected state.' He only altered his opinion when he began to spend some time with Ranjitsinhji, which included a week as a guest in Jamnagar in April 1909. Three weeks after that visit, Hill wrote to a superior: 'We have discussed the affairs of his state in great detail; and I am now convinced, not only of his willingness, and the earnestness of his intention, to take up his work seriously, but also of the fact that he possesses very high capabilities . . . He is capable, in fact, of taking his proper place as the leading Rajput chief in the province, and will come gradually to be looked up to by his brother chiefs as the one whose example should be followed. On one hand his early life and training have been a great handicap to him, and hitherto he was isolated and friendless in Kathiawar. He has, on the other hand, a warm nature which needs careful and sympathetic handling, and the results will repay this, for he has, by virtue of his position and his charming manner, a very considerable influence with other chiefs.'

For all the enthusiastic talk Ranji shared with Hill, few of his schemes for the enhancement of the state came to anything. But, in true princely fashion, not so his plans for himself. In December 1911, at the end of the year of severe drought, with annual revenue down to about £100,000 and his own allowance necessarily reduced to only £800 per month (almost a third of its original figure), he borrowed £36,000 to share in the spectacular Delhi Durbar to celebrate George V's accession. The money enabled him to arrive for the ceremony in a magnificent silver coach, although on the return journey to Jamnagar his specially chartered train was delayed five hours because the railway company insisted he pay cash in advance. This ill-timed and wanton extravagance was more than Hill's superiors could tolerate, and they promptly attached Berthon to the state as financial adviser.

The biggest mistake Ranji made during his first visit to England as Jam Sahib, in 1908, was to cross Lord Edward Winterton. Winterton, then aged twenty-six, was a nephew of Lord Hamilton, the former Secretary of State for India, and, being an Irish peer, had not been obliged to relinquish his seat in the House of Commons as Unionist MP for Horsham, when, the previous year, he had succeeded to his title and substantial estates in Norfolk and Sussex. Intolerant, quick-tempered and fearless at exposing injustice, he was one of the

211

rising young figures in parliament. In 1908, he had been president of Sussex County Cricket Club, and was originally on the organizing committee for the banquet in Cambridge held in Ranji's honour, but he was a notable absentee from the function itself in October because by then Ranji owed him the then not insubstantial sum of £100 for 'delapidations' on Shillinglee Park.

On principle, Winterton would have sued him for the money if it had been possible to do so under English law. Instead, he spoke to a number of people who had suffered similarly at the hands of Ranji, and began to rally support within the House. He hoped that if he could publicize what Ranji was doing, it would lead to an alteration in the law affecting the position of visiting Indian princes. He would have liked to get Ranji prevented from being allowed to return to Britain.

On 14 September 1909, during questions in the House on Indian affairs, William Joynson Hicks, a party colleague of Winterton, asked the Master of Elibank, the assistant private secretary to the Under-Secretary of State for the Colonies, 'Whether the Jam of Nawanagar is a ruling prince in India and whether such a Jam can only come to England with the permission of the Secretary of State?'

Elibank's reply was based on an answer prepared by the Political and Secret Department at the India Office: 'His Highness the Jam of Nawanagar is a ruling prince or chief governing his own territories under the suzerainty of His Majesty. The permission of the Secretary of State is not required to His Highness visiting England; but such visits would be arranged by Indian princes in communication with the Government of India.'

Another member of the opposition then asked if he was 'aware that this chief is alleged to owe a great deal of money to small local tradespeople in Sussex?' The question was disallowed by the Deputy Speaker, who said it did not arise out of the original question, but Joynson Hicks resumed the attack: was the assistant private secretary 'prepared to receive and consider representations from responsible members of this House before arranging any further visits of this prince?'

'I am afraid the answer I have given must suffice,' said Elibank. 'I have stated that these visits are only made in communication to the Government of India, not that there are any definite arrangements.'

These exchanges led to an acrimonious correspondence between Winterton and Hunt, Ranji's indefatigable solicitor, who remained unconvinced by Winterton's denials that he had inspired the interrogation of Elibank. Hunt protested that, since the question in the House was asked, all Ranji's Sussex accounts had been paid and that they had totalled under £500. He said that Ranji, before leaving for India, had instructed him to use dead stock amounting to about £1,000 to pay off outstanding debts, but unfortunately it had transpired that, in error, his client had not been informed that the stock had already been realized. 'I think that some allowance should be made for a person in the position of my client,' he continued, 'especially as, after his return to India, there were many state matters which had to be dealt with, and also that he was very seriously ill for several weeks in the spring of the year and unable to attend to any business.' (This last statement is not supported by the detailed accounts left by Hill, the Resident, of Ranjitsinhji's activities during the same period.)

Hunt attempted to put the debts into perspective by adding that Ranji, during his visit to England, had spent £15,000 in Sussex and a much larger sum in the country as a whole, and thus concluded that there was 'no foundation for the very serious and unfair attack intended to be made through the medium of the question in the House'. Nevertheless, he proffered a cheque for the long-overdue sum owing to Winterton.

Winterton was not interested in the money. Seven days after the first question, another MP asked a second. It related to the case of Premchand Keshavji being imprisoned without regular trial. This time Elibank had no information on the matter but said it was not policy to interfere in the internal affairs of Native States, except in cases of gross maladministration. If the matter warranted it, he added, the Resident attached to the state would report in due course. The government was clearly determined to block every avenue of attack Winterton came up with and, when a further MP was heard to ask if the grave disapproval with which members of the House viewed the withholding of information could be conveyed to the Secretary of State, Elibank had nothing to say.

Even by the time these questions were being asked in the House of Commons, Ranji had probably already decided when he would next be returning to Britain. Not long after his succession he was advised by the British that, at least until conditions improved in his beleaguered state, it would be best if such trips were not any more frequent than every four years, and it is an indication of how much he was missing life in England and the friends he had left behind there that he took the first opportunity available to him, and went back in 1912. The realization had also dawned that, despite his assertions at the end of his previous visit that he could continue playing cricket until he was fifty, at the age of thirty-nine he was facing his last chance to once more receive the acclaim of the crowds and to relive past glories.

Early in May 1912, soon after he had reached England and again been given an audience with the monarch, he was to be seen practising in the nets at Lord's. Although he had played little in the previous three years, from the first he announced he would play against the touring Australians if invited (England were to play concurrent Test series against South Africa and Australia as part of a triangular tournament) and he may have even harboured hopes of being asked to captain the side. Based in London and Cambridge, he took part only in southern matches, but his form leading up to the first of England's Test matches, against South Africa at Lord's on 10 June, was quite acceptable and when he did play for Sussex he captained the side ahead of the official appointee, H. P. Chaplin. He did not make a century during this period but produced some skilful innings in adverse circumstances. He made top score in three of Sussex's four championship innings in London towards the end of May and in his next match, against Oxford University in The Parks, he hit 75 before being stumped, despite being hampered by a sprained wrist. This last innings may have provided the evidence on which H. S. Altham, who was playing for the university, based his comments in A History of Cricket that Ranjitsinhji, 'in his later years discarded defence more and more for attack, and often played the innings of a pure hitter, only that it was backed throughout by his marvellously resourceful back-play'.

However, neither of Ranji's hopes were to be realized. England were captained throughout the summer by Fry, himself past forty and now playing for Hampshire, and Ranji was not chosen to play under him. Possibly, now that he was a ruling prince and a prominent representative of India, the selection of Ranji would have been regarded as even more inappropriate than it had been by some earlier. The day after the first Test ended, he played against Kent at Brighton and scored 128 in three and a half hours, not giving a chance until past his century, but in truth he was no longer the player he had once been, and this told against him. His eye had deteriorated and his bat was beaten more regularly than it used to be, while other balls were allowed to pass by unpunished. There was a tinge of nostalgia about his whole season. He had begun with a match at Fenner's, where he had not played in a first-class fixture for twelve years, and his hundred against Kent was noted to be his first at Brighton for almost eight years. As A. G. Gardiner was to lament: 'The Jam Sahib is forty, and, alas, the Jam Sahib is fat . . . his face wreathed in chubby smiles.'

Nevertheless, despite all this and despite continuing to be troubled by a sprained wrist, he discovered at times that the ball was finding the middle of the bat and that the old, exquisite timing had returned. They were, by their nature, vainglorious, bittersweet occasions, but that at the age of thirty-nine and after an absence of several years he could summon up from the depths of his experience such consummate exhibitions of batsmanship, demonstrated just what an extraordinarily gifted cricketer he must have been. Early in July, having been out first ball in his previous match, against Leicestershire, he made a century in two and a quarter hours for MCC against Cambridge University at Lord's. During the innings he began to score with some of his old freedom, and off one undergraduate's bowling in particular his leg-glance started to work especially well. In one of the intervals, the Cambridge captain told him he was breaking the young bowler's heart. 'Don't you like that shot?' Ranjitsinhji had replied. 'Then I'll hit him through the covers.' And when they resumed, he duly did.

Shortly after this, he appeared for the Gentlemen against the Players at the Oval and at Lord's, where, playing with Fry in a first-class match for what transpired to be the last time, he scored 55 in less than an hour. In his next match he produced a monumental display of 176 against Lancashire at Brighton, which contained several fortunate strokes, including playing the ball into his stumps when 71 without disturbing the bails, and lasted five hours fifty minutes, the longest innings of his career. He followed up with a beautiful exhibition on the first day of Sussex's match with the Australians, making 125 with shots all round the wicket, notably drives, which brought him twenty-two 4s and a 5.

That was another occasion he obviously savoured, for he seemed to lap up the adulation of the crowd and towards the end of his innings was playing so confidently that he began to nominate in advance, to his youthful and inexperienced partner Percy Fender, the strokes he intended to play. According to Fender, these included two leg-glances to long-leg and two late cuts to deep third man, each time for 2 runs, although the scorebook shows that after the early stages of his innings Ranji hit only one 2. There may have been an element of rivalry with the younger player in this, for just beforehand Fender had begun to hit out with spectacular results and was possibly starting to steal some of Ranji's thunder. Their partnership came to an end when Ranji was run out after playing a ball straight to mid-on, Fender sending him back. The next morning Fender walked into the amateurs' dressing-room in the Brighton pavilion to find the Jam Sahib sitting in one of the armchairs surrounded by the day's newspapers: 'You must have a lot of friends in the papers, young man. They all say it was my fault . . . and it was.'

The dressing-room armchairs, incidentally, had an interesting history. They were donated to the club early in the summer of 1912 by Ranji, and Sir Home Gordon remembered in 1939 that they were not paid for for many years. Ranji's subsequent explanation, according to Harold Gilligan, a regular Sussex player in the 1920s, in a letter to *The Times* in 1972, was that before leaving for India he had left money to pay all his outstanding bills with a 'friend', who had instead pocketed the cash.

Ranji's other bills during 1912 were amounting to more than pocket money. In June, while he was in Brighton taking his century off Kent, his solicitor was at the India Office in London being questioned by Sir James Dunlop Smith, the new political ADC, about his client's large English debts. During the course of the interview, Hunt identified some of them: £1,000 to the Lanchester motor company; £700 to a Cambridge firm; £900 to the Coupe Company for architectural designs and another 'considerable sum' outstanding from 1908, both of which Hunt had recently offered to settle with a sum smaller than the original claim; while £300 was owing to Redfern and Hunt themselves. The largest debt, an unspecified amount possibly running into several thousand pounds, was owing to Messrs King and Co. Importantly for Ranjitsinhji's reputation within government circles, however, Dunlop Smith considered that, 'unless he himself and his solicitors are lying, I think he has been steadily improving his position'. (In fact, Hunt had failed to mention some £3,300 still outstanding to Mansur Khachar.)

Ranji's reappearance in Britain had been noted by Lord Winterton, who began to renew his pursuit. George Greenwood, a Liberal MP, put a series of searching questions to Edwin Montagu, the Under-Secretary of State for India. Initially, they related to Ranji's repudiation of the claim against him by the Coupe Company, but effectively this was nothing more than a device to publicize his behaviour in general. Over three successive days Greenwood asked: 'Did His Highness claim to be above the jurisdiction of British law? Did he even acknowledge Coupe's claim existed? Did the India Office recognize it existed? If the India Office did, was there any way a creditor could obtain repayment?' Montagu managed not to give a direct answer to any of these questions but by the end was harassed enough to gratefully place the ball into Ranji's court by saying he was 'quite sure that His Highness will take such action as is demanded by his honour and that of the distinguished class to which he belongs'.

On 2 August, the day after the last of Greenwood's questions, Ranji made an appearance at the India Office himself, his first since his interview with Sir Curzon Wyllie in April 1908. He declared himself 'quite content' for any person to investigate his case with the Coupe Company. Shortly afterwards he agreed to pay them £500, only to then continue delaying payment. In September he received a letter from the India Office stating that Lord Crewe, the Secretary of State for India (whose office had claimed never to interfere in the financial affairs of the Native States), was himself prepared to advance him the £500. Ranji seemed genuinely moved by the offer, but said it would not be necessary and duly paid up, adding: 'After Scarborough I had a touch of influenza and consequently there has been a fortnight's delay in my reply'.

Ranji had ventured north for the Scarborough festival after playing only three matches in August, in which he did nothing exceptional. Off what proved to be the last ball he ever received at Brighton, during the match against the South Africans, he was stumped for 23 (made as Sussex lost their last 9 wickets for only 38 runs), the fifth time in eighteen innings during 1912 that he was dismissed that way. The festival games, in which he played for Lord Londesborough's XI against each of the touring sides, also proved to be a disappointment. Rain and a bitterly cold wind ruined the second match, with the South Africans, when wrapped in thick clothing Ranji batted only briefly, for 3 not out. Nevertheless, his record for the season was creditable: 1,113 runs at 42.81, an average that was bettered by only five players. Incidentally, Ranji's new personal secretary, Simms, who was able to play regularly, showed none of the problems encountered by his predecessor, MacLaren, in combining cricket with his job as he performed the double of 1,000 runs and 100 wickets.

In the autumn Ranji went to Scotland, where he stayed, at least temporarily, in Inveraray Castle and went shooting with Lord Lamington, the former Governor of Bombay, who had approved his selection as Jam Sahib, and King George V. He and Edith then spent several weeks at her father's rectory in Gilling, where one of his parting gestures was to give the local inhabitants a film show of the Delhi Durbar, before he finalized the acquisition of a beautiful residence in Staines, near London, where one of Edith's brothers, Clement, was now living. The house, which possessed extensive and magnificently laid-out grounds bordering the Thames, cost him £30,000. This new purchase was not announced until after he had left Britain in late January 1913.

Wild wrote that his return to India was, 'heralded by one of those many rumours that he was about to be married. In actual fact, he now had no intention of marrying, and he could afford to laugh at the many prophecies that his wife would be the daughter of a neighbouring prince, that she would be an Englishwoman, an Irishwoman, a Welshwoman, or any other nationality which rumour credited with the retention of his affections.' No doubt in an effort to confuse the issue further, Wild then suggested that Ranji had never actually been free to marry, having been betrothed in early life to a nobly born Rajput girl in a ceremony that no devout Hindu could ignore.

The prospects of Ranji ever enjoying the pleasures of life at Staines were soon to diminish fast. In August 1914 Britain declared war on Germany, and Ranji answered the call by putting the resources of his state at the disposal of the Empire, including his house at Staines, which was converted, at the expense of himself and the Maharajas of Kashmir and Patiala, into a forty-bed hospital for wounded officers.

Shortly afterwards, in November 1914, he left for the front, asking that Berthon administer the state in his absence. When he got to Bombay, he sent back for £1,000, saying he had forgotten to bring any money; Berthon replied that there was not that much in the treasury. It was announced he had been made an honorary major in the British army, but it was proving a problem to find work for the Indian princes, who were not allowed to take any risks. He had not been in France many days before he was given a week's leave in England, where he went to London and purchased several carriages at Tattersall's, explaining by way of apology in a letter to Berthon, who attempted to keep a tight rein on him through a badgering correspondence, that they were 'dirt cheap'. When he got back to the front, the winter was setting in and he began to suffer badly from asthma and chilblains. On 9 February 1915, he wrote to Berthon: 'We have only had two fine days in two months, and it has been cold. Of course, with quarters being so damp, and comforts being scarce and sanitation abominable, one naturally expects cold, but the worst of it is the rain, sleet, and snow. This has made exercising horses a considerable hardship. It is all right when anything happens, for you forget your own discomfort then. But such moments come few and far between except to the men in the trenches.' At the bombardment of Neuve Chapelle on 10 March, his general briefly let him go within a mile and a quarter of the allied trenches and inside the range of the guns.

In April, suffering from bronchitis, he was sent back to England and made a recruiting speech in Eastbourne of which he said: 'I felt so embarrassed, knowing that I had done nothing to deserve it.' In July he returned to France, and was made an honorary ADC, but was soon back, laid low by asthma.

On the last day of August he was a member of a shooting party that set out by car from the Red House, near Langdale End, on the peaceful Yorkshire moors. In addition to Ranjitsinhji the group included Edith, his old friend Dr Heasman, and Hunt, his solicitor, at whose suggestion they had come to shoot grouse over the Cross-cliffe estate of a Captain Palmes. It was necessary for them to leave the cars and cover the last three miles by foot. Ranjitsinhji and Edith occupied one butt, while some other members of the party were in a neighbouring one to their right. During the first few minutes, Ranji noticed that one of this group, a Mr Fisher, a local man, was bringing his gun round outside the boundary sticks. According to Wild's account, on one occasion Ranji had to bend down quickly himself and thrust Edith out of the way of a spray of pellets. He waved his arm at the man, but they were in the middle of a drive, so they all carried on.

It was then that Ranji was hit. Numbed, he tried to continue until the end of the drive, but searing pain brought him to a halt after three or four more shots (it would later be claimed he brought down a further ten birds). He put a hand to his face: there was blood streaming down the right side. Heasman examined the wound and it was clear the right eye was badly damaged.

Heasman told him to wait while they fetched one of the vehicles but Ranji could not wait and set out to walk the three miles to the cars. It was about nine miles to the nearest railway station, at Scarborough, from where they could take a train to Leeds, which had a general infirmary. The car jolted over the rough moor road towards Scarborough and all the time Ranji, who had attempted to make light of the wound and urged his friends to carry on, sat there, overwhelmed by the thought that he had lost the sight of one of his precious eyes. (Ironically, he had played his most recent first-class match in Scarborough, three years earlier; now, he must have wondered whether it would be his last.) The train seemed to take forever to make the journey to Leeds and once they got to the infirmary they had to wait until the evening for the specialist to get back from York.

It required only a cursory examination for the specialist to know what needed to be done. Two days later, on the morning of Thursday 2 September, Ranjitsinhji's right eye was removed.

It was a matter of some embarrassment to the authorities that, while so many of the nation's manhood was enduring the horrors of the trenches, one of its most famous figures should have been in a position to sustain an injury while grouse-shooting. As the news filtered into the press it was felt necessary to make some reassuring, if largely inaccurate, statements. The local newspaper, the *Yorkshire Herald*, said that Ranjitsinhji's return from France had only been brief and that his visit, which was practically unknown in the district, had been made in connection with military matters.

It was also stated that he intended to return to the front in two or three weeks, but he spent the next two months recuperating in Scarborough (though doubtless he also went to Gilling, which he was later reported to have visited frequently after the outbreak of war). Photographs discovered in Jamnagar recently by Alan Ross show Ranji at this time with his eye bandaged, in the company of two women, probably Edith and her sister, and apparently in good enough spirits. Gradually he became more mobile; on 26 October, he journeyed to Beckenham, Kent, to attend, in staff officer's uniform, W. G. Grace's funeral, and not long after was on his way to India for the marriage of his younger sister to Sumer Singh, the teenage Maharaja of Jodhpur. He did not return until after the war was over.

12

A MARRIAGE OF CONVENIENCE

B Y THE MID-1920S, Ranjitsinhji had everything an Indian prince could reasonably have desired. First, he had become very prosperous: he had always had princely tastes and was finally in a position to satisfy them. Second, having resumed his visits to Europe on a more regular basis in 1920, the first time he had been back for almost five years, he could now spend his time much as he wished, and for the rest of his life would be able to divide his year between the British Isles and India, picking the best of each climate. Born in an ill-lit corner room of a remote fort, by his early fifties he had risen to a position of worldly luxury.

In India, he possessed two main palaces in his capital. The magnificent eighty-room Pratap Villas palace, named after Pratap Singh (who had died in 1922), had been completed in 1915, although Ranji himself preferred to continue living in Vibha Villas, which he had developed considerably. He also had the modernized Lal bungalow as an additional, spacious guest house. He owned a summer house at Balachedi, on the Gulf of Kutch, and a shooting lodge at Kileshwar, in the Barda Hills – despite his eye injury, he retained much of his skill with a gun. There was also the massive Samana camp, near Sarodar, for hunting panthers, and a partridge shoot at Rozi Island. In addition to his country home in Staines, he bought for £60,000 in 1924 a lakeside castle on a 30,000-acre estate at Ballynahinch on the west coast of Ireland, ideal for fishing. All these places had been equipped with games rooms, tennis courts, swimming pools and such like, and filled either with fine Western art, jewellery and furniture, or with homely relics from his early days in England.

As a ruler, he had greater freedom – and in the eyes of other states,

222

more power – than ever before. Nawanagar had been elevated to a thirteen-gun salute state and had its political relations transferred from the Government of Bombay to the Government of India. He was in a position to provide magnificent entertainment, when the opportunity arose, for Viceroys, British and Continental aristocracy, or more simply old friends such as Sir Arthur Priestley and Charles Fry, who for several years acted as his private secretary. Three times he had travelled to Geneva as part of the Indian delegation to the League of Nations, set up to establish a framework for peace and international cooperation after the First World War. As a personal distinction he was entitled to a fifteen-gun salute and had been appointed a Knight Commander of the Star of India in 1917, and awarded the Grand Cross of the British Empire in 1919 and the Grand Commander of the Star of India in 1923. He had been given official permission to use the title Maharaja. He was also sufficiently wealthy for his visits to Europe to be no longer as troublesome as they had been in the past.

There were two main factors that had brought about this greatly improved situation. The first was that Ranjitsinhji had been assisted in the administration of Nawanagar by Lt.-Col. Berthon, his financial adviser, for several vital years of the state's development. Although it has been claimed that Ranji was the one responsible for the turn-around in Nawanagar's fortunes, it was actually during his year-long absence at the start of the war that Berthon, in his role as acting Administrator, began the process of rehabilitation that Ranji, in his inexperience, had earlier fought shy of. Berthon had replaced the slums of Jamnagar with new shops, houses and wider roads, and when money ran short had carried on with the clearing work.

Even after Ranji had been back several months, Berthon continued to stay in charge. Ranji, still recovering from the loss of his eye and apparently unable to face a return to his duties, preferred instead to travel around India visiting old friends, but matters came to a head in June 1916 when, having already borrowed £14,000 the previous year for his sister's marriage to the Maharaja of Jodhpur, he asked for a further large loan. The Government of India said it would consent to the request only on condition that Berthon was retained as Adminis-trator, and seemed keen to carry out the threat even after Ranji's reply that in that case, he did not want the loan. Ranji then went to Government House in Bombay and, according to Wild, declared that 'either the Government abandon the idea of the Administrator, or he himself would go'. Eventually, a compromise was reached, Berthon remaining attached to the state in a role ostensibly more minor than that of Administrator, while Ranjitsinhji, in return, was to receive more outward shows of favour. This situation remained until Berthon officially retired in 1920, although for a number of years after that he continued to act as close confidant and friend to the Jam Sahib.

In 1916 Berthon initiated various irrigation and relief schemes and though these were not complete by 1918, when a severe drought coincided with an influenza epidemic leading to the deaths of 22,000 people in the state, in the next year the first of a series of massive water tanks was completed. As a result, by the time of another poor rainfall, in 1923, there were sufficient reserves to prevent nothing more serious than a slight fall in revenue. Also, chiefly because of Berthon's influence, when the state finally began to acquire some capital, almost £750,000 was invested in four years into the War Loan scheme, and the Dwarka railway was finished in 1921.

The other thing that had materially improved Ranji's prosperity was the development of a port. Progress on the chosen site of Bedi, nearer to Jamnagar and more convenient than Salaya, the original suggestion of the British, had been slow and Ranji was only persuaded the scheme would be profitable when, in January 1918, the British agreed to suspend the customs line across the Kathiawar peninsula. The line was removed under a number of provisos, the main one being that states should adopt similar rates to those in effect at the Imperial ports. Work on Bedi had begun in earnest in 1917 and during the next ten years £490,000 was spent on the project.

The peninsula was in an important position and several trade routes were opened up to it. Nawanagar, meanwhile, did everything it could to encourage traffic: port charges were modest, labour and transit costs low, while the state bank offered low interest loans to merchants using the port. Bedi was soon thriving and was chiefly responsible for the dramatic rise in Nawanagar's revenue from £203,000 in 1916 to around £500,000 in 1925.

The Government of India watched this process with consternation. The rapid growth in the volume of traffic through Kathiawar had come at the drastic expense of the Imperial ports of Bombay and Karachi, and it began to suspect that some of the states were not abiding by the spirit of the original agreement. The government had always reserved the right to reconsider the position and, at a conference at Mount Abu in June 1927, proposed, among other things, that its officers be allowed to inspect port procedures. A few states, among them Nawanagar, refused to cooperate and as a result the government reimposed the customs line on three ports, including Bedi. Of course, despite the restrictions, it still proved possible to run them at a reduced profit.

Yet, for all his new found wealth and freedom, Ranji was still not content, still not able to enjoy life as he might. Part of the problem, perhaps, was that he no longer felt a strong enough affinity with the Indian people. Although he possessed some of their habits – ate their food, spoke their language, consulted their astrologers – he could not regard himself as one of them. Possibly like many ruling Indian princes, although worshipped blindly by the majority of his citizens, he was estranged from others, who had either been deprived of their lands or gone to work in more accommodating states. It was not insignificant that when he changed his choice of heir, as he did in 1915 to another nephew, he again did so in secret. The fact was that, emotionally, he was irrevocably tied to England, something which dated back at least to 1896, when he clearly felt so honoured at being selected to represent England at cricket. He seemed to like nothing better than to adopt the lifestyle of a member of the tweedy English aristocracy, and always appeared happiest in the company of the old friends he had made in Britain. As Jam Sahib, whenever he bid farewell to them all before sailing again for India, he invariably did so by extending earnest invitations to visit him, and his delight when they did so was apparent in the boyish pranks he would regularly play on them.

It was possibly a nostalgic affection for his past life in England that led him to attempt a return to first-class cricket at the age of forty-seven during his visit in 1920. Early on, King George V had made a polite enquiry as to whether he might play again despite now having only one eye. Later on in the summer, he had gone to watch several matches, including one at the Oval, where he had come across the broken-down, ageing figure of Bill Lockwood. Moved by the memories of their past encounters, he had given Lockwood a handsome present and introduced him to his friends as 'the greatest bowler I ever played against'. For some time he toyed with the idea of making a comeback (near the end of June he was to be seen practising at Lord's), and by late July the temptation to don the pads again in earnest was too great. Arthur Gilligan, one of the Sussex players, described what it was like when they learned that Ranji was to captain them against Essex: 'What a thrill went through us all. The news spread like wildfire, and the Jam Sahib's reappearance was the cause of a huge gate at Leyton. Press photographers came in their scores, reporters surged like flies trying to get a good story; in fact this was the greatest happening since the signing of the Armistice.'

Overweight and certainly no longer lithe, he went in at number eight, batted fifty minutes on a good pitch and not without skill gathered 16 runs (thirteen singles and a 3), but all his reactions were sluggish and he had to keep looking to play the ball away on the leg-side, the side of his good eye. Later, in the field, he had further difficulty focusing on the ball and, when not at slip, had to scheme to save himself exertion. Before an injured arm brought a swift end to his comeback he played two further games, as captain against Yorkshire at Headingley, where, with Sussex struggling for runs, he batted thirty minutes in the first innings and forty in the second, and against Northamptonshire at Hastings, but he could not improve on his modest score at Leyton.

To those few spectators who remembered him in his heyday, it must have been a pitiful sight, and even to those who had only heard of his great deeds the situation was not without its pathos. Walter Hammond was to write with feeling of Ranji's return, in his *Cricket My World* (1947): 'I suppose it was grand fun to meet all the old friends, to sniff the smell of bat-oil and pads and crushed grass, and to hear the affectionate thunder of delighted applause as his thousands of admirers saluted the one-time best batsman in the world. But it must have been pathetic, too, to find young and unknown bowlers coming up to him, out in the middle, contemptuously taking his measure, forcing him onto the back foot that had strolled victoriously down the pitch to "smell" at balls from a thousand greater than they . . .' Perhaps that was indeed what Ranjitsinhji felt, for, according to S. J. Southerton, the editor of *Wisden*, he was to explain that his only purpose in coming back had been a desire to write another book on cricket, with special emphasis on the art of batting with only one eye, but if that was so, the book never appeared.

By contrast to these strenuous efforts to rekindle the glories of his cricketing past in England, and his fondness in general of patronizing the game there, Ranji was to arouse criticism over his lack of interest in helping the Indian cricket authorities in their efforts to attain Test status for their country. Anthony de Mello, the first honorary secretary of the Board of Control for Cricket in India, which was set up in 1928, was to write in his *Portrait of Indian Sport*: 'It was natural that, when Ranji returned home, we should look to him for guidance on the road to cricketing recognition . . . It was right – indeed inevitable – that then, and at many times in the future, those who controlled Indian cricket should turn to Ranji. It was right that we should crave, and expect, his help and advice, that he should lend the weight of his great name and reputation to helping us along the way. In later years, as his nephew Duleepsinhji showed signs of being a player of almost the same class, that we should again approach Ranji with the request that Duleep be encouraged to bring his cricket talents to the aid of India. To all our requests for aid, encouragement and advice, Ranji gave but one answer: "Duleep and I are English cricketers." He could not have been more blunt . . .' De Mello was at a loss to explain Ranjitsinhji's attitude, but the fact was that Ranji could only conceive of Indians as British subjects, and failed to understand how they could wish to set up a national cricket team as a separate and rival entity to an English one – nor indeed, as we shall see, establish their country as an individual political unit.

Ranji might have been able to come to terms with his alienation from his countrymen had his intense loyalty to Britain not been stung by the disdain of its officials in India. It was this, most of all, that caused him to live in increasing bitterness. He felt entitled to be treated as one of them. Wild's biography cannot help but reveal the numerous petty squabbles he indulged in with the British authorities, or the disappointment he felt at being refused membership of the Bombay Gymkhana club, an exclusively English club which Ranji, with some justification in view of his standing in English society not so many years earlier, felt he ought to be entitled to join.

Although it did not excuse the prejudiced treatment to which he was sometimes subjected, Ranji was possibly treated as he was partly because his past record had finally spoken against him. The British suspected that he had only wanted an increased gun salute because, if a ruler was accorded fifteen guns, the Resident could not demand to see the state accounts; they knew that the transfer of Nawanagar's relations from the Government of Bombay to the Government of India had not been made without considerable acrimony; and they knew he had only achieved either through making himself notorious for demanding both.

The frustrating truth was that they would not take him as seriously as he would have liked.

There were other reasons for Ranjitsinhji's unhappiness. Although it may be thought that he and Edith Borissow could have happily continued their relationship on its existing basis, it had proved to be a situation in which neither of them found contentment or fulfilment.

It is not clear how much time they had actually been able to spend together during the upheaval of war. When Ranji returned to India late in 1915, Edith had certainly stayed behind in Britain. Two years later, in September 1917, the Reverend Borissow had died at the age of seventy-seven (among the wreaths at the funeral was one from 'Edith, Harold, Theo, Ronald, Frank and KSR'), and Edith and her sister, Beatrice, had left Gilling and moved first to nearby Hovingham and later to Staines, where other members of their immediate family already lived and where, of course, Ranjitsinhji himself had bought a house.

There are, however, at least two surviving photographs from Jamnagar which show Ranji in India in the company of a woman resembling one of those pictured with him after his eye accident, and who was therefore presumably Edith. One photograph portrays them on a shooting expedition, Ranji apparently quite late in life. The other, probably taken several years earlier, offers a semi-official pose, with Ranji and his companion seated on chairs in front of three men who may have been state officers. Both are elegantly dressed, Ranji in a western suit (although he is also turbaned, as he occasionally was, though he never learned to wrap one), the woman, her hair up, in a fine, long dress. They look very much a pair, Ranji with Popsey, the parrot, on his arm, she with a small dog on her lap. The most striking thing about the photograph is the ingrained sadness on the woman's face.

But, even if Edith did indeed visit Ranji in India, and did stay in the intimate arrangement of rooms in Vibha Villas palace already described, matters came to a head shortly after the war. The story, as Sewell recounted it in *Cricket Wallah*, was that: 'After the war and after the death of the father "Ranji" returned to England with the hope and intention of marriage. He brought (he told me) £100,000 to settle on the lady, who was to live, I think, in England. The lady, however, had transferred her attentions (so he told me in detail – a curious story it was) and refused. "Ranji" was terribly upset. There were endless "negotiations" but the lady, rightly sticking to her opinion, remained obdurate and did not consent to marry. I believe the engagement had lasted eighteen years. That was the end of it, but the two always remained friends.' Sewell also stated that the Reverend Borissow had finally been convinced of Ranjitsinhji's suitability to marry his daughter after there was a suggestion that Ranji, in taking the pellets that cost him his eye in the shooting accident in 1915, had saved Edith herself from being wounded. However, it is surely more significant that Ranji made no further attempt to secure Edith's hand in marriage until after her father's death, two years later.

Whether the account Ranji gave Sewell was an accurate one is open to doubt; for a start, it must be considered unlikely that he was ever in a position to find £100,000 to settle on Edith. Perhaps the truth was that Edith simply broke off their engagement because the cautious Ranjitsinhji had kept her waiting far too long. If this was the case, it would hardly have been surprising, for by 1920 she was forty-seven years of age. Little is known of Edith or of her personality, but to hold the position she did in Ranji's affections for so long with hardly any outward show or reward must have required strength of character perhaps in the end too much even for her, although it has to be said that the original delay came not from Ranjitsinhji but from her father.

During the early 1920s, she and her sister continued to live at The Limes in Penton Road, Staines, from where they busied themselves in the affairs of St Peter's Church and its parish. Ranji, when he subsequently stayed at his own house in Staines, was also to become involved in similar local affairs, occasionally staging church garden parties in his grounds, which suggests, as Sewell said, that he and Edith remained good friends.

He clearly felt the break-up as a great blow, one from which perhaps he never fully recovered. De Mello, searching for an explanation for Ranjitsinhji's neglect of India's sporting ambitions, wrote: 'Ranji's mind did not dwell amongst us in India. It was in England. And it is my understanding of this great and strange man that his heart was in England also . . . There was talk, too, of an unhappy love affair; and certainly, as an Indian prince, Ranji could not have married an English girl . . . Towards the end of his life Ranji gave the impression that he was disillusioned. Always, it seemed, he was waiting for something . . . waiting, with the calm patience of the true Indian, for something which, deep within himself, he knew he would never have. Not in this life, not ever.'

Occasionally, his patience ran out, giving way to deeply felt resentment. One such occasion, which obviously made an impression in the family, is known to the present Jam Sahib. It was sometime during the 1920s, and Ranji was in a car with some of his nephews, who were about to depart for England. As usual, he was sitting in the front, when one of the boys suggested that perhaps they ought not to go back to England because they might meet and fall in love with English girls and then have to endure the disappointment of not being able to marry them. Ranjitsinhji turned round sharply, looked his nephew directly in the face and said, in a barely controlled voice: 'And why should you not marry an English woman? Is she a monkey or something not human?'

In the absence of children of his own, Ranji began to live his life through his nephews and nieces. He effectively adopted them, bringing them up under his wing in the palaces of Jamnagar and often taking them with him on his trips to Europe. He sent them to British schools and universities and encouraged them generally to take a Western view of life. He was strict with them and forever impressed on them the need to uphold the family's good name.

Through his nephews, he was able to re-enact his cricketing past. In his early years as Jam Sahib he had coached them, in the cool of the evening, on the pitch in Jamnagar, and was a stern and unrelenting critic. During his visit to England in 1912, he placed five of them at public school, four at Malvern, a famous cricket nursery with some of the truest pitches in the country and the classroom of Geoffrey Foster and Harry Simms, who had been on his staff. Other nephews were to follow the pattern in the 1920s, when another four made their college XIs.

It was the fourth and youngest son of Jawansinhji who proved to be most in his uncle's likeness as a batsman. Duleepsinhji was eight years old when he began to be coached, and first played for Cheltenham, where his guardians were the ever more eccentric Charles Fry and his wife, around his sixteenth birthday, in 1921. Two years later, he captained the school and it was obvious that his talent was something out of the ordinary. There were similarities with Ranji: the stance, the powerful wrist-play, the harmony of movement and the certainty of judgment; the same instinctive brilliance as a slip fielder. But at eighteen his method was greater in range and orthodoxy. He had benefited from his uncle's experience and it was not by chance that he became one of the finest batsmen both on a wet pitch and of leg-break bowling.

Ranji was able to smooth the path for Duleepsinhji that he himself had found so rough. He supported him financially and sent him to Clare College, Cambridge, where he had no difficulty gaining his Blue as a freshman in 1925. He also made arrangements for him to qualify for Sussex by living in Eastbourne with Dr Heasman, now a member of the club's committee.

Duleep, as he became known, scored 75 in his first match against Oxford, and began in the county championship, in 1926, with 97 at Leicester and 115 against Hampshire at Brighton. The following year at Cambridge his batting immediately showed a greater maturity as he started by taking 101 off Yorkshire and 254 not out off Middlesex, still the highest innings played for the university. But a few days later he suffered a severe attack of pneumonia, was sent to Switzerland to recuperate and was unable to return to cricket until 1928.

A curious relationship developed between Duleep and his uncle. Ranji was forever instilling advice into him; above all, the need to be critical of one's own performance. When Duleep had his first run of bad form, during 1926, Ranji sent scathing telegrams to both him and his county captain, and on another occasion, when he was out for 93, cabled to enquire sarcastically, 'What was the matter with the other seven?' He seemed afraid to issue praise in case he turned the young man's head, though there became little danger of this as Duleep, who said he played the game only to please his uncle, rarely appeared to appreciate the true scope of his own powers and was often unable to do himself justice if he knew Ranjitsinhji was watching.

Further serious problems developed for Ranjitsinhji during the 1920s. The Indian National Congress, inspired by the fresh impetus given to the nationalist movement by the war years, had begun to show increasing hostility towards the princes, who, they felt, had no part in India's future.

Despite assurances from the British that their interests would continue to be safeguarded, Ranji had been quick to realize the dangers that lay with the advance of democracy and, aware that they were all coming under scrutiny, urged his fellow princes to put aside their age-old rivalries and unite. He harried the British with claims that the services of the princes during the war had not been adequately recognized, while heeding the advice of British government officials about the importance of being seen to introduce reforms (he instituted an Advisory Council of State, though it hardly ever met). Meanwhile, he played an active part in the formation and subsequent affairs of the Indian Chamber of Princes, a body which first convened in Delhi in 1921, but from the start ten of the most powerful states did not deign to take part.

He also tried to promote the princes' cause at the League of Nations in Geneva. As Fry, his private secretary at the time, wrote: 'Ranjitsinhji considered that he could do good work, since he had the means to do so, by bringing all the delegations into social contact; and he was desirous of proving to the representatives of the nations that Indians in general, and particularly the Indian princes, were very different from the mistaken notions commonly entertained of them.' He became a popular figure with other delegates through his munificent hospitality, though he perhaps only reinforced the notion of the princes as needlessly extravagant by spending over £1,500 in six weeks on entertaining during his first visit, presumably at the expense of the League. His party, which also included Berthon, managed to acquire influence beyond its real status in Geneva, for Ranji was only a late replacement on the Indian delegation in 1922 and the substitute delegate in 1923. Perhaps this was partly due to the exaggerated view of their importance held by Fry, who was held chiefly responsible for Ranjitsinhji making an early complaint at the first assembly, in 1920, that he had not been given precedence over representatives of the Dominions at a dinner.

One of Fry's tasks was to draft Ranjitsinhji's speeches, although, as he was to point out, Ranji 'had cultivated the art of reading out a prepared speech so skilfully that if you did not see he was reading you would have suspected him of speaking without his manuscript or even notes'. The most important speech Ranji had to make for the League was one he was asked to give on behalf of the British Empire in response to Greece's appeal for help following Italy's occupation of Corfu in 1923. It served to emphasize the League's intention to involve itself in the arbitration of such incidents and contributed to the Italians' decision to pull out, but the episode also illustrated the League's lack of practical political muscle, as the formal request for a withdrawal was left to come from the Council of Ambassadors, while the Greeks were nevertheless obliged to accept many of Italy's demands.

Not all of his speeches met with approval, although that was sometimes to his credit. In one, at the 1922 session, he spoke on the restrictions limiting the immigration of Indians into the colonies, and appealed to the South African delegates to help alter the attitude of their government on the issue. He said: 'The atmosphere and sympathy and good feeling with which this great assembly cannot fail to endow such an appeal will give that appeal a vivid human power such as it cannot obtain elsewhere . . . I should feel false to my fellow countrymen in India, and also to my fellow countrymen in South Africa, were I to neglect this unique opportunity of summoning to the assistance of their aspirations the spiritual power and the spiritual blessing of your sympathy . . . What is our ideal? What is our purpose? What is the very reason of our being? Let us have catholic justice and we shall have catholic peace.' Sir Joseph Cook, the former Prime Minister of Australia and its senior delegate that year, dismissed the comments as 'cheap claptrap', although when one remembers the way in which New South Wales had to waive a levy on coloured people entering the state before Ranji could play there during the 1897–98 tour, it appears that his country was hardly less guilty over this matter than South Africa.

It was during the 1920 session in Geneva that Ranjitsinhji learned from the Albanian delegation that their country was looking to fill its vacant throne and that the only requirements a candidate needed were that preferably he should be English and willing to spend £10,000 a year. Perhaps wishing above all to be seen to try to help, he came up with someone for their perusal, namely C. B. Fry. As nothing came of the meeting, it has been suggested that it was arranged merely as a joke at Fry's expense, although L. F. Rushbrook Williams, who succeeded to the position of Ranji's private secretary not long afterwards, was to deny this. Fry stated in his autobiography twenty years later that he felt Ranji could have found the necessary funds had he wished, but that he was reluctant to part with either his (Fry's) services or his company. While it was very likely true that he would have been loath to lose his old friend, the fact was that it would have been extremely difficult for Ranjitsinhji to find such a large annual sum and this must have been the overriding factor against Fry ever being selected. Whatever the exact circumstances of the affair, the two of them subsequently took great pleasure in recounting Fry's flirtation with the kingship of Albania.

Ranji also looked for support for the princes inside the House of Commons. Fry was encouraged in his ambitions to enter parliament, and in the first two general elections after the war came close to standing at Horsham and Worthing against Lord Winterton. The choice of opponent, surely, was no coincidence. Although politically slightly out of his depth, Fry was a Liberal candidate on three occasions, losing each time, though twice only narrowly. Ranji, while anxious to maintain an appearance of non-allegiance to any one party, came from the Continent to lend Fry support when he stood at Brighton in November 1922.

Then, in 1927, the All-India States Peoples' Conference was formed under the aegis of the Indian National Congress to provide leadership to popular movements in the states. The Conference published a series of pamphlets containing devastating, if overstated, attacks on individual rulers and it began with one on the best known of all princes, Ranji himself. He was accused of being an absentee ruler; of allowing neither freedom of speech nor liberty of person; and it was alleged there was inadequate legislation and a tyranny of taxation and monopolies. He was also charged with spending huge sums on entertaining friends and British officials. It was not the first attack levelled at him; the *Saurashtra* newspaper had long been identifying his public statements as specious, while the previous year a pamphleteer, Abhyankar, had published criticisms of him and distributed them around India and to British MPs.

Ranjitsinhji, like the majority of the princes, who had never seen their primary responsibility as improving the welfare of their people (nor had they traditionally been expected to do so), was ill equipped to stave off such assaults. Through various sources, though, he was able to produce a series of lengthy and detailed defences. The Times of India Press produced two works, *Jamnagar and its Ruler* (1927), by Naoroji Dumasia, styled as a tribute to many aspects of his reign, and

Nawanagar and its Critics (1929), a direct response to the Conference's pamphlet, answering each of its charges in turn. In 1931, for English consumption, Blackwood and Sons brought out Charles Kincaid's *The Land of Ranji and Duleep*. Ranji described it in his foreword as 'an accurate and in every way a trustworthy account' of his state's history, but although its author had spent a lifetime serving the British in India it owed more to Ranjitsinhji's view of the Nawanagar succession than to the government's own documentary evidence.

All these works portrayed him as an enlightened and responsible ruler, but even according to his own figures spending on public works did not amount to half his declared personal allowance. By his own admission no detailed state accounts were kept for fear of interference by the British, while it seems that large amounts of personal expenditure, much of which he felt was justified on grounds of maintaining the reputation of his state, were attributed to other areas. For example, it was rightly claimed that he had built ninety-eight miles of roads; what was not made clear was that eighty-six of them led from his capital to either the Samana camp or his lodge at Kileshwar. Also, he flatly denied having bought a luxury yacht in 1927, although the purchase had been widely publicized in the press at the time and a model of the *Star of India* can be seen proudly displayed in the main banqueting hall in Jamnagar to this day.

Ranji visited England in 1930 for the first Round Table Conference on India's future constitution. That year too he was asked to be president of Sussex CCC: for a man who had become apt to say that 'nobody is so soon forgotten as a successful cricketer', this was a welcome opportunity to step back into the limelight. In May he sent a telegram promising £1,000 to the club's funds, and in August contributed £50 to the benefit of Maurice Tate, son of the luckless Fred, but his proudest moment was to witness late in June, not long after his arrival from India, Duleepsinhji's brilliant 173 in four and three-quarter hours on the first day of his first appearance against Australia, which surpassed Ranji's own score on his Test début.

Despite the opposition of the ageing Lord Harris, Duleep had first played for England the previous year, against South Africa, although he was dropped after one match following objections from the Republic about the Indian's presence. Duleep's selection for the second Test at Lord's in 1930 had been ensured by some spectacular form, which included breaking Ranji's record score for Sussex with 333 in one day against Northamptonshire at Brighton.

The Lord's Test was Duleep's finest hour, but he was in a sense overshadowed by his uncle, who came to the match in full Indian dress, jewels sparkling from his tunic and turban. Accompanied by Archie MacLaren and the rest of his entourage, Ranji's entrance shortly before the start of play was a dramatic affair, while at the lunch interval he held court behind the pavilion and, looking every inch a Maharaja, was the chief attraction for the strolling crowds. He also paid a visit to the England dressing-room, where he made an equally striking impression on the players. One of them, Maurice Tate, was heard to confide admiringly: 'Cor, see Ranji – looks a veritable Hindu, don't he?'

Whatever he might have said about being forgotten, Ranji, one of the most potent and successful sporting figures there has ever been, still retained a powerful hold on the imagination of those old enough to remember his name, perhaps even to have seen him play. To their generation, who talked of the pre-war era as the Golden Age of Cricket, Ranji was an enduring image from a lost age. The person who best expressed this romanticism in these years of peace was Neville Cardus, the *Manchester Guardian*'s cricket correspondent. He wrote evocatively of Ranji's batting, although it can have been no more than a memory from a handful of visits as a youth to Old Trafford (Cardus admitted he barely went outside Manchester until 1912, when he spent the summer in Shrewsbury, and Ranji's last first-class match in the city was in 1904, when Cardus was sixteen).

The tantalizing proximity of two childhood heroes, Ranji, in all his princely finery, and MacLaren, seemed to captivate Cardus, whose opening words of his report on the Lord's Test of 1930 were:

A warm June sun cast a resplendent light on Lord's this morning. The old place was magnificent; we would get the sense of pomp and circumstance as we walked over the field before the first ball was bowled in the second Test match. In the crowd great cricketers of the past were to be seen; we could also feel the invisible presence of the ancient ghosts whose immortality is housed at Lord's.

He went on to compare one of Duleepsinhji's on-drives to the majestic manner in which the watching MacLaren used to execute the stroke, and commented: 'A dazzling leg-glance by Duleepsinhji let us understand who is his uncle. Ranjitsinhji, by the way, was present as his nephew scored a century in his first match against Australia.'

It is also interesting to note another passage in Cardus's account, when Duleep and Hendren were in complete command, which echoes his famous description of Ranji and Fry batting together: 'Hendren's vigour contrasted well with Duleepsinhji's suppleness. The difference between the two was that of the Orient and the Occident, between the slightly ambiguous and the utterly tangible.'

While Ranji admitted to basking in the reflected glory of Duleep's achievement, he nevertheless reserved some criticism for his nephew's performance, although it may have been prompted by nothing more than straightforward disappointment at him finally getting out. When play entered the last hour of the day, Duleep began to force the pace, and had already taken ten off the over when, at 6.15, he was caught at long-off. In the Long Room, as Duleep walked back across the turf and ran up the steps of the pavilion to a standing ovation, Ranji remarked about the final stroke: 'The boy was always careless.'

The climax to Ranji's year as president was a dinner he gave at the Metropole Hotel in honour of Sussex and the Australians on the Saturday of their match in Brighton at the end of August. (Earlier in the day Ranji had caused great excitement among the spectators by appearing at the ground, and Duleepsinhji was later to say, 'I then realized what a wonderful hold he had on the public imagination.') Despite the presence of the two teams, a sizeable proportion of the gathering was made up of Ranji and his contemporaries. One young England cricketer later recalled: 'The burden of the conversation was largely that cricket was a fine game, how well it used to be played and what a pity it was that nobody could play it any more.' A number of the older cricketers made speeches, MacLaren to the effect that the age of greatness was past, but Sir Home Gordon, perhaps suspecting that all these senior men were really expressing was the eternal envy of the younger sportsman, volunteered to reply and said there was nothing so depressing to the active cricketer as being run down in comparison with former players who were superior only by virtue of tradition. In support of his argument, he said that Duleep was a worthy successor to Ranji. He was cheered loudly by at least one section of the audience.

Among those in attendance that evening was Don Bradman, three days past his twenty-second birthday, who on his first tour of England had scored 974 runs in the Tests at an average of 139.14 and smashed several other major batting records, including Ranjitsinhji's tally of double centuries for one season. These two great batsmen, separated by thirty-six years and brought together for possibly the only time, had slightly different attitudes to each other. Bradman carried with him a story concerning Ranji which had served as an inspiration to him. It related how, when Hobbs scored his hundredth hundred in 1923, Ranji had sent him a gift inscribed, 'From a humble student of the game'; Bradman saw this as evidence that, however good a player you were, you could not absorb all there was to know about the game. Ranji said of Bradman: 'It was not thus in the heyday of Tom Richardson, Hugh Trumble and George Lohmann. Bradman's performances are not good enough to raise him to the standard of Trumper, Hill and Macartney, because he has no stiff bowling against him.' He was also to support, in a ghosted column for the *Daily Sketch*, the bodyline tactics of 1932–33 which were introduced to curb Bradman's phenomenal scoring: 'Jardine has no call to deviate from the tactics employed so far . . . Personally I don't believe that things are so dangerous as they are made out to be.'

When the match between Sussex and the Australians resumed on the Monday, someone chanced to produce an old press cutting and showed it to some of the players. It concerned Ranji's first appearance for England and in it he was reported as saying, in answer to some adverse comments about his methods, that the older generation were severe critics of the young and he hoped that in years to come he would be more generous.

Another revealing exchange that took place some time during 1930, involved the late 'Gubby' Allen, one of England's flagging bowlers that summer, who used to sit at matches with some of the famous former cricketers known to his father. One day Allen ventured to ask Ranji and Fry, during a pause in their conversation, 'Who is the greatest batsman of all time?' Another, longer pause was finally broken by Ranji: 'I think, Charles, that I was better than you on a soft wicket.'

During the last years of his life, Ranji became increasingly bitter at Britain's determination to proceed with reforms in India's constitution. His fears, though, were not altogether justified because the government had shown it was prepared to provide a form of self-government heavily weighted towards the princes. The princes themselves had even accepted, at the Round Table Conference in 1930, that the Government was publicly committed to giving British India a new constitution, that federalism should be the accepted framework and that their states should be involved, provided their own princely prerogatives were protected.

Ranji, however, was among those princes who continued to harbour doubts and fears about the future, particularly what the hostile Indian National Congress might have in store for them. His speeches contained frequent reminders of British obligations and employed the cricketing metaphors so favoured by the British themselves ('The Princes of India have been very old members of Great Britain's team and they have tried their best to play with a straight bat for the Empire'). Gradually the princes' initial enthusiasm for federation was dissipated, hopes of some further period of irresponsible rule grew, and impossible demands replaced the reasonable offers already on the table. They wanted, they said, complete immunity from supervision by a federal government.

Ranji, whatever he claimed, certainly had personal motives for delaying federation. The anti-British goods boycott begun by Congress had had disastrous consequences for the Imperial ports and provided an opening for fresh trade through his own port of Bedi, the treatment of which he continued to contest, though his repeated applications and appeals were rejected. During his final visit to England, in the summer of 1932, he revealed the benefit he had been reaping when he addressed a meeting, arranged by the Manchester Chamber of Commerce, of Lancashire businessmen interested in trade with India. He said: 'Over the last two or three years we in my state have trebled, if not quadrupled, the sale of Manchester goods because we felt that Bombay's stupidity was our opportunity.'

His attempts to obstruct moves towards federation continued until the end. During the last year of his life he acted as chancellor of the Chamber of Princes and was a delegate in 1932 at the third Round Table Conference, which ended in the parties failing to reach agreement (one of those sitting opposite him had been his old adversary Lord Winterton). Then, at the end of his term of office and just a week before he died, when he was asked to present his report of the Conference to the annual meeting of the Chamber in Delhi, he used the occasion to launch a withering invective against federation. He argued that there was no need for the Native States to take part – 'I have nothing but the friendliest and most brotherly sentiments for British India, and I hope she will attain her aspirations, but I hope she will do this without involving the states' – and repeated fears that 'the constitution will inevitably so work as to destroy the very principle of Indian kingship'.

However, before he could finish the speech he was brought to an abrupt halt by the chairman, Lord Willingdon, the Viceroy. Willingdon, who had himself played cricket for Sussex and whose acquaintance with Ranji went back nearly forty years, pointed out that these comments had nothing to do with the report he was supposed to be presenting. Ranji, stung by the rebuke, sat down and thrust away from him the papers on his desk. Although Willingdon smoothed over the incident with him later in the day, the other princes correctly interpreted it as proof of the government's resolve to stifle any opposition to federation.

While it is possible to be critical of Ranjitsinhji's behaviour in all this, it has to be said that he was doing no more than fighting his own corner – as were many others during these turbulent years in India's history – and doing so tenaciously by wielding the clout he undeniably possessed as still one of the most famous men in the Empire.

Ranjitsinhji died of heart failure at 5 a.m. on Sunday 2 April 1933 in the Vibha Villas palace at Jamnagar. He was sixty years of age. He had been confined to his bed, attended by an English doctor, for five days since returning from his trip to Delhi. During the previous three years he had suffered from heart and bronchial conditions; more recently he had also been troubled by the deteriorating sight of his remaining eye. His final illness was nevertheless sudden; preparations for his annual trip to the British Isles had been under way. His last visitors were reported to have been two of Duleepsinhji's brothers just hours before his death. Members of that morning's congregation at St Peter's Church in Staines were among the first to hear the news. Later in the day the people of Jamnagar lined the four-mile route to his funeral pyre, by when tributes were already coming in to the man who was said to have first put India on the map for the ordinary Englishman. Five months later, a thousand miles away near Allahabad, his ashes were scattered over the Ganges.

Ranjitsinhji left estate in England to the gross value of £185,958; in India, Digvijaysinhji, the second son of Jawansinhji, was installed as Jam Sahib within a fortnight. One of his earliest duties was to ensure that those best qualified to speak for Ranjitsinhji gave their assistance to the biography of him by Roland Wild, published by Rich and Cowan in June 1934. Ranji, perhaps sensing that he was nearing the end of his life, had authorized the publishers to commission the work and had stipulated that it should not be written by a famous cricketer so that his work for Nawanagar and India would not be obscured: in other words, it was to give to his life's events the proportions which he wished to give them. It was thus largely another defence of his reign, although another of its themes was that it had been his destiny to become Jam Sahib. Wild was a journalist and author who was only twenty-eight when Ranji died. He had travelled to India to carry out his researches but his style owes more to a newspaperman's enthusiasm than to a scholar's accuracy. But so far as his subject was concerned he performed the task well; so well in fact that when the *Morning Post*, a month after the book was published, picked up his implication that Ranjitsinhji's death was the result of a heart-breaking rebuff by the Viceroy, he was hard-pressed to lay the ensuing controversy to rest. As the 'official' work, it was to hoodwink those who read it for over fifty years. Wild lived on until January 1990, when he died in Canada at the age of eighty-five.

Edith Borissow must have had to hide her grief at his death as she had hidden her love when he was alive. She continued to live in Staines until her sister's death in November 1938, after which she moved back to Cambridge, the place where she had first met Ranji. There, in a house in Causewayside, she lived out her last years, financially not well off and, according to the present Jam Sahib, neglected by Ranji's family. She died there on 12 December 1942 at the age of sixty-nine. She was buried in Trumpington cemetery.

Several months after Ranjitsinhji's death, Lord Willingdon agreed to put the Kathiawar ports dispute to private arbitration and in 1934 it was announced that agreement had been reached. In January 1936, the Viceroy travelled to Jamnagar to unveil a statue in gilded bronze of the late Jam Sahib as a commemoration of his silver jubilee four years earlier.

Ranjitsinhji died fearing he had driven Duleep to an untimely death. Duleep had again been troubled by ill health during the winter of 1931 but, unaware that his illness was the onset of tuberculosis, determined to rejoin Sussex, whom he then captained, for the 1932 season. By August, when Sussex had become involved in a tense chase for their first county championship title, his health had worsened but Ranjitsinhji, holidaying in Ireland, sent a telegram telling him not to desert his men at a crucial time. Duleep played on only to collapse after the exertion of a match-winning innings of 90 at Taunton. He did not play again that season and was sent to a sanatorium in Switzerland, where he had a lung removed. He gradually made a full recovery, although Ranjitsinhji did not live to see it. Duleep was later medically advised not to resume first-class cricket, and, at the age of twenty-eight, his career was over. In 1936, he married a cousin of the Maharaja of Rajpipla, an alliance arranged by his uncle in 1929 and one to which he remained faithful, although he was subsequently to fall in love with a daughter of the Maharaja of Kapurthala. He lived until 1959.

Ranji was also survived by his three greatest friends in cricket, Charles Fry, Archie MacLaren and, by only eight days, Sir Arthur Priestley.

In 1934, two years after India had played its first Test match, the Board of Control for Cricket in India formed a competition between teams representing the provinces and the princely states, in order to help build a stronger national side. It was named the Ranji Trophy and in its third year was won by Nawanagar, which owed at least something to Ranjitsinhji's encouragement of local players such as Amar Singh. It is still played for annually.

In 1946 a new British government sent a cabinet mission to India to draw up plans for the transfer of power, and the princes were advised to organize themselves to fit into the revised constitutional framework. Lord Mountbatten, a member of the Royal Family, was appointed Viceroy specifically to carry out the transfer, which it was first announced would take place in June 1948 but which was later brought forward to August 1947. With no time to put their house in order, and riven by dissension, the princes were unable to rise to the challenge. The British hoped the succeeding Indian government would do their best to care for them. Twenty-four years after independence the privileges and privy purses of the princes were abolished.

To this day, Ranjitsinhji's bedroom in Vibha Villas has been preserved largely unchanged since the day he died, and is tended daily by one of the palace servants as though guarding a shrine's solitary spirit.

STATISTICAL APPENDIX

Ranjitsinhji in First-class Cricket

1. SEASONAL RECORD

Season	Matches	Innings	Not Out	Runs	Highest Innings	100s	50s	0s	Average	Posn in avgs
1893	12	19	2	439	58	0	3	3	25.82	24
1894	8	16	4	387	94	0	3	2	32.25	8
1895	21	39	3	1,775	150	4	11	0	49.31	4
1896	29	55	7	2,780	171*	10	11	1	57.92	1
1897	26	48	5	1,940	260	5	7	4	45.12	5
1897–98 (Aus)	12	22	3	1,157	189	3	6	0	60.89	1
1899	34	58	8	3,159	197	8	17	2	63.18	3
1899–1900 (US)	2	2	0	125	68	0	2	0	62.50	–
1900	26	40	5	3,065	275	11	10	2	87.57	1
1901	27	40	5	2,468	285*	8	10	4	70.51	3
1902	18	26	2	1,106	234*	3	3	3	46.08	2
1903	28	41	7	1,924	204	5	12	1	56.58	2
1904	24	34	6	2,077	207*	8	7	0	74.17	1
1908	18	28	3	1,138	200	3	4	1	45.52	7
1912	19	28	2	1,113	176	4	3	1	42.81	6
1920	3	4	0	39	16	0	0	0	9.75	–
TOTALS	307	500	62	24,692	285*	72	109	24	56.37	

Ranji's overall average stood as the highest for a complete career by an England-based batsman until G. Boycott (56.84) retired in 1986.

2. TEST MATCHES (all against Australia)

Season	Matches	Innings	Not Out	Runs	Highest Innings	100s	50s	0s	Average	Posn in avgs
1896	2	4	1	235	154*	1	1	0	78.33	1
1897–98	5	10	1	457	175	1	3	0	50.78	2
1899	5	8	2	278	93*	0	2	1	46.33	2
1902	3	4	0	19	13	0	0	1	4.75	12
TOTALS	15	26	4	989	175	2	6	2	44.96	

3. HIGHEST INNINGS

Score	Mins	4s	5s	6s	Match
285★	320	46	2	1	Sussex v. Somerset, Taunton, 1901
275	305	30			Sussex v. Leicestershire, Leicester, 1900
260	250	36		1	Sussex v. MCC, Lord's, 1897
234★	205	39			Sussex v. Surrey, Hastings, 1902
230	320	26			Sussex v. Essex, Leyton, 1902
222	250	35			Sussex v. Somerset, Brighton, 1900
220	205	34			Sussex v. Kent, Brighton, 1900
219	255	32			Sussex v. Essex, Brighton, 1901
215★	230	33			Sussex v. Cambridge University, Fenner's, 1900
207★	315	30			Sussex v. Lancashire, Brighton, 1904
204	300	29			Sussex v. Lancashire, Brighton, 1901
204	270	18			Sussex v. Surrey, the Oval, 1903
202	180	35			Sussex v. Middlesex, Brighton, 1900
200	345	20			Sussex v. Surrey, the Oval, 1908
197	250	32	2		Sussex v. Surrey, the Oval, 1899
192★	185	32	1		Sussex v. Kent, Tonbridge, 1900
189	265	23			Stoddart's XI v S. Australia, Adelaide, 1897–98
178★	180	21			Sussex v. South Africans, Brighton, 1904
178	285	26			Sussex v. Nottinghamshire, Brighton, 1899
176	350	23			Sussex v. Lancashire, Brighton, 1912
175	215	24			England v. Australia, Sydney, 1897–98
174		22			Sussex v. Surrey, Brighton, 1899
171★	200	19	1		Sussex v. Oxford University, Brighton, 1896
170★	230	21	1		Sussex v. Lancashire, Old Trafford, 1901
170		27			Sussex v. Essex, Brighton, 1897
166★	180	27			MCC v. Cambridge University, Lord's, 1904

Ranji made nine hundreds against both Lancashire (in thirty-three innings) and Surrey (thirty-six innings), six hundreds against Cambridge University (twenty-six innings) and five each against Gloucestershire (twenty-eight innings), Middlesex (thirty-five innings) and Yorkshire (thirty-six innings). His nine centuries against Surrey came in eighteen innings between 1899 and 1908.

Ranji scored a century in each innings of the same match once, 100 and 125 not out, for Sussex v. Yorkshire, at Brighton in 1896. All his runs were made on the third day of the match (he was 0 not out overnight) and he is the only batsman to perform the feat in a single day.

Ranji scored a century in a pre-lunch session on at least eleven occasions. His 180 runs – 54 to 234★ – during the morning session (150 minutes on the third day) for Sussex v. Surrey at Hastings in 1902, is a record for a match in Britain, while his 113 runs – 41 to 154★ – during the morning session (130 minutes on the third day) for England v. Australia at Old Trafford in 1896, is a record for an Anglo-Australian Test match. He was the first batsman to score a century before lunch in a Test.

With scores of 260, 275 and 285★, Ranji three times improved on the highest innings played for Sussex.

Over half of Ranji's first-class centuries (37 out of 72) were of 150 runs or more and his average century score was 156.

4. BOWLERS

The following bowlers took Ranji's wicket most often:

Times	Inns[1]	KSR's avg	Bowler	Teams[2]
13	43	46.33	E. Jones	S. Australia, Australians
12	37	50.17	W. Rhodes	Yorkshire, MCC, Rest
12	49	41.26	H. Trumble	Victoria, Australians
11	27	62.24	A. Mold	Lancashire, Thornton's XII, North
11	31	50.70	A. E. Trott	Middlesex, Rest
10	21	61.90	W. Mead	Essex, MCC
10	22	52.00	L. C. Braund	Surrey, Somerset, MCC
10	30	70.60	T. Richardson	Surrey
10	48	59.78	J. T. Hearne	Middlesex, MCC, Gentlemen of England
8	41	50.82	G. H. Hirst	Yorkshire, Rest

[1] *Inns*: innings in which Ranjitsinhji batted and the bowler bowled. It is not always certain that the two faced each other.

[2] The eight Englishmen in the table also opposed Ranji for the Players. The English amateur who took his wicket most often was J. R. Mason (Kent), six times.

Braund, bowling leg-breaks, accounted for Ranji ten times in fourteen innings, including nine times for 25 runs or less, between July 1901 and July 1904 – an astonishing record. However, this sequence also included the highest score of Ranjitsinhji's career, 285*, against Somerset at Taunton in 1901.

Trumble (off-breaks) dismissed him seven times in single figures and Mead (off-breaks and occasional leg-breaks) six times for 15 or less.

Other leg-break bowlers besides Braund and Mead caused Ranji occasional difficulties. A. Hearne (Kent and MCC) took his wicket five times for under 25 between 1896 and 1904, while J. W. Hearne (Middlesex and the Players) dismissed him four times in the only five innings in which he opposed him, all in 1912. A. O. Jones, of Nottinghamshire, claimed his wicket five times, twice at Brighton in 1900 and twice at Trent Bridge in 1901 – once in each match for 0.

Ranji rated W. H. Lockwood (Surrey and the Players) and Richardson among the best fast bowlers he faced. While they were at their height, his record against one or both of them was certainly only modest – an average of 22.95 in twenty innings – but from 1899 he averaged 111.92 from seventeen innings in which they bowled. Lockwood dismissed Ranji three times in twenty-three innings, twice for 0 in 1893. Two other bowlers he thought highly of were S. F. Barnes (Lancashire and the Players) and C. J. Kortright (Essex) but Barnes took his wicket only once in six innings (102, 105, 9, 144*, 6 and 55) and Kortright not at all in five (79, 7, 170, 219 and 230).

The spinners he acknowledged as the best he faced were, interestingly, three slow left-armers: in his early days, R. Peel (Yorkshire and the North) and J. Briggs (Lancashire and the Players), and later, C. Blythe (Kent and MCC). None had an especially distinguished record against him. Blythe dismissed him four times in twenty innings, Peel three in sixteen and Briggs three in eighteen. Ranji nevertheless rated Blythe ahead of Rhodes, who took his wicket far more often, although only once for a single-figure score and only four times for less than 38.

Apart from Jones and Lockwood (above), the only other bowler to dismiss him twice for 0 was G. L. Jessop, for Cambridge University in 1896 and Gloucestershire in 1901. J. B. King (Philadelphians, 1897) and W. Shipman (Leicestershire, 1912) each dismissed him for 0 with the first deliveries they ever bowled to him.

Ranji is one of only a few well-known batsmen never to be dismissed for a pair in first-class cricket. However, in a non first-class match, for Poona Gymkhana v Kathiawar at Poona in 1898, L. M. R. Deas dismissed him for 0 in both innings, each time third ball.

The following bowlers took Ranji's wicket most often in Tests:

Times	Inns	KSR's avg	Bowler
5	22	52.66	E. Jones
5	24	48.80	H. Trumble
3	8	86.00	T. R. McKibbin
3	19	29.00	M. A. Noble

Six bowlers took his wicket once: W. W. Armstrong (three innings), A. J. Y. Hopkins (three innings), G. Giffen (four innings), C. E. McLeod (seven innings), G. H. S. Trott (eleven innings) and W. P. Howell (fifteen innings).

Howell (Lord's, 1899) and Hopkins (Lord's, 1902) both dismissed him for 0.

5. DISMISSALS

Ranji's mode of dismissals during his career was as follows: caught 248 (56.62 per cent), bowled 118 (26.94), lbw 34 (7.76), stumped 20 (4.57), run out 18 (4.11); total 438.

E. Jones had him caught ten times (though never by a wicket-keeper); A. E. Trott bowled him six times (twice in both innings of a match); Trumble had him lbw five times (once in both innings of the Old Trafford Test in 1902), and Rhodes had him stumped three times.

6. GROUNDS

Ranji was once reported as saying that his three favourite grounds were Brighton, Lord's and Fenner's. It is hardly surprising that he should have said so: Lord's, with all its history and tradition, has natural attractions for any player, while Brighton and Fenner's possessed some of the shortest boundaries and truest pitches among first-class grounds in Britain, perfect for run-getting. On the two latter grounds in 1900 he amassed 1,721 runs at an average of 122.93.

After leaving university, Ranji's opportunities for playing in Cambridge were limited and his overall record at Fenner's was unexceptional (910 runs in nineteen innings, average 53.53, with three centuries). At Brighton, however, he scored over one-third of all his runs (8,860 in 154 innings, average 66.12) and thirty-two of his seventy-two centuries. At Lord's he made 3,420 runs in seventy-nine innings, average 47.50, with ten centuries.

7. HIGHEST PARTNERSHIPS

Runs	Wicket	Mins	Partner	Match
344[1]	7	260	W. Newham	Sussex v. Essex, Leyton, 1902
325	2	250	G. Brann	Sussex v. Surrey, the Oval, 1899
298	3	240	E. H. Killick	Sussex v. Lancashire, Brighton, 1901
292*	2	170	C. B. Fry	Sussex v. Somerset, Taunton, 1901
255	3	230	C. B. Fry	Sussex v. Yorkshire, Sheffield, 1904
252	2	160	G. Brann	Sussex v. Gloucestershire, Bristol, 1899
246	5	150	A. Collins	Sussex v. Kent, Brighton, 1900
237	1	140	E. G. Wynyard	MCC v. Cambridge University, Lord's, 1904
226	2	125	F. W. Marlow	Sussex v. Somerset, Brighton, 1895
213*	6	120	A. E. Relf	Sussex v. Lancashire, Brighton, 1904
207	5	160	J. Vine	Sussex v. Middlesex, Lord's, 1908
200	3	120	W. G. Grace	MCC v. Cambridge University, Lord's, 1894
197	3	100	C. B. Fry	Sussex v. Surrey, Brighton, 1900
196	3		C. B. Fry	Sussex v. Lancashire, Old Trafford, 1903
194	4	105	E. H. Killick	Sussex v. Somerset, Brighton, 1900
194	3		C. B. Fry	Sussex v. Leicestershire, Leicester, 1900
194	4	155	F. S. Jackson	Gentlemen v. Players, Lord's, 1904
192	7	100	G. R. Cox sen.	Sussex v. Surrey, Hastings, 1902

1. Ranji's partnership of 344 with Newham stood as the world record for the 7th wicket for fifty-two years and remains the English record, while his stand of 298 with Killick in 1901 still constitutes the best for Sussex's 3rd wicket. To the partnership of 246 for the 5th wicket in 1900 Collins contributed only 33, Ranjitsinhji making 220 of the 293 runs added while he was at the wicket.

For Sussex v. Surrey, at Hastings in 1902, Ranji (234*) added 160 unbroken for the 9th wicket with F. W. Tate in only seventy minutes.

8. BOWLING
Ranji took 133 wickets in first-class matches with his medium-slow off-breaks, at an average of 34.59 each. He also took 233 catches.

Bibliography

In the great majority of instances, the relevant sources have been identified in the text, but the following were generally useful:

ARCHIVE MATERIAL

India Office files
Jamnagar 1852–1884: recognition of Jaswantsinhji etc (R/2/708/8)
Death of HH the Jam Sahib Vibhaji in 1896 [sic] (R/2/724/88)
Jamnagar: Ranjitsinhji's file 1896–1901 (R/2/575/12)
Nawanagar: Investiture of HH Jam Sahib Jassaji (R/2/731/175)
Death of Jassaji and claims (R/2/676/20)
Ranji's claim to the throne (R/2/575/15)
Nawanagar 1908 (L/P+S/10/157)
and Annual Home Correspondence files and Political and Secret registers.

East Sussex County Record Office, Lewes
Official Sussex CCC scorebooks 1895–1920

BOOKS
Prince Ranjitsinhji, *The Jubilee Book of Cricket*, 1897
Prince Ranjitsinhji, *With Stoddart's Team in Australia*, 1898
P. C. Standing, *Ranjitsinhji Prince of Cricket*, 1903
G. W. Beldam and C. B. Fry, *Great Batsmen*, 1905
J. M. Framjee Patel, *Stray Thoughts on Indian Cricket*, 1905
Prince Ranjitsinhji, *Cricket Guide and How to Play Cricket*, 1906
H. H. Sir Bhavsinhji, Maharaja of Bhavnagar, *Forty Years of the Rajkumar College*, 1911
Naoroji Dumasia, *Jamnagar and its Ruler*, 1927
Charles Kincaid, *The Land of Ranji and Duleep*, 1931
Roland Wild, *The Biography of Colonel His Highness Shri Sir Ranjitsinhji*, 1934
H. S. Altham, *A History of Cricket*, 1926
C. B. Fry, *Life Worth Living*, 1939
Patrick Morrah, *The Golden Age of Cricket*, 1967
Michael Down, *Archie: A Biography of A. C. MacLaren*, 1981
Scyld Berry, *Cricket Wallah*, 1982
Alan Ross, *Ranji: Prince of Cricketers*, 1983
Clive Ellis, *CB: The Life of Charles Burgess Fry*, 1984
Charles Allen and Sharada Dwivedi, *Lives of the Indian Princes*, 1984

Bibliography

Philip Bailey, Philip Thorn and Peter Wynne-Thomas, *Who's Who of Cricketers*, 1984

Dictionary of National Biography, *Who Was Who* and *Wisden Cricketers' Almanack*.

NEWSPAPERS AND PERIODICALS

Cambridge Daily News, Cambridge Weekly News, Cricket: A Weekly Record of the Game, The Cricket Field, Strand Magazine, Sussex Daily News, The Times, Windsor Magazine, Yorkshire Herald.

INDEX

253

Index